THE Horticulture GARDENER'S GUIDES

PLANTS FOR SMALL SPACES

Clive Lane

HORTICULTURE
BOOKS
www.hortmag.com

A HORTICULTURE BOOK

Horticulture Publications, Boston, Massachusetts

First published in the US in 2005 ISBN 1-55870-749-2

Horticulture is a subsidiary of F+W Publications Inc. Company
Distributed by F+W Publications Inc.
4700 East Galbraith Road, Cincinnati, OH 45236
1-800-289-0963

Printed in Great Britain by Butler & Tanner Ltd
for Horticulture Publications, Boston, Massachusetts

Visit our website at www.hortmag.com

Commissioning Editor Mic Cady
Art Editor Sue Cleave
Production Director Roger Lane

Series Editor Sue Gordon, OutHouse Publishing
   Winchester, Hampshire SO22 5DS
Contributors Julia Brittain, Jo Weeks
Copy Editors Polly Boyd, Elizabeth Mallard-Shaw
Proofreader Audrey Horne
Indexer June Wilkins

American edition by
Craft Plus Publishing Ltd.
53 Crown Street
Brentwood, Essex CM14 4BD
Consultant Lynn M. Steiner, M.S. (Horticulture)

Contents

Introduction

The garden may be small and space strictly limited. The layout might be uninspiring and privacy a problem. But the urge to create a garden – somewhere to relax from the stresses and strains of a busy life – overtakes many of us, and then begins the daunting task of choosing suitable plants.

Plants for Small Spaces aims to provide the confidence and know-how to find beautiful, easy, and dependable plants for every aspect of a small garden or small space. It will take the uncertainty out of purchasing decisions and prevent expensive mistakes. As there is currently strong interest in traditional, English-style planting schemes, the emphasis is on plants that are appropriate for this type of garden. Many of the illustrations are of beautiful, old European gardens that exemplify this style and will inspire you to create your own homegrown version.

Flowering shrubs, popular perennials, scented plants, colorful annuals, and spring and summer bulbs are all here for you to discover. There are plants that look wonderful tumbling over walls or growing through shrubs, plants that make a bold statement standing out from the rest, and plants whose foliage will brighten a dull corner on a bleak winter day.

Here too are plants that are unusual or exotic and sometimes difficult to find. It is one thing to be a gardener and entirely another to be a plant collector, but most gardeners are interested in unusual plants and need to know how to keep these little gems happy.

Some of the plants that are included reflect my long fascination with cottage garden plants. These old-fashioned favorites are easy to grow and easy to propagate—often exactly the sort of plants that gardeners with small gardens are looking for. Other plants may at first glance appear to be unsuitable for a small area, but they feature because they can be trimmed and trained to look perfectly at home in a restricted space. Maybe they can earn their keep as focal points or be used to stunning effect in decorative pots and containers on the patio.

The variety and type of plants that can be grown in a restricted space is amazing. With a little help from *Plants for Small Spaces*, I hope you will be inspired to try many new things in those small places every garden has, whatever or wherever they may be.

Clive Lane

THE PLANTS IN THIS BOOK

Choosing plants for small spaces is not just a matter of buying whatever miniature plants you can find. Small spaces need clever design, and this will normally involve selecting plants of different types to give a good variety of shapes, textures... and sizes.

Generally speaking, the plants in this book are chosen either because they are compact, or adapt well to life in a confined area, or contribute something to the garden in more than one season, or act as a valuable accent in a planting scheme.

For a quick-reference guide to a season-by-season selection of some of the very best plants for small spaces, see 'Author's Choice: Top 20 Performance Plants' on page 186.

Availability

Many of the species mentioned are commonly grown, but others are rarer. Some are new cultivars and others are traditional British varieties, which, if you can find them, will give authenticity to your design. The following sources should help you on your way to your English-style garden:

Cistus Nursery, 22711 NW Gillihan Road, Sauvie Island, Oregon 97231, tel (503) 621-2233

Heronswood Nursery, 7530 NE 288th Street, Kingston, WA 98346, tel (360) 297-4172

Twombly Nursery, 162 Barn Hill Road, Monroe, CT 06468, tel (203) 261 2133

USDA HARDINESS ZONES

Most species described in this book will thrive in temperate areas (zone 7 and thereabouts) and the seasonal changes described apply to these areas. With the exception of annuals, zones are indicated next to each species name, and cultivars are suitable for the same zones unless otherwise stated. Remember that a plant's site can also affect its hardiness.

Zone	Avg. annual min. recorded temp.	Zone	Avg. annual min. recorded temp.
1	Below -50°F	7	0°F to 10°F
2	-50°F to -40°F	8	10°F to 20°F
3	-40°F to -30°F	9	20°F to 30°F
4	-30°F to -20°F	10	30°F to 40°F
5	-20°F to -10°F	11	Above 40°F
6	-10°F to 0°F		

To find your zone, see the USDA zone map on the back flap of this book.

SMALL-SPACE GARDENING

A small space is potentially the perfect garden. Intimate, unified, and undemanding, a compact area that is well planned offers opportunities and pleasures that larger gardens cannot. Everything is in close-up and subject to constant scrutiny. The need to avoid wasting space imposes its own constraints, but these can be an asset, not a limitation. The satisfaction of succeeding is immeasurable but, with the right information, and the right plants, not hard to achieve.

RIGHT: Harmonious planting in three dimensions

History of the small garden

All over the world and for centuries, man has created gardens, many of them in confined spaces. At first, enclosures tended to be small, simply because it was logistically impossible to make them otherwise; in the modern world it is a shortage of land, particularly in towns and cities, that ensures the predominance of small gardens.

A garden in the Japanese idiom—one of the classic design traditions.

The people who built early enclosures were more intent on security than on anything else, and since the only available materials were those they could source locally themselves, large enclosures were not feasible. These early "gardens" would have been little more than places in which to keep livestock or grow a few plants to feed them. Even within the castle walls of the more wealthy there was limited space for greenery.

However, while security was a prime reason for the creation of early enclosures, we know that, in China, gardens were being made solely for pleasure from around the fourth century B.C.; and Japanese gardening has a similarly ancient history. The ancient Egyptians and Greeks had ornamental gardens, too. As might be expected, these gardens reflected the conditions under which they were made. For example, ancient Egyptian gardens were re-creations of oases and always included water. They were not tiny, but were relatively small, and they were strongly influenced by the crop-growing traditions of the time, so plants were laid out in straight rows with paths between.

THE ORIENT AND THE ARAB WORLD

The creators of ancient Chinese and Japanese gardens sought to make them feel larger by using vistas and winding paths to make it impossible to view the entire garden from any one point. To blur the boundaries and express their reverence for nature, they linked the garden to the countryside beyond by making miniaturized landscapes complete with mountains, ravines, and waterfalls. The Chinese and Japanese are still masters at creating wonderfully peaceful, tiny gardens, and their design ideas have been emulated all over the world.

When the Moors invaded Spain in the eighth century, they brought with them many new ideas about gardens. In their own desert homelands, the practical need to have shade as well as good ventilation

Gardens like those of the Generalife and Alhambra in Granada, Spain, may be large and sumptuous, but they show the Moors' deep understanding of the use of the small spaces within them.

had led them to develop the "outdoor room," a courtyard surrounded by walls and usually filled with plants in pots. Water was always present in these rooms: like the Egyptians, the Arabs had a deep respect for this vital element. When they built gardens in Spain, such as those that still exist today in the Alhambra, they used this traditional layout but pierced the walls to provide views into the countryside. Unlike the harsh desert vistas that the Moors were used to, the scenery around cities such as Granada was beautiful, and the conquerors wanted to be able to look out on to the land they had won.

GREECE AND ITALY

The patio—such an important feature of modern small gardens—derives from the courtyard gardens of the Moors, but it was influenced by the gardens of ancient Greece. Like the Arabs, the Greeks created ways of extending the house into the surrounding garden through colonnaded passageways; the Romans adapted and used these designs in the building of their villas, taking them to northern Europe and Britain during the heyday of the Roman empire.

COTTAGE GARDENS

While British gardens have been influenced by trends from around the world, the English have also created their own unique small garden—the cottage garden. It emerged gradually, from around the ninth or tenth centuries, through the cultivation practices of the peasantry (which included the majority of the British population until the Industrial Revolution in the eighteenth century). These gardeners would have cultivated plants for food, but they would also have made use of any discarded plants from their employers' gardens, so a range of plants, from the exotic to the commonplace, would have been found growing side by side. Although the plants that are grown in cottage gardens have increased in number and variety, and the emphasis has shifted from the practical to the aesthetic, today's cottage gardens still have much in common with their more basic predecessors. Now, as

The English cottage-garden style has long been emulated all over the world. It remains a surprisingly useful source of pragmatic ideas on space-saving planting.

then, the aim is to include as many plants as possible in a very informal setting, with flowers and vegetables mingling and some plants choosing their own positions through self-seeding.

The cottage garden's longevity is perhaps explained by the fact that it was always the preserve of the poorer members of society. While other styles came and went among the fashion-conscious wealthy, farmers and other agricultural workers continued to garden for practical, rather than artistic, reasons; they could not afford to make changes for the sake of it, but gradually adopted new practices while retaining what was good about the old.

MONASTIC INFLUENCES

In Britain and northern Europe many of the first true gardens developed within the confines of the monasteries. Monks grew herbs for medicinal as well as culinary purposes; fruit and vegetables were cultivated for food, and flowers would have been useful for feeding bees. Early monastic plans show special areas dedicated to relaxation in the cloisters, and herb gardens with neat geometric beds intersected by pathways. Carthusian monks in particular were dedicated to gardening. They led solitary lives within individual cell-like rooms, each with a minute garden, which, it is believed, they were allowed to cultivate as they saw fit.

KNOT GARDENS

In Britain, during the reign of Queen Elizabeth I (1558–1603) gardening became more popular. The world had become safer and enclosing land was easier, so the gardens of the higher echelons of society became bigger. However, even then there was a tendency to divide gardens into small spaces, partly to create privacy

Early knot gardens were less intricately patterned than this, with flowers or herbs filling the spaces between the hedges.

and partly to maintain a sense of safety from the world outside. While Tudor gardens could extend to many acres, they were often intricate, to satisfy the period taste for detail. With their low, tightly clipped, interweaving hedges, knot gardens exemplified this, and such designs were embraced by garden makers all over the world.

The gardens of the general population, by contrast, were often more practical. In 1557 Thomas Tusser wrote *A Hundred Good Points of Husbandry*, which he addressed to the tenant farmer and his wife. In this we learn that small farmers had gardens that were quite distinct from the farmland, and that these were the wife's domain. These farmstead gardens might have contained flowers, but the emphasis was on productive plants.

GARDENING THE LANDSCAPE

Although European royal families and nobility had access to large parkland areas, it was not until the Renaissance in the fifteenth century that these were landscaped. In Italy, and later in France, the landscape was heavily manipulated in different ways according to local topography: multiple terraces were popular in Italy, while symmetrical woodlands and formal pathways and canals became widespread in France. These styles did not translate well into the English countryside; but elements were used and eventually gave rise to the development in the

eighteenth century of the English Landscape Movement, of which Lancelot "Capability" Brown is one of the best-known exponents.

It could be argued that, since this time, there have been two key types of garden: those that are arranged as open spaces, large or small, and those that are divided into parts. The latter is a more versatile approach because it can be adapted to fit the area available and it offers more possibilities to lovers of flowering plants.

BEDDING

American small gardens have their roots in colonial New England, where early gardeners fenced small areas around their homes to protect the plants from grazing animals. These gardens originally contained only useful plants, such as vegetables, fruits, and herbs, but later included ornamentals that could be used to decorate the home, both inside and out. The result was a charming, cottage-garden effect.

In Britain, the small garden space of today came about initially as a result of the Industrial Revolution. The need to house large numbers of employees near their place of work led to the development of row houses. These were built in many different sizes and styles, but most had a backyard, and some had a front area, too. The yards of the very modest row houses were perhaps intended for vegetable growing, but they also made it possible to explore the cultivation of ornamental plants. In both Europe and America, the grander ones were inhabited by well-off office workers and professionals, who filled their properties with fashionable bedding plants. Although these plants require work, as they must be replaced during the year, they were ideal for these gardens. The small space made it possible for the keen gardener to manage planting schemes that would be quite impractical on a large scale, and the plants themselves could be arranged precisely. Bedding was so popular and widespread that it has persisted in many gardens to this day. Municipal gardens, in particular, are bastions of traditional bedding. Here, flower beds are laid out in formal style like rugs decorating a green floor.

At the same time as the passion for bedding was at its height in Britain, some wealthier Victorians, tired of the dust and dirt of city life, began to show interest in the humble cottage garden, admiring it as the epitome of a simple idyllic life. Their enthusiasm boosted the slowly evolving cottage-garden style, although, for the average cottager, their interpretation of the joys of country living would have been somewhat fanciful.

A NEW NATURALISM

During the late nineteenth century in England, bedding plants began to fall from favor. This was the era of the plant hunter, and herbaceous perennials and shrubs from around the world arrived by the shipload. Through the efforts of nurserymen, many became widely available, but the years that gardeners had spent creating open parklands and then intricate bedding schemes had led to ignorance about growing these less showy plants in appropriate settings.

Seeking a new approach, William Robinson (1838–1935) began to experiment in using these new plants in naturalistic ways. His ideas were developed by Gertrude Jekyll (1843–1932), whose eye for detail and talent for combining plants and colors remains unsurpassed to the present day. This more natural approach to gardening was perpetuated by many subsequent home garden designers, who interpreted it in their own way.

Top right: A border inspired by the all-white garden at Sissinghurst in England.

Right: Contemporary urban design—Phil Jaffa's scheme for a London residential development, at the Chelsea Flower Show, London, 2004.

MODERN SMALL GARDENS

As space becomes increasingly precious, our gardens grow ever smaller, but that need not limit what we do with them. Today's designers, as well as those of the past, have widely differing approaches to these tiny spaces, and we can easily borrow and adapt ideas from them. With the ever-increasing shortage of land and its high cost, and the heavy demands that are made on our time nowadays, the small garden has to be the garden of the future.

Speaking botanically

Latin names, as opposed to common names, might seem complicated at first, but they are essential when it comes to accurate communication. A plant's common name may vary from one area to another. When it comes to using common names in a different country, the confusion is greater still, even when the same native tongue is used.

PLANT CLASSIFICATION

FAMILY In plant classification the flowering plants are divided into a number of families. Each of these families contains a number of genera that have similar characteristics. For example, the rose family Rosaceae includes not only the genus *Rosa* but also a number of other genera, such as *Amelanchier, Spiraea, Cotoneaster, Prunus,* and *Rubus*.

GENUS A botanical name consists of the genus and the species. The generic name (something like our surname), always starts with a capital letter and is a noun. It is often derived from names or terms found in an ancient language such as Greek, Latin, or Arabic. For example *Dicentra* is from the Greek *dis* (twice) and *kentron* (spur). Other generic names commemorate people, sometimes the person who first discovered the plant: *Kniphofia*, for example, is named after a German professor, Johann Kniphof; *Tradescantia* after John Tradescant and his son, gardeners to King Charles I of England.

SPECIES The specific name, or epithet, is more like our first name, except that it is written after the genus and always starts with a lower case letter. It cannot stand alone as a name and is not unique to that plant. As a Latin adjective, the specific name takes the gender of the generic name, so its ending agrees with the noun (although there are exceptions). The specific name is usually descriptive, telling us something about the plant.

Specific names fall into several categories, such as:

- **Describing origin:** by continent, country, region, for example *japonicus, -a,-um,* from Japan.

- **Describing habitat:** from mountains, woods, fields, water, e.g., *sylvestris, -e,* of woodland.

- **Describing the plant or a feature of the plant,** such as its size, habit, leaf shape, flower color, e.g., *fastigiatus, -a, -um,* erect growing, like a neat bundle of sticks.

- **Commemorating a botanist, plant collector, famous horticulturist, patron,** e.g., *davidii,* after 19th-century French plant collector Abbé Jean Pierre Armand David.

SUBSPECIES, VARIETAS, AND FORMA These are the botanically recognized subdivisions of a species

where distinct forms occur in the wild. These are variously known as subspecies (ssp.), varietas or variety (var.), and forma or form (f.). For example, *Euphorbia characias* ssp. *wulfenii.*

CULTIVAR A cultivar is a distinct form of a species that has been selected from wild or cultivated stock and has then been maintained in cultivation by vegetative propagation. In other words, all offspring come from one original plant or clone. The cultivar name is written with initial capital letters within single quotation marks, and follows the specific name. For example, *Astrantia major* 'Ruby Wedding'.

In gardening nomenclature, "cultivar" and "variety" are interchangeable. Often, too, "form" is used in a general way to refer to a variety, subspecies, or cultivar.

CLONE To all intents and purposes a clone is the same as a cultivar: a selection of single individuals maintained in cultivation by vegetative propagation. All offspring are identical to the original.

GROUP A group lies somewhere between a cultivar and the subdivision of a species. A cultivar shows little or no variation, having originated from one individual. Members of a group can show variation, but not enough to separate them botanically. So the *Viola riviniana* Purpurea Group includes forms of *Viola riviniana* with purple foliage that are not named as cultivars.

HYBRID Over the years, gardeners have interfered with nature by hybridizing species and, in some cases, genera. (Some hybrids have also occurred naturally where two compatible species grow together.) Where a hybrid has originated from a cross made between two  species, the new "hybrid epithet" is preceded by a multiplication sign. So *Osmanthus* × *burkwoodii* is a hybrid between *Osmanthus delavayi* and *Osmanthus decorus*. Where a hybrid's parents are unknown or very complicated, the genus name is followed by a name in single quotation marks, such as *Rosa* 'Albertine'.

In some cases, where two genera are closely related, it is possible to create a hybrid between them. In this case, the multiplication sign appears before the generic name. For example, × *Fatshedera lizei* is a hybrid between *Fatsia japonica* and *Hedera hibernica*.

NAME CHANGES

The naming of plants using botanical nomenclature is an ongoing process. As their knowledge increases, botanists find it necessary to make changes to nomenclature. It is important to remember that the numbers of plants introduced into cultivation in the last 200 years is vast, and it sometimes becomes apparent that plants which at first appeared similar are in fact sufficiently different to need separate classification. Hence name changes. Old

names, when they are well known, are often shown in parentheses after the new name, for example *Penstemon* 'Andenken an Friedrich Hahn' (*Penstemon* 'Garnet').

Two internationally accepted codes control all plant nomenclature. The botanical names (the generic and specific names) are covered by the International Code of Botanical Nomenclature. This is applied to wild and cultivated plants. The International Code of Nomenclature for Cultivated Plants covers the cultivar names and nomenclature, used in addition to the botanical name. This relates only to garden plants.

PLANT NAMES ARE FUN

Whether you are a natural linguist or not, botanical Latin is a satisfying language. Just as a feel for plants grows the more you work with them, so a feel for plant names develops over time. Not only are the names in a language that can be used anywhere in the world, they also provide immediately accessible information about the plant to which they refer. A few examples:

Specific epithet	Meaning	Example
compactus, -a, -um	compact, dense	*Deutzia compacta*
pumilus, -a, -um	dwarf	*Iris pumila*
humilis, -e	low-growing	*Chamaerops humilis*
micranthus, -a, -um	with small flowers	*Heuchera micrantha*
nanus, -a, -um	dwarf	*Betula nana*
minor	smaller	*Vinca minor*
minimus, -a, -um	smallest	*Ocimum minimum*

The fascinating subject of plant names and their meanings is fully explored in Horticulture's *Plant Names Explained*.

Making the most of your space

Some of the most wonderful gardens are created in the tiniest of spaces. Often it is the very smallness of the plot that stretches the imagination and impels the gardener to explore every possibility for maximizing every inch. But it is also true that lack of space limits choice, of both plants and hard landscaping—and in gardening, less really can be more.

BENEFITS AND PITFALLS

The wonderful thing about a small garden is that regardless of whether it is inherited and not to your liking, or new and a completely blank canvas, it need not take vast amounts of money or effort to make it suit your own taste and requirements. If you do splash out on expensive materials and choice plants, every item that is added to a small garden will work hard for its space and be worth the expenditure, whereas in a large plot all too frequently a costly expedition to the nursery does not result in much impact. However, from this it also follows that the plants in a small garden will be more clearly on show, so any mistakes will be more obvious.

ASSESSING YOUR GARDEN

If you are lucky, you will have a completely empty space to work with. It is much easier to create a garden from nothing than it is to battle with someone else's taste in hard landscaping or to work around the shapes and positions of their flower beds, patio, shed, and so on. Unfortunately, many of us have to do just this.

When you take on a garden it is tempting to begin planting right away, but before you do anything it is essential to make a thorough appraisal of the plot. The shape of your future garden depends on this stage, and it will save you time and heartache later. Take a long and dispassionate look at your space. Carefully consider its boundaries, any views—good or bad, the areas you like and do not like, and those that seem to melt into the background. Note any plants that you want to keep, even if they are in the wrong place at the moment. If you have inherited a garden there may be one or two mature shrubs or trees. Even if you don't like them, they give a sense of maturity to the garden and are worth retaining, at least until your own choices become established. Watch where the sun and shade are through the day and at different times of the year, and note the prevailing direction of the wind and rain. Dig down in various areas of the garden to discover what your soil is like (see pages 22–23).

Don't forget height, the all-important third dimension. Arbors, arches, and obelisks, as well as trees, can all take planting upward, making the garden feel more secluded and secure.

A seating area that feels like part of the house is a great asset, linking house and garden in a way that makes both feel more spacious. Here, a mixture of formal and informal planting helps to keep the area varied and attractive for the whole year.

PLANNING DECISIONS

First measure your garden, then take a pencil and paper and draw a plan of the space. This does not have to be a work of art, but it must be more or less to scale (perhaps 1:100), and it should include all the existing permanent features that you like or have to retain. Indicate the views and the sunny and shady areas. Next, make some photocopies. Now list all the things you want in your garden. Finally, try fitting them all into the space—this is where the copies come in handy. It is amazing how doing this will help you to crystallize your ideas. For example, you might want a garden shed but find that the only suitable site is where it will block your best view or where the evening sun shines on the garden. It is worth reassessing whether the shed is that important, or whether you could use the garage for storage instead.

A little imagination is all you need to create a bespoke pond or stream: water features need not be large, elaborate, or expensive.

THE SECRETS OF GARDEN DESIGN

Most of us know what we like in a garden, but we may not be sure why we like it. Gardens, like interiors, can be broken down into individual components, and doing this helps us understand how they work. Most of the key principles of garden design are self-explanatory and fairly obvious when you know what they are (see below). If you keep these principles in mind when you are making your decisions about plants, hard landscaping, and other features, you will increase your chances of producing a pleasing result.

PRIVATE SPACES

For the majority of us, the garden is the only outside accessible space that is private and our own. It is our chance to be able to breathe fresh air and be in touch

with nature in the way we choose, whether in the form of unstructured, untamed plants and rough, earthy paths or in the guise of chic, neat topiary and formal paving. The challenge in devising and planting a small garden is to make maximum use of the space while retaining a sense of privacy. Small gardens are often closely overlooked by neighboring properties, so this is important.

ALL WORK?

Think about how you are going to use the garden. The keen gardener will probably favor plants over man-made structures, but those who simply want to sit in a garden, and do a little weeding and deadheading when they are feeling energetic, will probably opt for fewer plants and

KEY DESIGN PRINCIPLES

- Unity—choose similar or matching materials and/or key plants to make a garden a self-contained whole rather than a collection of individual parts.

- Scale—ensure nothing is too big or too small in comparison to anything else.

- Balance—allow about two-thirds open space to one-third filled space.

- Perspective—things seem to get smaller and closer together the farther they are away from you. Use this to your advantage. For instance, put a relatively small statue at the far end of a short garden to make the garden seem longer.

- Light and shade—create areas of both, for three-dimensionality and interest.

- Texture and form—avoid monotony by making sure you have plants and structures that vary in texture and form, both contrasting and complementary.

- Color—make full use of color in plants and structures. Pale colors are calming, while bright ones are enlivening. Dark colors recede and light ones come to the foreground.

- Time—take account of the seasons so your garden looks good all year, and try to envisage it a few years from now when the plants are mature and the patio has aged. Allow space for plant expansion.

Gravel surfaces are always flattering to architectural planting, used here to create an effective focal point. The half-hidden terra-cotta urn completes a stylish, deliberately three-dimensional planting scheme, with imaginative use of color and contrasting plant forms.

THE FOUNDATIONS

Screens, shelters, boundaries, and views are the most important ingredients in a successful garden design. They are the backbone around which the rest of the garden can be created. In addition, all of them provide that essential element—height. Luckily for owners of small gardens, they are multipurpose, with a tallish boundary providing shelter and screening, or a carefully placed arbor or arch framing a view while also sheltering part of the garden.

In a small garden, the scale of these items is vital. Don't, for example, decide on a 30ft. (10m) pergola in a garden of the same length: all you will succeed in doing is dwarfing the space. Work out what size of pergola would look proportionally right. Aim for balance between your open space (patio, lawn, paths) and filled space (plants, structures, boundaries).

IN THE SPOTLIGHT

A small garden lends itself to artistic lighting, and for a relatively modest outlay, you can enjoy your garden well into the night, summer and winter. Think about lighting (and other electrical requirements) at the start as it will be easiest to install before you start planting. Light has a significant effect on the way we perceive space, so identify focal points (see page 19) that would benefit from the enlarging effect of spotlighting. Water can also be invaluable, not only for its light-reflecting qualities but for the soothing sound it makes when it is moving.

STYLE

Once you have a rough plan of what you want to do with your garden, the next step is to decide on a style that suits your taste. While style is reasonably definable, taste is more personal, and yours may well encompass several styles: perhaps cottagey at the front of the house, with roses round the door, but chic and practical in the backyard, with a patio and a barbecue. If you work all day in a stressful job, you may want a garden to be a serene and peaceful haven, but if you entertain a lot or you have young children, a more vibrant environment may be more suitable. Whatever your aim, be guided by the basic

more structures and hard landscaping. All gardens require work to begin with, but many—especially small ones—will eventually become as easy or as challenging to look after as their owner desires.

When it comes to paths, patios, and other hard landscaping, bear in mind that these are permanent features: even if they are not your key interest they need to be practical and goodlooking. When drawing up your borders, allow for access. It is almost guaranteed that a deep, fully stocked border will have the plants that need the most maintenance at the back; leave space for a narrow path and you will always be able to get in there.

A classic stone sundial makes a focal point amid a sea of drought-tolerant, Mediterranean-style plants. Taller perennials frame soft mounds and domes in harmonizing greens and golds.

CHOOSING A FOCAL POINT

Focal points give a sense of purpose and structure, attracting the eye then encouraging it to pause and linger. A focal point sited at the end of a garden's longest vista usually works well. If it is effective from more than one viewpoint, so much the better.

Lack of space means that a focal point in a small garden must work hard to earn its place. A small formal tree or topiary shrub, or a specimen plant in a striking container, makes an excellent focal point. However, dominant features in compact areas often have to be useful as well as attractive, in which case a garden seat, a pool, an arbor, or a summerhouse—built on a suitable scale—will do just as well.

Whatever your chosen object, plan its position carefully so that it appears to be an inherent part of the garden design rather than an afterthought. Resist the temptation to have too many focal points, otherwise the garden will look fussy and cluttered.

design principles (see page 16) when organizing the space, and then explore books, magazines, television programs, and other gardens for ideas and inspiration. Remember that ultimately the design of your garden must be right for your own particular needs, tastes, and lifestyle.

A SENSE OF PLACE

While the style you choose will reflect your personal taste, it is important to take account of the architecture and character of your home. Just as a traditional farmhouse kitchen with rustic tiles and wood floors would seem incongruous in a modern third-floor apartment, so sleek metal containers and a polished granite patio with bamboos and palm trees will look out of place in an old country garden. However, these ideas can be adapted so that they suit their environment without offending their owner's taste. For example, the sleek metal could be replaced with verdigris copper or rusting iron; the granite could be given up for stone, to match the country house, but with a few decorated or terra-cotta slabs included. By dispensing with the palm trees and blending the bamboo with other ornamental grasses and perhaps an elegant birch or maple, an attractive compromise is within your grasp.

THE ROLE OF PLANTS

Although some people might argue the case, generally it is agreed that gardens are about plants: hard landscaping is simply a frame for foliage and flowers. Plants therefore have a significant effect on the appearance of the garden and they play a crucial role in creating ambience. This is especially true in a small garden, where every inch counts. In a large garden, the eye is usually given a rest by swathes of lawn, and poor performers or favorite weaklings can be accommodated without detracting from the overall impression the garden makes. The small-scale

gardener does not have this luxury. However, if you choose carefully, you will find that the possibilities are endless: two or three trees, half-a-dozen shrubs, and a mixture of herbaceous perennials, bulbs, and bedding plants can reproduce a cottage garden, a tropical jungle, a wildlife haven, a modern room outside, or any other of the many variations there are on the basic garden theme.

The other thing to bear in mind is that you may have to exclude some favorite plants in order to accommodate others that will provide year-round structure and interest, which is essential in a small garden. For example, ever-greens (see pages 40–49) are needed if the garden is not to appear desolate in winter. There are plenty of beautiful evergreens that will do the job, and most have other assets as well as permanent leaf cover, so you should be able to find some that will make your compromise worthwhile.

Traditional or contemporary, formal or informal: choose your plants and plan your planting scheme to reflect the style you are aiming for.

Obscuring parts of a garden so that you can never view it all at once is an established way of increasing the sense of space. But you can go further by playing specific visual tricks. One of the oldest methods of doing this is *trompe l'oeil*, which deceives the eye into seeing more than there is. It is particularly effective in a small courtyard where walls can be painted with country scenes that recede into the distance, or hung with mirrors whose reflections give the illusion of gardens beyond. However, birds have a habit of flying into mirrors, so they should be placed where the flight path is relatively short. Growing leafy climbers beside and across them will also limit problems.

Clever use of perspective also helps to maximize the feeling of space. For example, if a winding path is made narrower as it reaches the end of the garden, it will make the distance that the path covers appear greater than it is. Dividing the area into several compartments using trellis with latticework of progressively smaller size the further the panels are from the house will have a similar effect.

Climbers, shrubs, and perennials work at different levels here to provide screening and give good ground cover.

MULTILAYERING

The value of multilayering cannot be overestimated in a small garden where space is so precious. Imagine sitting out on a patio on a sunny day, the paving stones hot and bright; now imagine a vine-entwined arbor to one side, hiding you from the house next door, and a clematis-clad arch to the other, inviting you to get up and walk through it to admire the plants that furnish the far reaches of your garden. Quite apart from the sense of security and seclusion such structures provide, they maximize the number of plants you can grow because they make use of more than one level.

Increase the layered effect with window boxes and hanging baskets (these can be secured to walls and fences, as well as hung from arbors and arches), and consider constructing raised beds. All are particularly useful close to the house, perhaps on or around the patio, because they bring the plants nearer your eyes and nose. Raised beds should contain a few "anchor"

Hortus Conclusus, which won a Gold Medal for its designer Christopher Bradley-Hole at the Chelsea Flower Show 2004. Sophisticated but simple, the garden was full of innovative ideas for a sleek, contemporary look.

SPACE-SAVING PLANTING

The planting space in a small flower border can be effectively doubled or trebled by "layered" planting through the seasons. This offers the double advantages of saving space and extending the season of interest.

Plant daffodils, tulips, and other spring bulbs beneath mat-forming herbaceous perennials such as *Alchemilla mollis* (zone 4–7) or hardy geraniums, which will flower in early summer. Summer annuals such as poppies, pansies, celosia, and cosmos can follow as these fade. After the bulbs have finished flowering, the other plants will hide their unsightly dying foliage. Later still, plants with interesting, long-lasting seed heads could take center stage.

The space beneath deciduous shrubs is ideal for spring woodland flowers such as primulas, violas, and pulmonarias, which can bloom in the sunshine before the shrub comes into leaf but will appreciate both the shade cast by the shrub's leaves in summer and the protective blanket of the fallen leaves in winter.

Some climbers (such as less vigorous varieties of clematis) will happily scramble up through the branches of deciduous spring-flowering shrubs, giving them a second season of interest after their own blooms have faded. Clematis grown in this way will have their own ready-made support and will appreciate the shade that their host casts on their roots.

Remember to feed, mulch, and water adequately where several plants are growing close together in this way.

plants that stay in place all year round (evergreens will make the most impact), but otherwise these contained planters are best regarded as seasonal. With careful planning, it is relatively easy and inexpensive to have successional color—you could even change the palette each time. If the plants that you are removing are long-lived and have proved their worth, find them some space in the main garden where they can recuperate and perform again next year.

CLEVER DISGUISE

If you have a clear view of an unattractive feature, such as a telephone pole, just outside your property, it is often a reasonably easy matter to hide it, or at least distract attention from it. Perhaps you could do this with a well-positioned tree somewhere in the foreground. Alternatively, place an attractive feature, such as an arch, between your house (or main viewpoint) and the pole. Use the arch as a support for a choice climber or two, perhaps a clematis (pages 76–77) and a climbing rose (pages 80–81) for a traditional cottage-garden effect. In a very short space of time you will find that your eye is drawn more to the arch than it is to the pole. Further careful planting will add to the distraction until you no longer notice the pole at all.

Practicalities

One of the advantages of a small garden is that it is possible to carry out all essential maintenance, such as weeding, deadheading, pruning, and feeding, in just a few hours each week, leaving you with enough time simply to enjoy the space or plan alterations and improvements. To ensure that your garden is easy to look after, it is wise to take a few precautions and make some practical arrangements at the outset.

SOIL OR SPOIL?

Get to know your soil. It will be your plants' prime carer, so time spent nurturing it will pay dividends. Even in a small area there can be dry places and very damp places. Find these by digging down during dry weather, then again after a rain shower. Where drainage is very poor, consider putting in land drains or planting moisture-loving or bog plants.

Buy a simple soil tester from your garden store and establish whether you have acid, neutral, or alkaline soil. The acidity, or alkalinity, of soil is known as its pH and is measured on a scale of 1 to 14—1 is very acidic, 7 is neutral, and 14 is very alkaline. Although many plants are happy in a variety of soils, some—camellias and rhododendrons, for example—do not tolerate alkaline conditions. Choose plants that suit your soil, rather than attempt to adapt it, unless you plan to grow the plants in containers or perhaps a raised bed filled with suitable soil.

Improve the soil generally by digging in humus-rich material, whether in the form of well-rotted manure, spent mushroom compost, or garden compost. For most plants, it is difficult to overdo soil improvement. Do it at least twice a year, if possible, by applying a layer of mulch (see page 31)—and locally whenever you plant something new.

If your soil could more accurately be described as builder's rubble (a common problem with newly built houses), it may be worth removing the top 12in. (30cm) or so where you want to make flower beds, replacing it with a mixture of bought topsoil and

KNOW YOUR SOIL

There are three main types of soil: sandy, clay, and loam. They usually occur in combination, so you might have sandy loam or clay loam. Soil type affects plant growing conditions.

- **SANDY** Light, gritty, allows water to drain very rapidly, which removes nutrients as well; tends to be dry and very hot in summer. Easy to dig and quick to warm up in spring. To improve sandy soil, dig in well-rotted compost or manure; this increases moisture retention. Mulch with a 2–3in. (5–7cm) layer of well-decayed compost in spring to prevent moisture evaporating, replenish nutrients, and keep the soil cool.

- **CLAY** Heavy and sticky when wet, hard when dry, easily waterlogged, usually rich in nutrients. Generally cold, slow to warm up in spring and hard to dig. Add organic matter or coarse compost to improve the passage of water and air. Liming helps the soil particles to bind together, forming larger air spaces; do not fertilize for at least one month before liming and for three months afterward.

- **LOAM** The ideal soil, a balanced mixture of sandy and clay soils, easy to dig throughout the year, warms up early in spring but is slow to cool down in fall, retains moisture and nutrients. It feels almost velvety to the touch. Loam varies and is often classified as light, medium, or heavy, depending on the ratio of clay to sand. Well-decayed compost or manure is a useful addition to increase fertility levels and moisture-retentive properties.

Almost any experienced gardener will confirm that organic matter is the key to a good soil, improving texture, retaining moisture, and feeding the plants. Spread compost or manure, which must always be well rotted, as a mulch (left) or work it into the soil (right).

organic matter. Alternatively, build up a collection of containers. These are valuable design features in their own right and also offer the opportunity to grow plants that are outside the range of your soil's pH, so that you can grow camellias, for instance, even if you have alkaline soil. Use rain-water for watering as tap water will gradually change the soil back to its natural pH.

WATERING FACILITIES

A conveniently sited water butt saves both water and work, and can easily be screened (left). If you have a lot of pots, an automatic watering system (right) may prove to be a worthwhile investment.

Something that is best considered early in the process of creating a garden is the provision of watering facilities. A space full of plants, even a small one, takes some watering in summer—and it is rarely practical to rely on the kitchen faucet. Consider having at least one rainwater tank, perhaps to collect water from a shed roof, and think about installing soaker hoses when you make

your flower beds. Perforated with tiny holes, these hoses deliver water just where it is needed—around the roots of the plants. If you are planning to have a number of containers, think about automatic waterers for these, too.

BOUNDARIES, PATHS, AND PATIOS

Whether the boundaries you inherit or plan are walls, fences, or hedges, do ensure they are attractive and secure before you start to train climbers over them or plant up flower beds in front—by then, it will be too late to make any repairs or other alterations. Outdoor paints are available in a wide range of colors, and it is worthwhile considering whether these would enhance your garden plans. New timber, whether natural or tanalized (pressure-treated), is easily painted. This will also increase its longevity. Take time to fix wires and trellis securely in place so that you don't have to do it later, when this will involve a fight with your plants.

Even in a small garden a hedge can be an excellent way of dividing an outdoor space as well as enclosing it.

Not so long ago, color in the garden meant only plants. Now, outdoor paints offer a whole spectrum of instant color, whether bold or, as here, subtle and subdued.

Some hedging plants are good for attracting wildlife, such as birds and butterflies. However, hedges do require space—often more than you think—and must be kept within their bounds in a small plot. Be sure to consider maintenance and what you will do with the trimmings. Take time at the outset to select hedging material that is suitable for a small space (see pages 37 and 38). A carefully planned and maintained hedge will be an asset for many years.

Be prepared to spend money on your paths, patios, and driveways. Hard landscaping, too, is going to be in place for a long time, so invest in a design you really like. Also bear in mind that the cost of putting the material down is more or less the same whether the material is expensive or cheap. Be sure the contractor knows exactly what you want (it is a good idea to outline the work involved on paper and base the contractors' estimates on that). Be prepared to keep a contingency fund to pay for small alterations as the work progresses, if you feel these are necessary. During construction, if you don't like the way something has been done, say so; after all, it is you who are going to be living with it. A good builder will be prepared to make adjustments. Before beginning any

Evergreens—such as ivy trained on a trellis—are an effective and simple way to create a living screen without eating up precious ground space.

LAWNLESS GARDENS

Most gardeners like to have a certain amount of open space in the garden. This complements the planted areas, providing a horizontal plane to their vertical one, quite apart from providing access to the plants and giving you somewhere to sit and enjoy the garden. In addition to the patio, the other traditional open space in a garden is the lawn. Before you opt for one (or decide to retain an existing one) be realistic: to look good, lawns require excellent drainage, full sun, regular mowing, and frequent feeding, raking, aerating, weeding, edging, trimming, and watering. Remember that in small urban gardens, which may be overshadowed by buildings or trees, all too often lawns do not do well. Now consider the alternatives— gravel, paving, decking, rubber matting (for play areas), and so on. If they are properly installed, the maintenance they require is minimal, perhaps an occasional sweep or a quick run around with an outdoor vacuum. And, with careful planning—for example, omitting a few paving stones—you can plant them with feature specimens or small groups of plants. In gravel, you can even allow self-seeding.

correction

major construction, find out where services such as water, gas, and electricity lines are to avoid damaging these and check local building regulations.

CATERING FOR PLANTS

If you are making new borders, or altering existing ones, mark them out on the ground at an early stage in your plans (remember to allow for maintenance access). Remove sod if necessary and turn them over to at least the depth of your fork, deeper if possible, removing weeds and improving the soil.

Containers are always invaluable, whatever the size of your garden. Their main drawbacks are that they need frequent watering and occasional feeding, and their occupants may eventually outgrow them. However, they also have many advantages over borders: they can be moved into and out of sight as the plants they hold come into flower and go over; they can be filled with a potting medium that exactly suits the plants; they need less weeding than borders; they can be

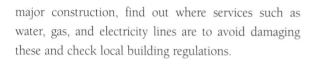
Match the vigor of climbers to their support. Late-flowering clematis (left) need annual hard pruning, which helps control their size, while spring-flowering *Clematis montana* (right, trained through *Rosa* 'Nevada' and into a tree) is best kept for places where it can ramble unchecked.

placed on patios and in difficult areas where plants may not grow, such as dry shade under large trees; they bring the plants nearer eye and nose height; and they can be attractive in themselves.

GROWING UP

Vertical interest is vital in any garden and especially a small one (see also page 72). There is no need to limit climbing plants to fences and walls: make use of the house, garage, and shed, perhaps a summerhouse or greenhouse, arbors, arches, gazebos, and obelisks. The list is endless, and all should be considered. There are many types of dedicated frame for climbing plants on the market. These are usually made from wood or metal and come in a wide range of styles. In addition, wooden self-assembly garden buildings are reasonably easy and quick to construct.

Buying your plants

There are three main aspects to owning plants: deciding which ones to buy, picking healthy specimens, and then looking after them properly so that they do well and give you pleasure. Although none of this is difficult, you can improve your chances of success by arming yourself with a few important pieces of information.

MAKING A LIST

All gardening books and gardeners will tell you the same thing: "Don't go to the garden store without a list of what you want to buy." This is excellent advice, but none of us follow it—we are all prone to impulse buys. However, when you first start to plant a garden, or part of one, you should compile a list of key inhabitants. Make a simple plan of your garden and draw rough outline shapes in the borders to show individual specimens and groups of plants. Think about trees and shrubs first. In small areas you may have space for only one tree and a few key shrubs, but this makes it doubly important that you choose wisely. Remember to include evergreens, for year-round interest. Choosing the right plant for each spot takes time, so make full use of this book for inspiration.

HAPPY TENANTS

When making your list, take into account a plant's preferred growing conditions. Although some plants will grow almost anywhere, most have strong preferences as to

A good garden center is one of the best places to see and compare a wide range of plants before you buy.

When choosing new plants, try to bear in mind how they will look with their neighbors. Consider potential color harmonies, seasonal partnerships, and effective contrasts in shape and growth habit.

light and moisture. Generally plants that flower relish sunny sites with moist, well-drained soil, but some do not object if they have sun for only part of the day. And many other plants thrive in shade. Their flowers, even if they are not the showiest, are welcome for the brightness they bring to a quiet corner. Nor are flowers essential. Ferns, for example, have beautiful foliage in a range of colors and they love shade. Among suggestions for a wide range of conditions, this book has many ideas for dark corners.

IS IT WARM ENOUGH?

Before you buy a plant, be sure to determine whether it will survive in the climate in your garden. The USDA hardiness zone information is normally a safe indicator of whether a plant is a good choice for your garden. With the exception of plants normally grown as annuals, zone information for the plants in this book is provided next to each species name. Cultivars are suitable for the same zones unless otherwise stated. To find your zone, see the map on the back flap of this book. Plants that are half-hardy and tender in your zone will usually thrive outside through the warmer months but either die when the weather gets cooler or survive the cold only if they are given protection, such as heavy mulching, or are dug up and stored under cover. If you really like a plant, give it the best protection you can and see what happens.

INVASIVE SPECIES

Many useful plants become invasive pests in favorable conditions. Examples in this book include *Anthriscus sylvestris*, *Fallopia baldschuanica*, *Glechoma hederacea*, *Hedera hibernica*, *Lupinus arboreus*, *Pseudosasa japonica*, *Rosa rubiginosa*, and *Sinarundinaria murielae*. Be aware of the invasive plants in your state (see the APWG website at www. nps.gov/plants/alien), and try an alternative.

27

BUYING CONTAINER-GROWN PLANTS

When you buy a plant, make sure it is healthy. The leaves and branches should be a good color and shape, not discolored or distorted (unless the plant variety dictates

this). There should be a good collection of roots, with not much loose potting mixture (as seen left), but the plant should not be potbound (this means no potting mixture is visible and the roots wind tightly around each other).

GARDEN SUPERSTORES

The majority of plants are bought at garden superstores. These places are the department stores of the gardening world, stocking everything from plants, seeds, and potting mixture to tools and garden furniture. The great advantage of buying at a garden superstore is that you can see the plants in leaf and in flower, season by season.

What size should I buy? A larger shrub makes an instant impact, while a smaller specimen is cheaper and establishes more quickly but requires patience. They will probably be the same size after a few years.

For plants that are not in flower or leaf, illustrated labels give a very good idea of what they are like, and there are usually knowledgeable staff on hand to answer your questions. For the less decisive among us, garden superstores also offer the chance to wander up and down the aisles trying out different combinations of plants, before making a purchase. They provide a simple way of choosing quality plants at competitive prices.

SUBSTITUTES

It may be that you have a specific plant in mind when you head for the garden superstore—one you have read about, perhaps—but you should always be prepared to consider a close substitute. By insisting on the exact variety you set out to buy, you may end up turning down a better plant. For example, *Spiraea japonica* 'Goldflame' may have been recommended to you by someone who is not aware that 'Goldflame' has now been superseded by *Spiraea japonica* 'Firelight', a superior variety whose colorful foliage does not revert to plain green.

Spiraea japonica 'Firelight'

SPECIALTY NURSERIES

Once you are captivated by gardening, you may want to investigate the possibilities offered by specialty nurseries. These are usually run by enthusiasts for enthusiasts, and they often specialize in a particular plant type: alpines, country garden favorites, old roses, exotics, and so on. As specialty sellers are often small and family-run, they may have limited opening hours, so it is wise to telephone ahead to obtain directions and to make sure the nursery will be open when you arrive.

One of the best ways to find out about nurseries near you is to look in regional source books or magazines. Searching online for plants on the internet is another good way of locating sources of information on specialty nurseries.

MAIL ORDER

Using mail order is another way of purchasing plants, bulbs, and seeds. You can buy even fairly mature trees by mail. The drawback is that you cannot see the plants before you buy them. Nevertheless, you can usually rely on established mail-order nurseries to supply good-quality stock.

SOCIETIES AND OPEN GARDENS

Many gardeners find plant sales are an irresistible draw. Interesting cuttings, divisions, or seed-raised plants, often from specimens found in the garden, may be on offer at bargain prices.

Several of the larger gardening societies have annual plant sales that are open to the general public. Like the specialty nurseries, these sales offer the valuable chance to acquire the rare and unusual. Some societies also publish seed lists from which you can make purchases of hard-to-find specimens very cheaply.

Private gardens large and small, open to the public for charity, are a wonderful source of ideas and inspiration, and sometimes of treasures on the plant stall too.

LONGEVITY

Plants have different natural life expectancies, and this often affects the growing conditions they prefer.

• **Annuals** complete their entire life cycle (that is, grow from seed, flower, and die) in a single growing season. The term is also loosely used to refer to many tender perennials and some hardy plants that grow from seed and flower in a single season. Although there are exceptions, most annuals prefer a sunny spot in well-drained soil. In fertile soil they will produce lush foliage but few flowers.

• **Biennials** usually flower in the second growing season after their seed has been sown. After the second year, some biennials die and self-seed, while others hang on for another season, or even longer. Most biennials enjoy the same growing conditions as annuals.

• **Perennials** are any plants that live longer than two years. However, the term is usually used for more or less nonwoody long-lived plants. They enjoy a wide range of growing conditions: rich soil, dry soil, damp soil, poor soil, full sun, deep shade, partial shade, dappled shade—there is a perennial for every spot. Herbaceous perennials die down in winter but regrow the following year.

• **Shrubs and trees** are woody perennials, although rarely described as such, and are either deciduous or evergreen. Unlike herbaceous perennials, they do not die back each winter but build on one season's growth in the following year. There is a tree or shrub for almost any situation you can imagine.

29

Maintaining your plants

Most plants are easy to look after, but there are a few pitfalls that should be avoided and some basic cultivation techniques that are useful to know. Once you get your plants home, make sure you give them what they need. They will reward you by performing to the best of their capabilities.

PLANTING

Before planting, prepare the area well (see pages 22–23) and give the plant a thorough soak in its pot for a few hours. Dig a roomy hole and break up the soil at the bottom, mixing plenty of well-rotted organic matter such as compost into the surrounding soil. Most plants, except annuals, will also benefit from a handful or two of slow-acting fertilizer mixed in at this point.

Place the plant in the hole, normally at a level where the garden soil, when firmed, just covers the top of the

potting medium in the root ball. Firm the soil well with your foot, working in toward the root ball, to provide stability and eliminate air pockets around the roots. Water in adequately to settle the soil. All plants need time to get their feet into the soil, so give them plenty of water and keep their surroundings free of weeds until they have settled in. The soil near walls and fences can be very dry, so plant 12in. (30cm) away and be prepared to water frequently. With trees, climbers, tall perennials, and some annuals, you also need to provide support.

Always make the planting hole just a little bigger than you think is necessary.

Break up the soil at the bottom of the hole and mix in some well-rotted compost.

Place the plant carefully, with the top of the potting mixture just below the soil surface.

Settle the soil firmly around the root ball, ensuring there are no air pockets.

Tread the plant in gently with your foot to ensure it is in good contact with the soil.

Check the plant is straight, firm, and at the right level, and water it in.

FEEDING

As well as mulching with garden compost (see below), it is often beneficial to apply a general-purpose fertilizer over your whole garden in spring and once or twice through the growing season. Check the requirements of individual plants before treating all in the same way, however, as feeding is something of a balancing act; clematis, for example, are well known for their hunger so need regular meals, while many herbs, silver-leaved shrubs, and annuals grow better if they are hungry.

MULCHING

Mulching flower beds and containers is well worth the effort. This involves adding a layer of gravel, bark, compost, or other material over the soil to prevent moisture evaporating and weeds growing; in the case of the compost, it also improves the soil. Mulches can produce a sense of visual unity, especially valuable while your plants are becoming established. Choose your mulch to suit the style of your garden. For a natural look, bark is very effective. Remember, however, that bark rots down, and while this is happening it will rob nutrients from the soil, although eventually it will improve overall fertility. Gravel is excellent for a contemporary effect and lasts

TYING AND STAKING

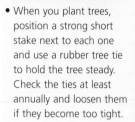

- Young trees, tall plants such as delphiniums and many dahlias, and most climbers need to be staked or fixed to supports. If you neglect this, you may find your precious plants drooping and broken if there is a spell of wet, windy weather.

- When you plant trees, position a strong short stake next to each one and use a rubber tree tie to hold the tree steady. Check the ties at least annually and loosen them if they become too tight.

- Tie in climbers as they grow: do this regularly and it is an easy, therapeutic job; leave it for too long and coping with the enmeshed stems of plants such as clematis will be very hard work.

- With herbaceous plants it is always more satisfactory to provide support before the plant starts to grow rather than after staking

has become necessary. Position grow-through supports or use bamboo canes and horticultural wire or twine, tying the plants in as necessary. Remember to allow room for increasing girth, if appropriate.

WATERING—SOME FACTS

- Sufficient water is essential for healthy plant growth.

- Too much water can kill plants by suffocating their roots; this is more likely to happen if they are in containers without good drainage or in continuously damp soil (unless they are bog plants).

- Plants need minimal water during their dormant period—usually winter.

- During dry weather, or with containers, it is better to water before plants start to wilt.

- Hanging baskets and other summer bedding containers may need watering more than once a day, even if it rains.

- Always "deep-water" plants so that moisture gets right down to the roots. A quick spray will only wet the soil surface and will not reach the roots.

much longer than bark. If you buy it in bulk, it is relatively inexpensive. Horticultural fabric can be laid under loose mulches and is excellent for reducing the growth of perennial weeds. It can be tricky to plant through, however, so do all your major planting before you add the decorative mulch on top—it is irritating to plant through mulches that are lighter in color than the earth, such as gravel, as some soil inevitably ends up on top.

WEEDING

Weeds compete with your ornamental plants for sunlight, nutrients, water, and space for growth. They may also attract pests and diseases. You do not have any space in a small garden for such trespassers, so eradicate them, along with their roots, as soon as possible. Do not let them flower and go to seed, or they'll soon be back in even greater numbers. The best approach is to dig them up, roots and all. Most gardeners would agree that weeding is a rewarding job, and it does get easier every year as the weeds reduce in numbers.

PRUNING

Pruning of woody plants is usually carried out to keep them in check, make them look tidy, remove dead branches, or improve flower or fruit production. However, it is not essential to prune. If you are going to prune, it's best to do so regularly, from an early stage in the plant's life, and immediately after flowering—unless,

Cutting back a buddleia in early spring. Your best friends when pruning are sharp pruners, a keen eye, and a grasp of the principles involved.

of course, you are growing the plant for fruit. Take your time, and always make your cuts just above healthy buds as this will ensure that the stem stays alive, discouraging disease from entering via the cut. Nevertheless, most plants are very forgiving; roses, for example, have been shown to respond just as well to brutal chainsawing as to careful removal of individual stems.

PESTS AND DISEASES

Healthy, well-grown plants usually shrug off disease and can cope with the occasional aphid infestation. Although, in small areas, it is tempting to use pesticides, it is better to encourage and maintain a population of natural predators, such as ladybugs, ground beetles, wasps, and honey bees, who will do the work for you. Ladybugs have an enormous appetite for aphids, while

ground beetles love slugs and snails. Many natural predators are also extremely efficient at pollinating flowers. Their diet is not confined to insects; in fact, many have periods in their life cycle when they require nectar and pollen, so try to have a succession of suitable flowers in the garden from early spring to fall, to provide them with food. Ants may prevent predators from controlling aphids, so keeping them in check should be a high priority.

DEADHEADING

Deadheading is a relaxing task for the evening, as you wander around enjoying your garden. It involves removing the old flowers from plants, particularly annuals, but also roses and many perennials. As well as keeping the plant looking good, if it is done on a regular basis it encourages more flowers to be produced. Sometimes the "head" doesn't even need to be "dead"—sweet peas, for example, should have most, if not all, of their blooms cut on a more or less daily basis, otherwise they quickly go to seed and stop flowering. Use this time as an opportunity to check on the health of your plants, too.

GETTING MORE PLANTS

Propagating is often quite straightforward and is an easy and very satisfying way to get more plants from those in your garden or that of a friend.

Seeds harvested fresh often germinate well, eventually proving a cheap and convenient source of plants either to fill gaps in your own borders or to give away. Above, the annual love-in-a-mist (*Nigella*).

Many plants can be raised from seed. Annuals are easily grown in this way; perennials, shrubs, and trees will obviously take longer to produce plants that are big enough to make an impact in the garden. Cultivars, hybrids, and doubles do not come true from seeds and must be propagated by division, or cuttings.

The simplest way of propagating many herbaceous perennials is to break a large clump up into smaller ones. Dig the clump up in fall or spring, then remove the stronger, younger outside sections, either by pulling them apart or by cutting them away with a sharp knife;

Dividing perennials—here primulas (left) and astilbes (right)—may look brutal, but it benefits the plants as well as increasing your stock. Replant some of the best pieces after improving the soil.

make sure there are a few roots on them. In the case of tough roots, like those of hostas, it is easier to use an old bread knife to saw them into pieces. Most herbaceous perennials respond well to this treatment and actually benefit from being divided every three to five years.

During the summer some shrubs and perennials, such as penstemons, can be propagated by taking soft-wood cuttings. Look for soft shoot tips that have grown in the current year and cut them off about 3in. (7cm) long. Trim them below a leaf joint and remove the lower

Taking penstemon cuttings in summer. Kept shaded and watered, many softwood cuttings will root in a satisfyingly short time while the weather is still warm.

leaves with a sharp knife. Generally it is sufficient to leave two leaves. Dip the cuttings into a hormone rooting powder (this enables the cut surfaces to form roots rapidly), and pot them up, watering in with a fungicide solution. Cover the cuttings with a very thin, clear plastic sheet, secured with a rubber band, then put the pots in a sheltered, shady position or cold frame. They should have formed roots in six to ten weeks.

Tender perennials such as argyranthemums and geraniums (pelargoniums) are propagated in the same way, except that the cuttings are usually taken in late summer and there is no need to cover them with plastic. Just place them on a shady window sill, out of direct sunlight. Even if you think you don't need more plants, this is a good way of ensuring that you have replacements, should any not survive until next year.

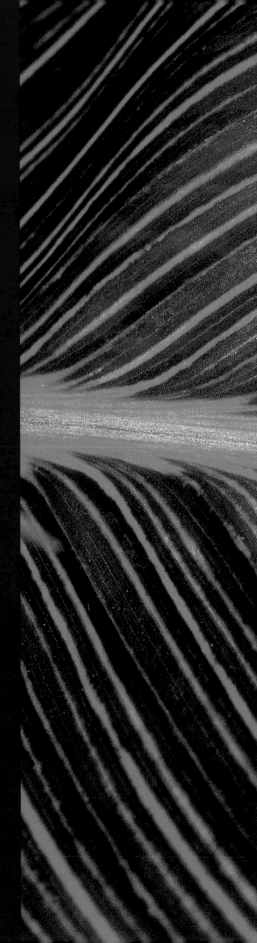

STRUCTURE AND FOLIAGE

Structural planting and clever use of foliage are among the key things to get right when organizing any outdoor space, but they are all the more critical when that space is not large. A well-planned framework will carry a garden through the whole year, providing a reassuring backdrop to the shifting seasonal displays as well as taking center stage during winter.

RIGHT: *Canna* 'Tropicanna'

Trimmed and trained

The craft of clipping plants to shape them into useful or ornamental garden features of our own choosing goes back a very long way. Today, topiary still has its place in almost every kind of garden, whether you want to create a formal focal point or hedge, a living archway, a space-saving fruit tree, or a witty piece of sculpture to enliven an outdoor space.

Simple topiary shapes are the most effective in a small space, pulling a design together, acting as focal points, and giving the garden valuable "green architecture" throughout the year.

simple geometric forms. With clever design, these can visually link buildings to the greenery around them, bringing house and garden into close harmony. Pyramids, cubes, or spheres of clipped greenery can be used singly as focal points, in pairs to define an entrance, or in a double or single row to frame a view or lead the eye in a particular direction. Their smooth, uncomplicated surfaces make an excellent foil to the bright, exuberant planting of summer. In winter, they will change the mood of the garden entirely, looking pleasingly formal when thrown into contrast by low winter sunshine and magical when covered in frost or snow.

Container-grown plants that have already been shaped for topiary are

The Romans enjoyed sculpting shrubs into geometric shapes or imaginative ornaments, and practiced the art of topiary in the gardens of the villas they built in Britain. The Roman *toparius*, or topiarist, worked with **laurel** and **box**, but perhaps not with **English yew**, the plant acknowledged to be one of the best for the job. Pliny the Elder, writing in the first century A.D., described cypress topiary representing fleets of ships and elaborate scenes of hunting expeditions.

Leafing through books or magazine articles on topiary will confirm that there is no limit to what can be sculpted from evergreens. Topiarists through the ages have enlivened their gardens and amused passersby with their eccentric art, from a fanciful teapot to a group of huntsmen, and from a snail to a full-size steam locomotive. In Britain, the cottage garden has always been the traditional place for this kind of topiary.

A more contemporary application of topiary in small spaces is to sculpt neat,

LEVENS HALL

With more than 100 fanciful sculptures in yew and box, the world-famous topiary garden at Levens Hall in Cumbria, England, originally laid out in the late 1600s, may be on a very grand scale, but it is full of inspiration for how to use topiary and what to plant with it.

OTHER EVERGREENS FOR TOPIARY OR HEDGING *Berberis darwinii* • *Ilex crenata* 'Golden Gem' •

widely available in garden centers. Because of the time factor, they are more expensive than other plants, but the results are instant. Alternatively, you may wish to create your own topiary. Purpose-made wire or plastic frames can be purchased to use as a base for standard topiary shapes. Or, with a piece of chicken wire and a little imagination, you can create an entirely original work of art in box or yew.

The ultimate compact fruit trees, "stepovers" can be used to edge borders and paths. Being horizontal, the wood ripens well in the sun, generally resulting in surprisingly abundant crops.

TRAINING STANDARDS

The "standard"—a vegetable lollipop—has long been a familiar garden feature, fashionable at different times for roses, fuchsias, wisteria, bay trees, box (below), lemons, and many other plants. Standards are in some ways ideal for small areas, freeing precious planting space at ground level and introducing height to a planting scheme without adding too much bulk. As with topiary, it is costly to buy ready-trained standards, but with a little patience you can train your own.

Choose a young plant with a straight central stem and tie this to a straight supporting cane. Pinch back the side shoots to keep them small as the main stem grows; when it reaches the required height, pinch out the growing point. The top will bush out; keep pinching back the new shoots to keep this bushy. Lastly, remove the side shoots from the main stem. Once they are established, standards require only occasional maintenance pruning.

TRAINING TREES

Other traditional pruning forms useful for plants in small spaces include the training of trees into cordons, espaliers, and fans. A useful introduction is the "stepover"—a knee-high tree trained horizontally, ideal for edging a kitchen-garden bed. Commonly used for fruit trees, especially **apples** and **pears**, all these pruning and training techniques create a two-dimensional plant trained against a wall or tied to a purpose-built, freestanding wire support. Plants trained in this way can be an aesthetic addition to a garden, but they also have a practical use. Branches that have been trained horizontally against a wall or fence take up a fraction of the space needed for a full-size tree. Increased exposure to sunshine and warmth mean that the trees generally tend to flower and fruit more freely, and the fruit is earlier to ripen and easier to harvest.

The techniques involved, explained in any good book on pruning, can be applied successfully to a great variety of ornamental garden plants including **pyracantha, chaenomeles, camellias,** and **climbing** or **pillar roses.**

HEDGES FOR SMALL GARDENS

Hedges tend to take up valuable space, especially as they age. However, a well-made hedge, either on a boundary or as a dividing feature within the garden, is sometimes the only way to achieve a desired effect. Growing hedges is also a very effective way of filtering strong winds to provide shelter.

Good evergreens include *Buxus sempervirens* (box) (z. 6–9), *Taxus baccata* (yew) (z. 6–7), *Lonicera nitida* (z. 7–9) and *Lonicera nitida* 'Baggesen's Gold', *Escallonia* 'Apple Blossom' (z. 8–10), or *Rosmarinus officinalis* (rosemary) (z. 8–10).

For a dwarf hedge to edge a border or path, or for a knot garden, use the dwarf form of box, *Buxus sempervirens* 'Suffruticosa' (z. 6–9), *Teucrium chamaedrys* (z. 7–9), *Santolina chamaecyparissus* (z. 6–9), *Berberis thunbergii* f. atropurpurea 'Atropurpurea Nana' (z. 4–8), the holly *Ilex crenata* 'Convexa' (z. 5–7), or a compact lavender (left).

37

Plants for hedging and topiary

Hedges and clipped evergreens are an excellent way to manipulate garden space, combining the organic earthiness of plant material with architectural form and function. However, many commonly used hedging plants are quite unsuited to small spaces. They grow too fast, taking up too much valuable space and depriving adjacent plants of light, water, and nutrients. Some also dislike the hard pruning that may be needed if they outgrow their space. But careful selection of more appropriate plants can make a hedge or specimen shrub that will be an asset for many years.

Box balls of different sizes introduce a semiformal element that gives unity to a design.

Although *Taxus baccata* (zone 6–7), the yew, grows extremely large in the wild, it is an ideal topiary or hedging plant that is particularly suitable for a small garden. The qualities that make it so useful for garden architecture include its attractive dark, dense foliage, its longevity, and its determination to flourish in the face of repeated clipping. It is hardy and will even survive in zone 5 in some protected areas.

Taxus baccata grows easily in a wide range of soils, thriving as it does on the poor ground of its native habitat in Britain's alkaline regions. However, it will not tolerate long-term water-logging, so on a very damp site you will have to install drainage or grow a different plant instead. Other than this, yew is fairly undemanding. Hedges usually need to be clipped only once or twice a year, topiary more frequently to ensure crisp outlines.

One important thing to note about yew is that it is toxic and should not be used for hedging that livestock can reach. Birds love its red, fleshy berries (arils) but do not digest the poisonous pip. Like certain other poisonous plants, yew contains chemicals that have pharmaceutical uses, and compounds extracted from it are processed for use in the treatment of cancers.

There are numerous variations and named cultivars of yew. A distinguished cultivar is *Taxus baccata* 'Fastigiata' (Irish yew). The branches grow upward and it develops into a slim, columnar bush. It needs occasional clipping to keep it that way as it ages, for its girth tends to spread eventually. The golden Irish yew, *Taxus baccata* 'Fastigiata Aureomarginata', grows even more slowly and provides a lighter alternative.

Numerous other yew cultivars have been selected because of their habit, golden leaves, or yellow berries.

Other plants subjected to the regular clipping required for hedging or topiary respond with varying degrees of success. Not all will suit a small garden: some are too vigorous; others have large leaves that can look out of scale. The shrubby honeysuckle *Lonicera nitida* (zone 7–9) is small leaved, neat, and easy to clip but it tends to flop if grown beyond a height of about 5ft. (1.5m), and it needs frequent clipping, perhaps every two weeks in the growing season. The holly *Ilex aquifolium* (zone 6–9), with its shiny, clear foliage, is a good topiary plant, but in a small garden choose one of the less prickly varieties. See also page 44.

The ivy *Hedera helix* (zone 4–9) is a good choice for a tight space, where it can be trained on fencing or trellis and kept trimmed and tied in, to create a narrow evergreen screen, known as a "fedge." Ivies with long runners can be trained onto a framework to make an arch, or grown on wires or trellis flush against a wall, trained and clipped in a formal design. Variegated ivies are particularly effective (see page 75).

Taxus baccata

Hedera helix 'Green Ripple'

Lonicera nitida 'Baggesen's Gold'

BOX BLIGHT

This comparatively new fungal disease is a serious threat to mature box plants in gardens across much of Europe, although it is still rare in the United States. The problem usually manifests itself initially as spots on the leaves. Subsequently the stem tissue is attacked. Small branches are killed and the leaves drop off.

There is currently no completely effective chemical remedy for box blight, and the best control is simply to prune off and destroy infected material immediately. Often plants do in fact recover.

PLANT PROFILE

Box (Buxus)

The topiary plant that is usually mentioned in the same breath as yew as part of the formal gardening tradition is *Buxus sempervirens* (zone 6–9), the common box. Like yew, this is a British native plant, but box differs in being broad-leaved. The small evergreen leaves can withstand repeated and heavy pruning, so it is an ideal candidate for topiary— although its unusual foxlike smell, particularly noticeable in late winter, is not to everyone's taste.

There are many box species and cultivars. Some are suitable for tall hedging and are used to create living walls for "garden rooms," while others are better for edging or rock gardens. Different kinds are used to suit conditions in the United States, Europe, and Asia.

The dwarf *Buxus sempervirens* 'Suffruticosa', slow growing and with dense foliage, is the form of box most often used as a formal edging for paths and beds, or for knot gardens.

The very hardy, dwarf, dark green *Buxus microphylla* 'Winter Gem' (zone 5–9) is ideal in areas with harsh winters. Spreading wider than it is tall, it is good for edging or shorter hedges.

Buxus sempervirens 'Elegantissima' is ideal for small spaces, bringing brightness on dull winter days and, clipped into a neat dome, a touch of formality to summer planting. (See also page 41.)

39

Evergreens

Evergreen foliage becomes a principal player in the autumn garden as the leaves of other plants fade and fall. The function of evergreens as architectural plants is critical in winter, and they can look spectacular when covered by hoarfrost or snow. Some evergreens, as a bonus, have fragrant winter flowers, or a cheery display of berries. With lengthening days, their role changes again, and they become a glorious green background to the emerging display of colorful spring bulbs and summer perennials.

Hoarfrost always brings a touch of magic to the garden—especially effective on evergreens with shapely leaves, like hollies, ivies, and conifers.

Evergreens come in all shapes and sizes, from majestic trees to slender shrubs and low-lying ground cover. There is an evergreen for almost every situation. The majority of evergreens are trees and shrubs: woody-stemmed plants that normally retain most of their foliage throughout the year. However, evergreens are not necessarily woody. There are a number of very useful soft-stemmed perennials, such as certain hellebores, euphorbias, and irises, that offer valuable greenery as well as structural interest in the garden in winter.

Among the most traditional of evergreens is the Mediterranean sweet bay or bay laurel, *Laurus nobilis* (zone 8–9). Introduced into British gardens in the 16th century, it has retained its place as one of a handful of indispensable evergreens, making a dense shrub that is naturally pyramidal in shape. The aromatic leaves, used as a flavoring in cooking, are a warm shade of green, so the plant never looks dejected on gloomy winter days. It tolerates clipping well but, like other broad-leaved evergreens, it is best trimmed back with secateurs rather than shears, to prevent leaf damage. Bay

is often grown in containers, where it can either be allowed free rein or be trained and clipped as a cone or standard: it is often used in this way, to good effect, in town gardens and other limited spaces. Bay is ideal in mild coastal regions, for it is slightly tender, especially in its early years, when it benefits from a sheltered site and protection from severe frosts. This applies especially to plants grown in containers. Even a mature specimen can be damaged in an exposed position, although the shrub will usually survive, producing new shoots from the base in spring.

Another good shrub that likes shelter in cold areas is *Rhamnus alaternus* 'Argenteovariegata' (zone 8–9). This plant was originally from Portugal but has been cultivated in gardens for hundreds of years. Since rhamnus is one of the most handsome of all variegated evergreens, it is worth giving this shade-tolerant, fast-growing, bushy plant a choice spot in the border, perhaps near a wall that will protect it from the coldest weather. Rhamnus can be left unpruned or trimmed to shape. Its leaves are green but have gray marbling and irregular creamy white edges. Look

Rhamnus alaternus 'Argenteovariegata'

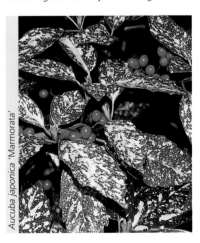

Aucuba japonica 'Marmorata'

out for any shoots that have reverted to plain green, and cut them off promptly to prevent them from taking over the bush. Rhamnus also looks good in flower arrangements.

One of the most familiar variegated evergreens in the garden is *Aucuba japonica* (spotted laurel) (zone 7–10). This very hardy but deceptively tropical-looking plant, with large, gold-splashed leaves, is ideal for brightening shady corners and courtyards. Popular in Victorian gardens, it is a versatile foliage shrub and has returned to favor (and particularly to floristry) in recent years. It is one of the most trouble-free, shade-tolerant evergreens, withstanding dry soil and content to be pruned to size (like bay, with pruning shears) if necessary. Aucubas will usually grow to 6–10ft. (2–3m) if left untrimmed.

Golden-variegated *Aucuba japonica* 'Crotonifolia' is particularly bright, with more gold than green on its finely mottled leaves. Other good forms are *Aucuba japonica* 'Marmorata', with heavy yellow blotches on the leaves, and the distinctive *Aucuba japonica* 'Picturata', which has a big yellow central streak on each leaf. For a different winter effect, plant the plain-leaved *Aucuba japonica* 'Rozannie', which gives a striking display of scarlet berries if it has a male partner. Aucuba flowers, usually dismissed as insignificant, are minute but subtly beautiful and well worth close inspection.

Almost equally tolerant of difficult conditions is the slow-growing silver-variegated box *Buxus sempervirens* 'Elegantissima' (see page 39). With its neat habit and dainty foliage, this is one of those invaluable plants that look good all year. It is excellent in a container: start with a small plant, or even two or three in a group, and plant them out in the garden when they mature.

The foliage of *Azara microphylla* 'Variegata' (zone 7–9) is very similar to

ARCHITECTURAL EVERGREENS

Some areas of a garden—perhaps a driveway, or areas close to windows and doors—are seen just as much in winter as in summer. It is worth giving some thought to the look of these areas in the dormant season and investing in a few plants that will give a faded summer flower bed interest and structure through the winter months. Combine bold architectural plants with low-key evergreens for a really stylish effect that will give pleasure and look smart every day of the year.

Euphorbia characias ssp. *wulfenii* (z. 8–9) This is a stunning plant for year-round interest in a sunny place, particularly if it is given a sheltered spot such as at the foot of a wall. In late winter, the stems, with their glaucous evergreen leaves, begin slowly to unfurl into what will eventually become massive yellow-green spires in spring. Cutting out the flowered stems in early summer is the only attention required.

Fatsia japonica (z. 8–9) Although fairly hardy, fatsia could be taken for a subtropical plant, with its big, shiny, hand-shaped leaves. They contrast well with small-leaved evergreens such as ferns or *Lonicera nitida* 'Baggesen's Gold' (see pages 39, 43). Fatsia is best grown in a sheltered site in moist, compost-rich soil. Happy in shade, it also makes a good plant for the house or in a conservatory that gets little sun.

Yucca filamentosa 'Bright Edge' (z. 5–8) Like fatsia, this suggests warmer climates but is, in fact, hardy. Its eye-catching fans of swordlike foliage, striped green and brilliant gold, bring sunshine and structure to a winter border even on gloomy days. It is happiest in a sunny, well-drained position and will succeed in gritty compost in a large pot.

Cordyline australis 'Purple Tower' (z. 7–11) This striking, exotic, and slightly tender evergreen is only for a very sheltered, warm, well-drained spot, but it is sure to provoke comment if successful. Its broad, sword-shaped leaves are a subtle shade of purple, a color seldom seen in the winter garden. In cold weather, wrap it in burlap or tie its leaves together to protect the crown.

Azara microphylla 'Variegata'

Viburnum tinus 'Variegatum'

Choisya ternata 'Sundance'

Osmanthus heterophyllus 'Goshiki'

that of the silver-variegated box, with its small leaves prettily edged with cream. The azara is a more tender plant but compensates by having a delicious fragrance. Tiny yellow flowers, without petals but with numerous conspicuous stamens, appear on the undersides of the twigs in early spring, giving off a powerful vanillalike perfume on mild days. *Azara microphylla* (zone 7–9), the hardiest plant of this tender South American genus, forms a small dainty tree with glossy evergreen foliage.

A larger-leaved but also slightly tender variegated shrub, magnificent when kept in good shape, is *Viburnum tinus* 'Variegatum' (zone 8–9). Its leaves are olive green, with cream-colored edges, and are borne on vivid red stems. This viburnum needs protection from cold winds and makes the best shape when grown against a wall. Its pink buds open to creamy white flowers from midwinter to early spring and are followed by blue berries.

With any luck, you will get not one but two seasons of fragrance from *Choisya ternata* (zone 8–10), the Mexican orange blossom. This superb, drought-tolerant Mexican native produces scented white flowers in late spring and early summer, and frequently again in the fall. The glossy, evergreen, neatly oval-shaped leaves

are aromatic too. This is an easy plant to keep trim for small gardens, and it appreciates the shelter of a confined space. The hybrid **Choisya 'Aztec Pearl'** has proved to be a very popular shrub, with elegantly divided foliage and pink-tinged flowers, while the dazzling **Choisya ternata 'Sundance'** has leaves of bright gold. The attributes of these two attractive plants have been combined in the more recent cultivar **Choisya 'Goldfingers'**.

Smaller than choisyas, but also fragrant and attractive in the garden, is **Sarcococca confusa** (zone 6–8), the Christmas box, with small, shiny, dark green leaves and tiny white flowers that fill the winter air with a strong vanilla perfume. Glossy black fruits follow.

Scented flowers as well as handsome foliage characterize another wonderful group of slow-growing evergreen shrubs,

osmanthus. They are useful for all-year screening and combine well with other border plants, thriving on fertile, well-drained soil in dappled shade. The excellent and fairly hardy **Osmanthus × burkwoodii** (zone 6–8) forms a dense bush that bears small, finely serrated leaves and scented, long-stalked, little white flowers, rather like those of jasmine, in spring. One of its parent plants, the similar **Osmanthus delavayi** (zone 7–10), is also robust. **Osmanthus heterophyllus** 'Goshiki' (zone 6–9) is a striking plant, with gold-mottled leaves similar in shape to those of holly. The young foliage is attractively bronze tinged, while in **Osmanthus heterophyllus** 'Purpureus' (zone 6–9) the new leaves are purple, maturing to green with a purple cast. This is a useful evergreen shrub in a planting scheme of rich red and purple shades.

EVERGREEN GROUND COVER FOR SUNNY SITES *Erica carnea* • *Hebe cupressoides* 'Boughton Dome' •

Pieris japonica 'Little Heath'

Viburnum davidii

Highly colored young leaves are one of the main reasons for choosing **pieris**—but only if your soil is acidic and you can give it the conditions that suit its rather fussy nature. Many pieris grow quite large, but there are a number of dwarf cultivars of *Pieris japonica* (zone 5–8), including the dainty but hardy *Pieris japonica* 'Little Heath'. Mature foliage, which is variegated green and creamy white, is accompanied by new growth of a soft coral-pink. White flowers bloom in spring. It will be happiest out of strong sunshine but dislikes deep shade.

A handsome, dark-leaved, dome-shaped evergreen, similar in size to pieris, and good to plant beside it, is *Viburnum davidii* (zone 7–9). Slender, shapely, grooved leaves are not its only asset. Clusters of white flowers in early summer are followed by red-tinged young foliage and then, if the shrub has a pollinating partner, winter berries in a surprising shade of bright blue appear. It is compact and needs little attention.

Similar in size to the viburnum is the honeysuckle *Lonicera pileata* (zone 6–8). It offers no such seasonal conjuring tricks but is certainly worth considering. Its small leaves are attractively arranged and make a good foil for a variety of other kinds of plants, such as climbers, while covering the ground very efficiently. Its relative *Lonicera nitida* **'Baggesen's Gold'** (zone 7–9) is more familiar, providing a welcome splash of sunshine all year. Like many golden-leaved plants, it needs sunlight to keep its bright color. It can be clipped into a formal shape or its tiny-leaved golden shoots can be allowed to stray among the larger, darker leaves of a carefully chosen neighbor such as sweet bay or bay laurel (*Laurus nobilis,* see page 40) or a purple elder (*Sambucus,* see page 52).

The good dwarf shrub *Pittosporum tenuifolium* **'Tom Thumb'** (zone 9–10) earns its space in even the smallest of gardens. Its young foliage starts green and matures to bronze-purple. For most of the year its uniform

Hebe 'Red Edge'

purplish leaf color is a valuable foil to hot colors. Sedums, red tulips, penstemons, heleniums, and zinnias are all good in its company.

There are many types of hebes. Some are very compact, with small, densely packed foliage, and make good ground cover. *Hebe rakaiensis* (zone 6–8) is a neat, mid-green, dome-shaped bush, varying little all year, except when it bears white flowers in summer. It is unlikely to grow to much more than 3ft. (1m) in any direction, but it can be trimmed in spring or after flowering. Smaller, gray-leaved, ground-cover hebes include the stalwart *Hebe pinguifolia* **'Pagei'** (zone 6–8) and *Hebe* **'Red Edge'** (zone 8–10). Like most hebes, these prefer a sunny position out of cold winds.

GOOD COMPANIONS

Pittosporum tenuifolium 'Tom Thumb' (1) (z. 9–10) looks good at almost any time of year combined with flowers in strong shades of red. Try it with *Penstemon* 'Andenken an Friedrich Hahn' (2) (z. 7–9).

Let some straggly shoots of *Lonicera nitida* 'Baggesen's Gold' (3) (z. 7–9) wander among the foliage of the purple-leaved *Physocarpus opulifolius* 'Diabolo' (4) (z. 2–7).

Iberis sempervirens • *Juniperus horizontalis* 'Wiltonii' • *Ruta graveolens* • *Santolina* • *Sempervivum* •

Holly (Ilex)

Everyone is familiar with the classic Christmas holly *Ilex aquifolium* (zone 6–9), with its dark, glossy foliage all year round and its festive scarlet berries in winter. Although slow-growing to begin with, it is a valuable structural plant, which does well in shade and looks good either as a specimen shrub or a hedge.

Some of the variegated hollies are also very familiar. *Ilex × altaclerensis* 'Golden King' (zone 6–9) is one of the best, looking handsome all year and producing abundant red berries. While not entirely prickle-free, it bears relatively smooth leaves. The opposite is true of *Ilex aquifolium* 'Ferox'. The leaves of this distinctive plant and its variegated forms have short, sharp spines on their upper surfaces as well as on their edges. These "hedgehog hollies" are all male clones, so although they produce no berries themselves, they are useful as pollinating partners, since most of the variegated hollies are female. Just one male plant per garden will normally be sufficient to ensure berries every year.

Hollies will usually produce more berries in a sunny position, although the plants themselves are very tolerant of shade.

If you have room for only one holly, try the self-pollinating cultivar *Ilex aquifolium* 'J.C. van Tol' (z. 6–9). This has dark, shining, almost spineless green leaves and will produce an abundance of red berries all by itself.

Ilex aquifolium 'Pyramidalis' (z. 6–9) is a handsome, free-fruiting fastigiate (upright) clone with green stems and variously spined leaves. It will eventually reach some 20ft. (6m) tall but grows slowly and can be trimmed if necessary. It makes an unusual hedge, if space permits. A golden-variegated form is available.

Ilex × meserveae 'Blue Prince' (z. 5–8) is one of several very hardy cultivars known as 'blue hollies'. They are ideal for small spaces, being more compact than *Ilex aquifolium*. Their young stems are purplish while the dark green leaves have a definite blue tinge.

OTHER GOOD HOLLIES

Ilex aquifolium 'Argentea Marginata' (z. 6–9) Its white-edged leaves make this a good partner for pastel colors.

The slow growing *Ilex aquifolium* 'Ferox Argentea' (z. 6–9), the silver hedgehog, is an ideal feature plant for a small garden; it carries rich purple twigs and leaves with creamy white margins.

Ilex crenata 'Golden Gem' (z. 5–7) Slow growing and compact, with small golden leaves and black berries. Attractive in winter and spring; makes a good container plant and an excellent, dwarf, clipped hedge.

Ilex × meserveae 'Mesgolg' Golden Girl™ holly P.P.A.F. (z. 5–8) A female "blue holly" with yellow fruit; forms a broad pyramid.

Evergreens for ground cover

Although sometimes maligned for its association with dull public areas, evergreen ground-cover planting can be invaluable in gardens. Its main practical role is to provide a carpet of evergreen foliage that restricts weed growth and helps prevent moisture loss from the soil. But if you choose the right plants, ground-cover planting becomes a pleasing and positive element of the garden picture.

Easy ground cover for all seasons: *Cotoneaster dammeri*.

Extremes of dry shade are always a planting challenge, but with thorough soil preparation and well-chosen plants it is almost always possible to make really worthwhile improvements to the look of such problem areas. More open sites with richer soil lend themselves to a whole host of inventive and attractive ground-cover possibilities.

The irrepressible *Euonymus fortunei* cultivars (zone 5–8) are available in many different shapes, sizes, and colors. Two compact, bushy forms—the golden-variegated *Euonymus fortunei* 'Emerald 'n' Gold' and the white and green *Euonymus fortunei* 'Emerald Gaiety'—are both much used in difficult sites, but when grown well they are really good plants. Although they prefer some sun, they are surprisingly tolerant of inhospitable growing conditions and make dense ground cover to a height of some 2ft. (60cm). For added seasonal interest, they can be interplanted with flowering perennials that will weave among their foliage.

For carrying color from summer into the fall and early winter, there is no better ground-hugging evergreen than *Cotoneaster dammeri* (zone 5–7). Use it to clothe difficult banks or to create a splash of late-season color in shaded, poor ground under trees. Its abundant scarlet berries are carried on long, trailing shoots, which can be pegged down with wire to encourage them to root and make denser cover. Partners to weave

among it might include a variegated form of *Hedera helix* (ivy; see page 75) or the periwinkle *Vinca minor* (zone 5–8), which are both excellent plants for shaded areas; their foliage will brighten even the darkest corners.

A prostrate evergreen that gives a splash of color at a different time of year

is *Ceanothus* 'Centennial' (zone 7–10). Its glossy foliage mixes well with silver-leaved plants, such as *Convolvulus cneorum*, giving a second season of interest—important where space is at a premium. Like all ceanothus, it needs the sun to flower well, producing a sheet of dazzling violet-blue in early summer.

EVERGREEN CLIMBERS AND TRAILERS

Useful where year-round screening is required, evergreen climbers can be grown on trellis or fences and up walls, provided the masonry is sound. Some will also spread themselves out over the ground in front of the wall or fence, and in a confined area are particularly valuable as "anchors," linking horizontal and vertical space.

Euonymus fortunei 'Silver Queen' (z. 5–8) A useful variegated evergreen shrub that is happy to climb or scramble and looks good against brickwork. Its unfolding leaves in spring appear rich, creamy yellow, later becoming dark green with a broad, creamy white margin.

Hedera helix (common ivy) (z. 4–9) These hardy, self-clinging climbers are indispensable for winter interest but must be used with care because of their creeping habit and penetrating stem roots. Most of the cultivated varieties are less vigorous than the species. Many are attractively variegated, such as the silvery *Hedera helix* 'Glacier' (right) or the striking *Hedera helix* 'Oro di Bogliasco', formerly known more aptly as 'Goldheart'.

× *Fatshedera lizei* (z. 8–11) Not a true climber, but valuable for its bold evergreen leaves, this is a bigeneric hybrid between *Hedera* and *Fatsia japonica*. Although it is often seen as a houseplant, it is quite tough and shade-tolerant but dislikes cold winds and will benefit from the shelter and support of a wall. It looks most effective growing near feathery plants such as the evergreen *Cryptomeria japonica* 'Elegans Compacta' (z. 6–8).

EVERGREENS TO GROW UNDER DECIDUOUS SHRUBS *Liriope muscari* • *Luzula sylvatica* 'Marginata' • *Polystichum setiferum* • *Saxifraga* × *urbium* • *Tellima grandiflora* • *Tolmiea menziesii* 'Taff's Gold' •

Ajuga reptans 'Catlin's Giant'

Helleborus foetidus

Pachysandra terminalis

The woodland wild flower *Ajuga reptans* (zone 4–7) is a low-growing evergreen perennial with shiny leaves and underground stolons that like to colonize bare ground. A natural woodland plant, it is happy in light shade beneath deciduous trees and shrubs and at border edges, preferring moist soil but tolerating temporarily dry conditions in summer. Many cultivars are available, with a range of flower and foliage colors. *Ajuga reptans* 'Catlin's Giant' is an especially large variety, with violet-blue flowers and handsome deep purple-bronze leaves. It combines beautifully with most yellow spring-flowering bulbs. To establish ajugas in new places, simply dig up and move some of the little plants that grow along the trailing stolons—an easy job for any time of the year.

Although they are not generally considered true evergreens, two species of hellebore that tolerate shade are invaluable for covering bare ground with welcome greenery in winter, namely *Helleborus foetidus* (zone 6–8) and the similar *Helleborus argutifolius* (zone 6–8). Their pale green flower heads contrast pleasingly with the attractive dark green palmate leaves. The flowers usually begin to open early in the new year, much to the delight of any bees that may be around on mild days.

Euphorbia amygdaloides var. *robbiae* (zone 7–9) is a good plant for difficult places in the garden. It has glossy, forest green foliage and lime yellow flowers that gradually unfurl above the leaf rosettes in early spring. Partners for a dry-shade planting scheme might include *Iris foetidissima* (zone 6–9), with its spiky evergreen foliage and vermilion winter fruits, *Galium odoratum* (sweet woodruff) (zone 5–8), or one of the more robust vincas (periwinkles), whose dark blue flowers complement all euphorbias.

In shady places that are not too dry, *Pachysandra terminalis* (zone 5–8) is another useful and attractive plant for evergreen ground cover. It makes a dense mat of foliage, about 8–12in. (20–30cm) high, and produces tiny greenish white flowers in spring.

GOOD COMPANIONS

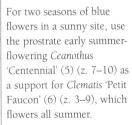

A good partner for *Euonymus fortunei* 'Emerald Gaiety' (1) (z. 5–8) in semi-shade is the purple-leaved violet, *Viola riviniana* Purpurea Group (2) (z. 5–8). Or interplant the euonymus with the dark-flowered *Vinca minor* 'Atropurpurea' (z. 5–8) or the summer-flowering *Viola* 'Belmont Blue' (z. 6–8).

Early spring partners for shade: *Euphorbia amygdaloides* var. *robbiae* (3) (z. 7–9) and the equally tolerant, vigorous, mat-forming woodlander *Galium odoratum* (sweet woodruff) (4) (z. 5–8).

For two seasons of blue flowers in a sunny site, use the prostrate early summer-flowering *Ceanothus* 'Centennial' (5) (z. 7–10) as a support for *Clematis* 'Petit Faucon' (6) (z. 3–9), which flowers all summer.

Heathers

Where space in the garden is tight, a few carefully chosen heathers, integrated into a mixed planting scheme, can prolong the season of interest and fill color gaps with a rainbow of foliage and flower hues. Heathers are quite easy to grow but prefer sunny sites. They are useful as ground cover and in perennial borders, in rock gardens, and as container plants. Their tiny flowers have a wonderful honey fragrance, and they are highly attractive to bees and other insects.

There are two main groups of garden plants that are commonly called heathers. Most of those that flower between fall and spring belong to the genus *Erica*

(heaths), while summer-flowering heathers are all cultivars of the single species *Calluna vulgaris* (zone 4–7), known as true heather. The two groups have much in common. Most need acidic soil, but the exceptions include the winter-flowering heaths, those extremely useful garden plants.

Plant all heathers in spring or fall. They have very fine roots and, although established plants are quite drought-tolerant, young ones will soon die if allowed to dry out. Use special lime-free potting mix when planting heathers in containers. Trim the plants occasionally to prevent them from looking straggly.

The low-growing *Erica carnea* 'Adrienne Duncan' (z. 5–7) is a heath with dark bronze-green foliage and carmine red blossom. Its flowering (midwinter to mid-spring) coincides with that of *Erica carnea* 'Springwood White' (see below).

Erica carnea 'Eileen Porter' (z. 5–7) is one of dozens of compact winter-flowering heaths that give successional color right through winter into spring. The bicolored blooms of this cultivar give an overall rich, carmine red effect.

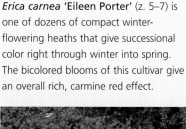

Erica × *darleyensis* 'Silberschmelze' (z. 4–7), sometimes known as 'Molten Silver', is often considered the best white winter-flowering heath. Its mid-green foliage is cream-tipped in spring, and its flowers usually begin to open in early fall, continuing for several months.

OTHER GOOD HEATHERS

Calluna vulgaris 'Dark Beauty' (z. 4–7) Fairly compact plant with dark green foliage and semidouble, deep pink flowers that darken with age.

Erica carnea 'Springwood White' (z. 4–7) Produces strong trailing growths packed with masses of long, urn-shaped white flowers on bright green stems.

Erica × *darleyensis* 'Furzey' (z. 4–7) Bears deep rose pink flowers from late fall through to spring, when the dark green foliage develops pink tips.

Calluna vulgaris 'Wickwar Flame' (z. 4–7) is good for small gardens because it is colorful for most of the year. Looking somewhat wild when young, it matures into a dense, tight mound of unusual foliage, burnt orange yellow above and lime green below, deepening to fiery red in winter. The summer flowers are lavender pink.

Conifers

Conifers form a distinctive group of mainly evergreen trees and shrubs. They have great presence in a garden and can be a striking and stylish feature, even in a small space, provided you choose the right kinds. The consequences of a wrong choice can be unfortunate in many respects, so when buying conifers more care must be taken than when selecting almost any other group of garden plants.

For winter structure, group conifers with other plants of contrasting form and texture.

Garden centers and nurseries offer an immense range of conifers, which vary in color between green, gray, silver, gold, purple, or blue, and may be conical or dome-shaped, pendulous, upright, or prostrate. The foliage of some varieties consists of bundles of long needles, such as those of pines, while others have short, often sharply pointed leaves, for example junipers and firs. Most conifers are evergreen, although a few are deciduous, and they can be slow- or fast-growing. They may be trimmed and shaped, or allowed to shoot upward and outward in whatever direction they please.

There are conifers to suit any size of plot. As gardens continue to shrink in size, there generally tends to be less space for trees. However, well-chosen, compact conifers, planted singly or in groups depending on the space, can be a year-round asset to a garden. They need little or no pruning and tend not to be affected by pests or diseases.

The first consideration when making your selection is the ultimate size. Many conifers make huge trees very rapidly, and for a small garden you need to be quite certain that you are buying something at the opposite end of the scale. The best way to ensure this is to buy from a good garden center or nursery, and check the labels with extreme care. Remember that true dwarf conifers grow slowly and are expensive to produce, so be prepared to pay accordingly. A compact conifer may cost more in the first place, but if it is a true, named variety, it will give pleasure, and will be almost maintenance-free, for many years.

Be wary of any conifers for sale at discounted prices. Some outlets save on costs by selling kinds they can quickly grow to a good size. These look-alikes, which are not true dwarf conifers, will soon outgrow the space intended for them and can be very unsatisfactory to prune and expensive to remove.

Garden conifers come in a rainbow of year-round colors that can be used in many garden situations. Golden foliage is cheering on gloomy days, and for a small space perhaps the most suitable golden conifer is the rather elegant *Chamaecyparis obtusa* 'Nana Aurea' (zone 4–8). It grows very slowly to about 6ft. (2m) tall, but it is neat and narrow. An alternative, *Chamaecyparis lawsoniana* 'Golden Showers' (zone 5–7), will reach about twice that height.

Abies lasiocarpa var. arizonica 'Compacta'

OTHER CONIFERS *Cupressus macrocarpa* 'Woking' • *Juniperus sabina* 'Tamariscifolia' • *Pinus mugo* 'Mops' •

Cryptomeria japonica 'Elegans Compacta'

Taxus baccata 'Repandens'

It is a more solid-looking shrub, with golden-tinged foliage.

Purple and bronze hues are harder to find in conifers, although there are a few valuable examples. A shrub that is quite unlike anything else in the garden is the feathery *Cryptomeria japonica* **'Elegans Compacta'** (zone 6–8). With green foliage in summer, turning bronze in winter, it is a good foil for plants with more solid, architectural foliage, such as spiky phormiums or

Juniperus communis 'Compressa'

Fatsia japonica (zone 8–9). It enjoys a sheltered spot with good soil, and if it grows too large, it can be pruned hard.

For blue coloring it is hard to beat the slow-growing fir *Abies concolor* **'Compacta'** (zone 4–7). Perhaps the bluest of all conifers, it has long, flexible, powder blue needles and eventually makes a striking 10ft. (3m) specimen. Another dwarf fir to try is *Abies lasiocarpa* var. *arizonica* **'Compacta'** (zone 5–7), which forms an effective silvery blue cone. For a neat cone in bright green, the perfect plant is the dense, bushy spruce *Picea glauca* var. *albertiana* **'Conica'** (zone 2–6).

Fastigiate conifers—those with a slender, upright habit—are invaluable in restricted spaces because they can create height and serve as accents or focal points in a design, without taking up much lateral space. Several junipers are just right for this purpose. They tolerate most conditions, are particularly good in dry, sunny sites, and offer the added attraction of aromatic foliage. The slender and neat *Juniperus communis* **'Hibernica'**, (zone 2–7) unlikely to reach much more than 10ft. (3m) tall, or *Juniperus scopulorum* **'Skyrocket'** (zone 3–7), about twice that size, are

good examples. A similar juniper on a miniature scale suitable for the tiniest of plots, at scarcely 3ft. (90cm) tall, is *Juniperus communis* **'Compressa'** (zone 2–7). None of these are likely to exceed 20in. (50cm) in diameter.

Where space is less critical, there are some excellent conifers that grow quite slowly but eventually reach the size of a small tree. A most distinctive example (if correctly labeled—check you are buying the real thing) is *Abies koreana* (zone 5–7), which will produce wonderful cones in violet blue, even when young.

For good ground cover, try the prostrate conifers that spread laterally. *Tsuga canadensis* **'Cole's Prostrate'** (zone 3–7) is one such, while the slightly larger *Taxus baccata* **'Repandens'** (zone 6–7) does better in dense shade or on dry soils. This prostrate yew, which grows about 2ft. (60cm) high, has deep green needles and long, spreading branches that droop at the tips. Yews are poisonous and should not be grown near livestock, but they are so tolerant of poor conditions, including alkaline soil, pollution, or deep shade, that many gardeners consider them indispensable in planting schemes.

Abies koreana

Pinus pumila 'Glauca' • *Taxus baccata* Fastigiata Aurea Group • *Tsuga canadensis* 'Jeddeloh' •

Seasonal foliage

A framework of well-chosen shrubs, with a small tree or two if space allows, makes all the difference to a garden. Flowers come and go, creating their own spectacular effects, but foliage that changes subtly through the seasons is crucial to a well-furnished, comfortable look. All through the year, planting schemes benefit from the judicious use of colored foliage. Green, gold, silver, purple, and variegated shrubs open up endless design possibilities as they combine with other plants. Choosing good foliage and using it well is a key part of garden planning.

The many cultivars of *Acer palmatum* (Japanese maples) (zone 6–8) have long been recognized as some of the finest shrubs and small trees for foliage form and fall color. Most of them grow slowly, remaining manageable in size for many years. Some cultivars are more fussy about growing conditions than others, but the basic requirements are shelter from cold winds and rich, moist, well-drained soil. Many cultivars dislike alkaline soil, but others are slightly alkaline tolerant. Japanese maples can be grown in large containers—a useful

The Japanese maples are among the best shrubs for all-season foliage color, ending the year in a blaze of reds and golds.

An inspirational border like this would not be possible without colored foliage. Purple, bronze, and silver leaves are the best companions for hot colors.

50

MORE SHRUBS FOR FOLIAGE COLOR *Cornus mas* 'Variegata' • *Cotinus coggygria* 'Royal Purple' •

alternative, particularly if the garden soil is not suitable. Grown this way, they look especially good on gravel.

Acer palmatum 'Bloodgood' is a popular, airy form and is perfect as an accent plant for patios and gateways or standing alone as a feature. Its dramatic deep color lasts well, intensifying to fluorescent red in fall. It thrives in part shade, slowly maturing to a height of some 15ft. (5m). Another very well-established form, *Acer palmatum* 'Ôsakazuki', has handsome large, deeply divided green leaves, which take on the most remarkable red hues before dropping in fall. A third outstanding, tried and tested variety is the coral bark maple, *Acer palmatum* 'Sango-kaku' (sometimes labeled as *Acer palmatum* 'Senkaki'). Excellent for a small garden, it is attractive at all times of year, changing from coral red shoots set off by warm yellow leaves in spring, through summer green, and then to wonderful shades of soft gold in the fall. Its all-year-round credentials are completed by its winter twigs and bark, which are a bright coral red that

USING COLORED FOLIAGE

Purple and bronze Use with hot colors such as reds and oranges, or to give substance and depth to a border in pastel colors. For dramatic contrasts, plant as a backdrop to golden or silver foliage.

Gold Lively and fresh combined with dark blue, deep violet, and white in spring. Invaluable for brightening gloomy corners—although some golden-leaved plants will become greener in too much shade.

Silver Grow in hot, sunny places to create a Mediterranean effect. Often suitable for the top of retaining walls and good in gravel. Effective planted with reds and dark blues. Silver-leaved plants show up best at dusk.

Variegated Use sparingly to avoid a muddled, "busy" effect. Plant where they will be seen at dusk, when white variegation, in particular, really stands out. Striking in shade, or for enlivening plain walls, or planted among greenery.

deepens in cold weather. Site the shrub in part shade, in a conspicuous place where you will be able to enjoy its distinctive winter bark after leaf fall.

For foliage interest, the most useful of the many different types of **berberis** are the purple-leaved cultivars of the deciduous *Berberis thunbergii* (zone 4–8). The compact forms are ideal for tight spaces, and their small leaves are perfectly suited to planting schemes on a reduced scale. *Berberis thunbergii* 'Atropurpurea Nana' is a charming dwarf cultivar, reaching only 2ft. (60cm) or so in height and spread, and can be tucked into many different kinds of planting to great effect. *Berberis thunbergii* 'Helmond Pillar' is a tall,

slender exclamation mark of a shrub, growing to approximately 5ft. (1.5m) tall. It creates a fine focal point and is especially effective as a structural element in perennial plantings. Three of these narrowly upright cultivars can be grouped together if there is space. Both 'Atropurpurea Nana' and 'Helmond Pillar' have foliage of a very good deep red-purple. If they are left unpruned, they produce small pale yellow or orange spring flowers, followed by tiny berries of sealing-wax red, tucked under the leaves. With the approach of winter the foliage becomes steadily redder, eventually falling to expose the berries, which sometimes remain on the spiny twigs until spring.

Cotoneaster atropurpureus 'Variegatus' • *Philadelphus coronarius* 'Aureus' • *Spiraea japonica* 'Firelight' •

Ornamental elders (Sambucus)

Sambucus nigra (common elder) (zone 5–7) is a coarse shrub, suitable only for a wild garden. However, a number of its cultivars and relatives share its tough constitution but have very ornamental foliage and are refined enough to earn their space in a small garden.

Sambucus grow in most soils, thriving in alkaline conditions, and are fully hardy. With their amazing powers of regeneration after being cut back, these elders can be grown in much the same way as perennials—cut almost to the ground in the dormant season and allowed to regrow each year. This is the best way to manage them in a restricted space because,

apart from limiting their size, it encourages them to produce bolder, better foliage. It also allows spring-flowering bulbs and perennials to be packed into the space around their feet. These will appreciate the shade of the elder foliage later in the year. Mulching around the shrubs in winter will help ensure that they have enough nutrients and water to make all their growth anew every year.

Other foliage shrubs that can be treated in the same way include the fine purple-leaved cultivars of *Cotinus coggygria* (zone 4–8) and *Corylus maxima* (zone 4–8), and some of the shrubby willows (*Salix*) (zone 2–9).

Sambucus racemosa 'Sutherland Gold' (z. 3–7), with its beautiful bright, fernlike foliage, is among the best golden-leaved shrubs. Unlike some others, it will tolerate full sun without scorching. This elder has a graceful habit and its foliage holds its color well. Hard pruning every year in late winter will produce bolder leaves and keep the plant compact enough for most small gardens.

Sambucus nigra f. *porphyrophylla* 'Eva' (also known as *Sambucus nigra* 'Black Lace') (z. 5–7) has dramatic, dark foliage. Prune in late winter for best foliage, or leave to form pink buds and fragrant flowers in early summer, with purple-black berries later. Other dark elders include *Sambucus nigra* 'Guincho Purple' and 'Black Beauty'.

Not often seen, but so easy to grow and to propagate that it is worth searching for, is the white-variegated elder *Sambucus nigra* 'Marginata' (z. 5–7). It is ideal for lightening a dull corner where the soil may be less than perfect. If fed and watered well, and pruned hard in late winter, it will produce its handsome foliage in abundance.

OTHER GOOD ORNAMENTAL ELDERS

Sambucus nigra 'Aurea' (z. 5–7) Useful, easy-to-grow foliage plant with golden leaves. Very hardy.

Sambucus nigra f. *laciniata* (z. 5–7) An exceptionally graceful cut-leaved elder, with finely divided foliage.

Sambucus nigra 'Pulverulenta' (z. 5–7) Bears mid-green leaves that appear to be dusted with flour.

Sambucus nigra f. *porphyrophylla* 'Gerda' (also known as *Sambucus nigra* 'Black Beauty') (z. 5–7) A relatively new purple-leaved elder. Its very dark foliage does not lose its dramatic color in the summer but actually gets darker.

Sambucus racemosa 'Plumosa Aurea' (z. 3–7) Cut-leaved golden foliage. Does best in light shade.

Silver-leaved shrubs

Most silver- or gray-leaved shrubs need plenty of sunshine. Generally, they are very drought-tolerant, because of the waxy bloom or fine hairs on their leaves that help them to retain moisture. These plants are normally tolerant of cold but not if they have too much moisture in winter, so give them a free-draining position. Most do very well on alkaline and poor, sandy soils. They do not need routine feeding.

Silver foliage shows up well at dusk, in the same way as white flowers, so these plants are extremely effective in a place where they can be admired as a ghostly presence on summer evenings. The shimmering foliage of some silver-leaved shrubs stays beautiful in winter, and many are at their most luminous in late summer and fall. Some silver-leaved plants, for example lavender and santolina, have aromatic leaves.

Convolvulus cneorum (z. 8–10) is a choice small shrub growing to no more than 2ft. (60cm) high. It has silver foliage with an unusual satiny sheen, and clusters of pink buds that open to white, funnel-shaped flowers. It needs a sheltered, sunny position on light soil.

As a neat, compact shrub for well-drained soil, santolina or cotton lavender is hard to beat. If pruned annually, *Santolina pinnata* ssp. *neapolitana* 'Edward Bowles' (above) (z. 8–10) forms a neat, gray-green dome of aromatic foliage with creamy white flower heads.

Helichrysum splendidum (zone 7–10) The stems and leaves of this surprisingly hardy little shrub have a slight camphor scent, and its canary yellow button flowers in summer have a faint perfume. Apart from a spring clipping to keep it neat, it needs little care.

OTHER GOOD SILVER-LEAVED SHRUBS

Brachyglottis (Dunedin Group) 'Sunshine' (formerly *Senecio*) (z. 8–10) Grown more for its leaves—silvery gray becoming greener as they age—than for its harsh yellow flowers.

Hebe pinguifolia 'Pagei' (z. 8–10) Prostrate, evergray, ground-cover shrub with small gray-blue leaves and short spikes of white flowers.

Helianthemum 'Rhodanthe Carneum' (z. 5–8) One of a handful of helianthemums with gray leaves. Pale pink flowers.

Helichrysum italicum (z. 8–10) Universally known as the curry plant because of its aromatic leaves (see page 129). Feathery sage green leaves, small bright yellow flowers.

Lavandula angustifolia 'Hidcote' (z. 5–8) Probably the most well-known lavender, and one of the best. Deep violet flowers.

Potentilla fruticosa 'Manchu' (z. 2–7) A useful dwarf potentilla with silvery leaves and white flowers.

Salix exigua (coyote willow) (z. 2–9) Slender, grayish brown branches and linear, silvery, silky, minutely toothed leaves.

Salix lanata (z. 2–9) A very hardy, compact deciduous shrub with rounded, silvery leaves and charming catkins.

Teucrium fruticans (z. 9–10) A fine corner or wall shrub with long, graceful stems and soft lavender blue flowers.

Physocarpus opulifolius 'Diabolo'

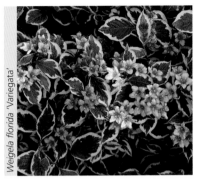

Weigela florida 'Variegata'

The many different kinds of plants that belong to the genus *Cornus* (the dogwoods) contribute a great wealth of attractive and valuable features to the garden: variegated, deep green, or gold foliage; flowers borne in late spring; brilliantly colored fall foliage; and bright red winter stems or interesting bark. Many dogwoods grow very large, but several cultivars of *Cornus alba* (zone 2–8) are easy to keep under control by annual pruning, so gardeners with limited space need not be deprived of these valuable shrubs.

Cornus alba 'Aurea' has golden foliage. Its leaves are plain, while those of *Cornus alba* 'Spaethii' are gold-and-green-variegated. One of the most attractive and easiest to use in mixed plantings is *Cornus alba* 'Sibirica Variegata', with its white variegation. Prune in spring by removing the oldest stems at the base, to encourage the shrub to produce more young growth, which has the brightest winter color.

For a garden with a little more space, *Cornus alternifolia* 'Argentea' (zone 3–7) is a star among white-variegated shrubs. Its tiered branches are covered with small leaves edged consistently with creamy white, giving a wonderful light, airy effect—stunning against a backdrop of dark evergreen foliage.

Physocarpus opulifolius (zone 2–7) is a thicket-forming, deciduous foliage shrub with papery bark and well-shaped leaves resembling those of the cranberry bush (*Viburnum opulus*). Although not ideal for the tightest spaces, two forms with colored foliage are particularly good in mixed plantings and like the dogwoods are very useful plants for damp gardens. The cultivar *Physocarpus opulifolius* 'Dart's Gold' is true to its name in spring, although by summer the leaves are more of a lime green color. Its purple-leaved relative, *Physocarpus opulifolius* 'Diabolo', has very dark foliage, which looks wonderful with almost any other plant in the garden. As with the dogwoods, cut out the oldest stems at the base each year to encourage straight new growth with good leaves.

Weigelas (zone 5–9) are good, accommodating shrubs that fit in almost anywhere. They are particularly valuable for compact urban gardens. Several new cultivars have recently been introduced, but the rather dainty, slow-growing *Weigela florida* 'Variegata' is still a winner for its beautiful cream-edged leaves. Fragrant, funnel-shaped flowers, deep pink with a paler inside, are produced in early summer. Another excellent, tried and tested cultivar is *Weigela florida* 'Foliis Purpureis', with its unusual and attractive bronze green foliage and darker flowers.

To keep weigelas tidy without losing their graceful shape, prune them after flowering, cutting out the oldest shoots that have flowered.

Cornus alba 'Sibirica Variegata' is truly a shrub for all seasons: attractive white-variegated foliage, summer flowers and glowing cherry-red stems in winter.

Compact deciduous trees

Garden trees may be grown for the color and form of their foliage, for their attractive flowers, their autumn fruits, or their interesting bark. Any tree will also make a valuable structural contribution to the garden's design. In a small area a tree must be compact and work extra hard throughout the year to earn its keep.

One of the prettiest and most popular of all compact trees is *Pyrus salicifolia* 'Pendula' (willow-leaved pear) (zone 4–7). This elegant and attractive tree has graceful weeping branches and slender, willowlike leaves, which are white-felted in spring, later changing to gray-green. Creamy white spring flowers are followed by small, hard, inedible fruits. In small spaces, where it may be the only tree, it will flatter either

The graceful willow-leaved pear, *Pyrus salicifolia* 'Pendula', is deservedly popular as one of the prettiest of small trees. Its small creamy white flowers appear in spring.

CROWN THINNING

Useful space can often be made available under existing trees by professional crown thinning of their canopies. Selected branches are carefully removed to allow more air, light, and rainfall to penetrate, enabling plants to be grown under the dappled shade of the branches. In a small space this is worth considering from an early stage with trees such as birch and sorbus. Often successful planting can be achieved right up to the trunk of the tree if the canopy is kept light and open.

a hot color scheme using red and bronze, or cottagey flower beds planted in pastels and grays. It is a classic ingredient of white planting schemes.

The **willows** (**Salix**) include some of the largest and most vigorous garden trees as well as one of the very smallest. Suitable for even the smallest space is *Salix caprea* 'Kilmarnock' (zone 4–9),

a miniature weeping willow. Sometimes seen as a ground-hugging shrub, the plant is often grafted onto a standard to form a small tree about 6ft. (2m) tall. In early spring the branches are covered with large, silvery catkins which develop golden anthers. Although not long-lived, it is the ideal small-scale accent on a patio or beside a garden pond.

Ornamental cherries (**Prunus**) are a wonderful sight in early spring, with

their clouds of pink or white blossom. One very suitable for small gardens is *Prunus serrulata* 'Kiku-shidare sakura' (Cheal's weeping cherry) (zone 5–9), an attractive little tree with very double, rose pink flowers. The leaves, bronze at first, later become green and glossy. *Prunus × subhirtella* 'Autumnalis' (zone 5–8) flowers in mild spells all through the winter, opening a few flowers at a time from late fall to spring. *Prunus cerasifera* **'Newport'** (zone 3–8) bears pale pink flowers and purple leaves. It makes a dramatic backdrop to planting in shimmering silvery tones or combined with sultry colors in summer.

All these ornamental cherries should thrive in well-drained soil, in sun or shade, but they dislike cold winds and waterlogged ground. Avoid pruning them unnecessarily, especially in winter, since cuts can encourage bacterial and fungal diseases. Recent years have seen an increase in bacterial canker and other problems in *Prunus*, so in areas where cherries are susceptible it may be better to choose other kinds of tree.

Whitebeams and **rowans** (*Sorbus*) can make fine garden specimens, often combining good foliage with spring or summer flowers and autumn fruit. Many grow too large for small gardens, but some are more compact, for example *Sorbus* **'Autumn Spires'** (zone 6–8), a newcomer with an upright habit and large hanging clusters of yellow-orange berries that complement the spectacular yellow and flame red color in the fall.

Abundant autumn berries are also a striking feature of several **hawthorn** (*Crataegus*) relatives (zone 4–7) that grow to approximately 25ft. (8m) tall;

Amelanchier canadensis 'Lamarckii'

these trees are very useful where space is limited. *Crataegus persimilis* **'Prunifolia'** is a small, broad-headed, hardy tree with clusters of pretty white flowers in early summer. The glossy, oval leaves really come into their own in fall, when their rich orange and scarlet colors outshine those of most other thorns. The spines, although sparse, are long and sharp, so do not plant it near a path or seating area. It is happy in most soils and succeeds on alkaline soil.

Gleditsia triacanthos 'Sunburst'

A similar small thorn tree for difficult soils is *Crataegus laevigata* **'Paul's Scarlet'**. A good alternative to a cherry, this compact tree bears clusters of rosy red flowers in late spring and rich green foliage on spreading branches. It is widely available and easy to grow.

Autumn fruit is a feature of another group of compact trees, popular in the northern United States, the **ornamental crab apples** (*Malus*) (zone 4–7). There are many to choose from, but not all have good enough foliage to sustain interest outside the flowering and fruiting seasons. The graceful *Malus transitoria*, however, is beautiful all year round. Its arching branches carry attractively divided leaves and starry pink and white spring blossom. Its autumn color is also good, with rich yellow foliage and masses of tiny golden yellow crab apples. The tree needs fertile soil in a sunny position.

Despite their brief flowering season, **amelanchiers** are a versatile choice for small gardens and are especially useful for damp soils. *Amelanchier canadensis* **'Lamarckii'** (Juneberry or snowy mespilus) (zone 4–8) is a good

Malus transitoria

OTHER COMPACT DECIDUOUS TREES *Acer griseum* • *Betula pendula* 'Youngii' • *Cercis siliquastrum* • *Cydonia oblonga* • *Malus* × *scheideckeri* 'Red Jade' • *Malus toringo* ssp. *sargentii* • *Mespilus germanica* •

Crataegus persimilis 'Prunifolia'

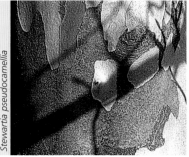
Stewartia pseudocamellia

of atmospheric pollution. It can be pruned hard, if it becomes too large to fit comfortably in the available space.

Although it will ultimately grow much taller than the other trees in this book, and is therefore not suitable for very small gardens, *Stewartia pseudocamellia* (zone 4–8) is an ideal

garden tree because, with four seasons of beauty, it earns its space. Silky buds break into beautiful white flowers in late summer. The foliage changes to soft, reddish purple, or red and orange in the fall, dropping to show off a beautiful trunk with flaking bark all through the winter.

garden species because it is so beautiful at blossom time, as is the similar *Amelanchier × grandiflora* (zone 4–7). White flowers, generously produced in loose racemes, appear as the coppery pink leaves begin to emerge. The foliage later becomes green and finally a good orange-red in the fall. Small, juicy, black fruits (which are edible when cooked) are an added bonus in summer. You may come across *Amelanchier canadensis* (zone 3–7), a multistemmed, upright-growing bush. The names (and that of *Amelanchier laevis*) are sometimes confused in garden centers, and it may be worth establishing whether you are being offered a tree or a multistemmed shrub. Amelanchiers prefer sun but they are tolerant of some shade.

For a stunning foliage tree, especially for partially shaded situations, it is hard to beat *Gleditsia triacanthos* 'Sunburst' (zone 3–9). Its light canopy of golden, fernlike leaves looks wonderful with deep blues and purples planted nearby. A good town tree, it has rather brittle branches so it needs a sheltered place and it is fairly tolerant

CONNOISSEUR'S CHOICE: FLOWERING TREES

Sorbus vilmorinii (z. 6–8) Dainty rowan with creamy white flowers in summer, followed by pinkish red berries that turn white and last well into winter. Fernlike foliage turns red in the fall.

Prunus 'Okame' (z. 6–8) A very early-flowering hybrid with a dense mass of rosy pink blossom and attractive fall foliage.

Prunus maackii 'Amber Beauty' (z. 2–6) A compact, narrow tree with little white flowers in spring. Named for the color of its glossy, flaking bark.

Styrax japonicus (Japanese snowbell) (z. 5–8) A beautiful, slow-growing tree with white, bell-shaped flowers in early summer, followed by distinctive, long-stalked seed capsules. If possible, plant the tree where the flowers can be viewed from beneath.

Parrotia persica • *Prunus serrula* • *Pyrus calleryana* 'Chanticleer' • *Robinia × slavinii* 'Hillieri' • *Sorbus aria* 'Lutescens' • *Sorbus hupehensis* • *Sorbus* 'Joseph Rock' •

Exotics

Global warming, a desire to grow plants that recall vacations in warm climates, the excitement of growing something unusual: these are some of the reasons why gardeners are turning to plants that, not so long ago, were considered hothouse rarities. Although some are large and vigorous, these plants often thrive in the protected microclimate of gardens in southern states. Even a small space must allow itself an occasional showstopper, and in temperate climates exotics hog the limelight only temporarily, for the warmest weeks of the year.

The unusual warm pink color and rich bronze purple foliage of *Canna* 'Shenandoah' are a winning combination that guarantees the plant a starring role in any sunny border.

Exotic need not mean difficult, and many of these plants are less demanding than you might expect. They need basic care, such as careful watering and protection from strong winds and harsh weather, but in return for these small attentions exotics will bring extraordinary diversity, richness, and color into the garden. Varieties that were once obscure and difficult to obtain are sold by a growing number of nurseries and garden centers, inspiring once-skeptical gardeners to be more adventurous.

Cannas (zone 7–10) are one form of exotic that was popular many years ago, during the Victorian fashion for subtropical bedding. These tender perennials mix well with tall plants of many other kinds and are ideal for a central role in a border with hot colors. Cannas have never lost their ability to shock when used well in mixed planting schemes. Their big, banana-like leaves emerge from the upright stem in a tight roll and then unfurl, often with amazing speed in warm weather. The gladiolus-like flowers are typically big, brassy, and bold, blooming for several months in late summer and until frosts begin in the fall. The leaves may be variegated, bronze, or plain green, and the flowers come in various combinations and shades, always on the "hot" side of the color spectrum.

The remarkable variegated forms look good in any situation, including pots and containers. The best may well be *Canna* 'Tropicanna', sometimes sold as *Canna* 'Durban', with stunning leaf coloration of red veins picked out against a background of dark purple. The flowers are orange. Many excellent cannas have purple or bronze foliage. These include the tricky but sought-after cultivar *Canna* 'King Humbert', whose dark bronze purple foliage is a perfect foil for its scarlet flowers. For a more subtle color scheme, choose *Canna* 'Shenandoah'. This combines bronze foliage with large flowers of a soft, deep pink. Dwarf cannas can be found in some nurseries, and these include *Canna* 'Lucifer', one of the smallest at only 2ft. (60cm) high, with two-tone flowers in red and yellow.

Cannas do best in a fertile soil in full sun but will grow in most soils if they are kept reasonably moist. In mild winters in favored areas cannas, like dahlias, will often survive if left in the ground, especially if given a protective mulch. To be on the safe side, however,

Canna 'Lucifer'

Cordyline australis 'Torbay Dazzler'

Brugmansia suaveolens

lift some of the rhizomes of each kind in the fall and store them in a dry, cool, but frost-free place, in case those left in situ die. To increase your stock, divide canna rhizomes every second or third year. They multiply reasonably well in summer, and splitting them up will give you a useful supply of new plants and prevent the existing ones from becoming congested.

Like cannas, **cordylines** (zone 7–11) also featured in Victorian bedding. Today they are usually seen in pots or as accent plants in sheltered borders, though the species *Cordyline australis* will eventually grow into a mop-headed tree in the right conditions. They need well-drained soil in a sunny place. In winter the more tender varieties may need protection: tie the leaves loosely into a bunch to protect the vulnerable growing tip.

More named varieties appear all the time as breeders strive to achieve more unusual colorings and variegations. Varieties worth seeking out include *Cordyline australis* 'Torbay Dazzler', a small, erect, variegated form, boldly striped in cream and green, and *Cordyline australis* 'Sundance', which is tinged with red. The darkest cordyline is 'Purple Tower' (see page 41).

A totally different star of the summer garden is the unmistakable **brugmansia** (formerly datura) (zone 10). Angels' trumpets, as they are also known, have become more familiar with the increasing popularity of sunrooms, but they quite happily spend the summer outside provided they are kept frost-free in a greenhouse or sunroom in winter.

These are imposing woody perennials, and one of them in a large container on a patio will steal the show. Though far from compact, brugmansias are so dramatic when grown well that they are worth accommodating if possible. Try training one as a standard, with a bare trunk to 6ft. (2m) or so, to economize on ground space (see page 37). The large, dangling, 'angels' trumpet' blooms come in a range of shades from white through cream and yellow to peach, orange, pink, or red. *Brugmansia × candida* 'Grand Marnier' is popular, free-flowering, and versatile, with scented, pale orange-yellow flowers. Scent is one of the best things about brugmansias, so place them where the fragrance can be enjoyed as you sit outdoors on a balmy summer evening. Varieties said to have the best perfume include the white-

flowered *Brugmansia suaveolens* and *Brugmansia × cubensis* 'Charles Grimaldi', which has large, soft orange flowers. *Brugmansia versicolor* grows into a small, graceful tree up to 8ft. (2.4m) tall, with enormous white flowers that age to peach.

Brugmansias enjoy good living, with plenty of water in the growing season. Despite their rise in popularity, the plants are very toxic if ingested, so it is advisable to grow them out of the reach of small children and pets.

Unlike brugmansias, many of the **phormiums** (zone 8–10), or New Zealand flaxes, stand up very well to more extreme weather, taking occasional frost, strong sunshine, and sea breezes in their stride. The two available species each have a number of cultivars, and there are many hybrids. As you might expect, the colored varieties are smaller and more tender than the common green forms. They need a more sheltered position, especially those with yellow in the leaves, but are worth a little extra trouble. *Phormium cookianum* ssp. *hookeri* 'Cream Delight', a statuesque plant with gracefully arching leaves, is a tried and tested, popular cultivar, handsomely striped in creamy yellow and dark green. *Phormium* **'Sundowner'**, a more upright hybrid, is green with glowing tones of pink and bronze.

Alongside cannas and phormiums, ornamental gingers are among the best exotics for temperate climates. Used imaginatively in mixed planting, they can make a garden look genuinely tropical, suggesting fragrant, spicy foods and sultry evenings. **Hedychiums** (zone 8–11), the most reliable group of gingers, have showy, usually scented flowers and lush green tropical foliage. Large blooms in shades of red, yellow, orange, or white emerge from the top of a tall, canelike stem, perfuming the air.

Exotics on the brink of hardiness, they are perhaps best avoided by gardeners who require guaranteed success, for only trial and error will determine which of these plants will succeed in a particular garden—and even that can vary from year to year. However, a few hedychiums can be grown outside, surviving brief periods of freezing conditions if mulched or grown among evergreen foliage for protection. In cold areas grow them in pots or tubs, sunk into a border or displayed on the patio. They can then be moved easily in doubtful winter weather. In the growing season hedychiums like

Hedychium densiflorum

Abutilon 'Kentish Belle'

Fremontodendron 'California Glory'

Abutilon vitifolium 'Tennant's White'

VIEWING EXOTICS

To get some ideas for exotic planting, visit either a public conservatory or one of the many specialty nurseries in the southern states.

Exotic plants flourish in many public conservatories, even in winter. In some specialty nurseries in southern locations, exotics such as agaves overwinter happily outdoors. Cannas, tender salvias, satin-leaved astelias, towering blue echiums, and huge agapanthus bask in the borders, combining with the palm trees to give the impression of a garden from very much warmer climes.

---

comfortably warm temperatures, plenty of water, and a monthly feed. Most do best in bright, part shade rather than hot sunshine. They may not bloom in their first year, but be patient: they will ultimately be spectacular.

Good varieties include *Hedychium coccineum*, a tall, slim species with fragrant, scarlet-orange flowers which, though not large, grow in a dense cluster, to telling effect. Its cultivar **'Tara'** has larger flowers but little scent. *Hedychium densiflorum* is among the hardiest gingers: look out for its cultivars **'Assam Orange'** and the very fragrant, pale yellow **'Stephen'**.

Also of variable hardiness are the **abutilons** (zone 9–11), a large group of fast-growing shrubs related to hollyhocks and hibiscus and with equally beautiful flowers. The plants undoubtedly earn their space if they can be admired at close range. Hanging like bells, or of a more open saucer shape, they bloom over a long period and come in a good range of rich colors: scarlet, crimson, white, lavender, and

yellow. The slender stems carry maple-shaped leaves, attractively variegated in some forms. Most of the abutilons are evergreen, growing rapidly to 6ft. (2m) or more in rich, well-drained soil.

Many abutilons are too tender to grow outdoors, but others are tough enough to survive all but the harshest winters, provided they are planted beside a warm wall or in a sunny, open position in a mild, coastal garden. None are out-and-out hardy but, like many tender shrubs, they will sometimes shoot up again from the base when they appear to have been killed by frost, so do not be too hasty in digging up any winter casualties: wait and see.

One of the hardier species, worth trying in the open border, is the South American *Abutilon vitifolium*. It is short-lived but should last for a few seasons, growing to 10ft. (3m) or so. With the satin sheen of its flowers, and gray-green leaves, it resembles the mallow, a close relative. The cultivar *Abutilon vitifolium* **'Tennant's White'** has many large white flowers,

SPACE-SAVING SPIKES—COMPACT PLANTS WITH A VERTICAL HABIT *Iris pallida* 'Variegata' •

while *Abutilon × suntense* 'Jermyns', has dark mauve blooms. *Abutilon* **'Kentish Belle'** is a compact shrub with beautiful flowers of soft apricot orange. The attractive but considerably more tender *Abutilon megapotamicum* **'Variegatum'** has leaves that are freely spotted with yellow.

A flamboyant shrub of reasonable size for a warm, sunny wall is the **fremontodendron**, sometimes known as the flannel bush. *Fremontodendron* **'California Glory'** (zone 9–11) is possibly the best cultivated form, with many large yellow flowers all summer. Fremontodendrons require very well-drained soil, are surprisingly resistant to cold, and will not need watering once established, growing quite happily in alkaline soil. In favorable conditions they can make up to 20ft. (6m) of growth, though they tend to be short-lived and can sometimes die almost overnight. As the roots are shallow, it is a good idea to stake the young stem after planting. Take care handling the plant because hairs from its leaves and stems may irritate eyes and skin.

Their African origins and tropical appearance put **kniphofias** (zone 6–9) with other exotics even though many of them are quite hardy. This amazing group of highly ornamental plants ranges from dwarfs to giants, flowering at different times, from early summer until the frosts. Flower colors range from reds and oranges through yellow to lime green and cream, not forgetting the two-toned yellow and coral red forms that gave the genus its everyday names of red-hot poker and torch lily. These old-fashioned types are the hardiest and most reliable, tolerating neglect and often seen among the stalwarts that have managed to survive in long-abandoned gardens.

Everyone knows red-hot pokers, but these old favorites have undergone something of a modernization in recent years, as enthusiastic breeders have come up with more and more compact, hardy cultivars in many different colors. *Kniphofia* **'John Benary'** is a good coral red, while the slender **'Jenny Bloom'** is in more subtle peaches-and-cream hues. Yellow pokers include the excellent golden *Kniphofia* **'Bees' Sunset'** and green-tinged **'Percy's Pride'**. If you like the idea of the older, two-tone, large pokers, *Kniphofia uvaria* **'Nobilis'** is the star: 6ft. (2m) tall and flowering in late summer and fall. More compact pokers in the traditional colors include **'Atlanta'**, **'Samuel's Sensation'**, and **'Alcazar'**.

Kniphofias need sun, and soil that does not lack moisture in the growing season, but has sharp winter drainage. Cut down the flower stalks as they fade, but leave the foliage to protect the crown in winter. Discard old foliage in spring, leaving the emerging new leaves in the center of each clump intact.

Kniphofia uvaria 'Alcazar'

SUCCULENTS FOR INDOORS AND OUT

For an exotic garden on a small scale, there are no better or more trouble-free plants than the succulents. Echeverias, aeoniums, aloes, and agaves all come in a fascinating range of shapes, sizes, and colors. Planted in interesting containers, a collection of these drought-tolerant plants, perhaps arranged with a cactus or two and a couple of dwarf grasses in pots, immediately lends an exotic touch to a sunny porch or patio.

Although they do not like to go short of water for too long in summer, one requirement of these natives of the world's dry places is good drainage, so plant them in gritty, free-draining potting mix. They will be happy to spend the winter indoors, kept fairly dry on a sunny windowsill. If they outgrow their space (and some do reach a large size in their native habitats), they can be planted outdoors in beds and borders for a summer season, though most will not withstand wet, cold winter weather.

Recommended varieties

Aeonium 'Zwartkop' · Agave victoriae-reginae · Aloe variegata · Crassula falcata · Echeveria secunda var. glauca

Kniphofia caulescens • Kniphofia 'Little Maid' • Phormium 'Bronze Baby' • Sisyrinchium striatum •

Grasses and bamboos

Grasses and bamboos are well established as popular garden plants. From tiny sedges to towering canes twice the height of a man, these versatile plants are known and used increasingly, both in mixed plantings and as stand-alone features. Very effective in achieving a clean, contemporary look, grasses and bamboos come in a palette of subtle colors, and there is one for every situation—sunny or shady, damp or dry.

GRASSES

Grasses have a low-key beauty quite unlike that of other garden plants. They have many excellent qualities. Used in drifts or individually, they can often complement the shapes and colors of the plants around them, opening up numerous design possibilities with their different forms and textures. They can provide vertical accents, neat edgings, and low ground cover, either performing steadily for much of the year or effecting temporary changes of scene. Many grow happily in containers, making them useful for patios and for filling temporary gaps in borders. They are especially valuable in late summer and fall, when they may well be highlighted by low, golden sunshine. A select few even look lovely long into the winter, holding their shape to become a key garden feature, especially when rimed by hoarfrost.

Many perennial grasses will go from strength to strength, growing more beautiful each year. For long-term use in a small space, it is usually better to choose grasses that form tidy clumps, rather than the running, rhizomatous types that invade their neighbors and become a nuisance if not kept in check.

Miscanthus (zone 5–9) are among the stateliest of grasses. The larger varieties would be overpowering in a small garden, but fortunately some of the more compact cultivars are among the

Miscanthus sinensis 'Morning Light'

Cortaderia selloana 'Pumila'

best. The striped *Miscanthus sinensis* **'Morning Light'** is stunning in a white border or as an accent plant against a darker background. *Miscanthus sinensis* **'Zebrinus'** has horizontally banded leaves and looks good in dappled shade. Both grow to about 4ft. (1.2m).

Like miscanthus, **pampas grass** (*Cortaderia selloana*) tends to be big and bulky. However, sometimes a large plant with a presence is needed for a particular effect in a small space and, with its great silky plumes held aloft on long stalks, pampas grass can make a telling feature. *Cortaderia selloana* **'Pumila'** (zone 6–9) is a good variety of moderate size so is more suitable for limited spaces. It has creamy white flowers on stems up to 5ft. (1.5m) tall.

Another tall grass worth considering for any garden is *Stipa gigantea* (zone 6–9). It has such an airy habit that it

almost appears to be taking up no space at all. Its oatlike flower heads, golden all summer, mature to a paler color and continue to look beautiful into winter. Its smaller relative *Stipa tenuissima* (zone 8–9) is equally attractive, with fine, silky leaves that just demand to be touched. Both these grasses work well in a sharply drained mixed border in full sun. For a damper, shadier situation, a good light and feathery grass would be *Deschampsia cespitosa* 'Goldtau' (zone 4–9).

Grasses like the stipas that stand well into the winter months are especially deserving of space in a small garden. For a sunny position, another such would be *Calamagrostis* × *acutiflora* **'Overdam'** (zone 5–9), with variegated young leaves and upright stems that support airy, purplish flower heads. For all-year interest generally, the evergreen

GRASSES FOR SHADE   *Carex elata* 'Aurea' • *Carex morrowii* 'Fisher's Form' • *Carex pendula* •

sedges (*Carex*) are difficult to beat. One of the neatest, suitable for the edge of a border or for gravel in partial shade, is **Carex conica 'Snowline'** (zone 7–9). This has tufts of white-variegated leaves no more than 6in. (15cm) high, while the similar **Carex oshimensis 'Evergold'** (zone 5–9) is larger, with gold variegation. Other carex have a fountainlike arrangement of leathery leaves. These varieties are good all-year plants in containers or at the corners of borders; they include the resilient, tawny **Carex buchananii** (zone 7–9).

Fescues (zone 6–9) are smaller grasses, with needlelike leaves in finely textured, usually silvery blue clumps. They are lovely with sedums, silver-leaved plants, and dwarf spring bulbs, and enjoy the same well-drained conditions, either in a bed or in containers. The best forms are **Festuca glauca 'Blaufuchs'** and **Festuca glauca 'Elijah Blue'**.

For a plant to attract attention in late summer, choose one of the fountain grasses (*Pennisetum*). These all have wonderful fluffy flower heads and thrive in full sun, preferring poor, gravely soils. **Pennisetum setaceum** (zone 9) has rusty green foliage and fuzzy, pinkish flower spikes. It is tender and sometimes grown as an annual. The colors are much deeper and more intense in its cultivar **'Rubrum'**. Related perennials include **Pennisetum orientale** (zone 7–9), a neat, tufted plant with bottle-brush flowers, and the diminutive **Pennisetum**

GOOD COMPANIONS FOR GRASSES

Mix *Pennisetum orientale* (1) (z. 7–9) with annual or perennial flowers in the bright, hot colors of late summer, for example *Helenium* 'Moerheim Beauty' (2) (z. 3–8).

Beneath deciduous shrubs, the bright evergreen leaves of *Carex oshimensis* 'Evergold' (3) (z. 5–9) contrast pleasingly with *Pachysandra terminalis* (4) (z. 5–8).

Grow *Stipa gigantea* (5) (z. 6–9) near a bronze- or purple-leaved shrub such as *Cotinus* 'Grace' (6) (z. 5–8). Site the plants where low evening sunlight will shine through them.

alopecuroides 'Little Bunny' (zone 5–9). These are hardier but seldom keep their flower heads through the winter.

In the front rank for its remarkable, hairy flower heads is **Hordeum jubatum** (zone 5–9), descriptively called squirrel-tail grass. A kind of barley, it is best treated as an annual and is likely to self-seed. Unfortunately, it disintegrates after a few weeks but, while they last, the seed heads are truly eye-catching, especially in low sunshine late in the day.

A favorite annual grass, good for cutting as well as in borders, is the fast-growing but short-lived **Briza maxima** (quaking grass). The distinctive, shiny, buff flower heads hang from hairlike stems, catching every passing breeze and remaining decorative for some time before shedding their seeds. Best grown in groups for impact, quaking grass may be sown in situ and may well self-seed. Gather a few flower heads to dry for use in winter arrangements.

Pennisetum alopecuroides 'Little Bunny'

Hordeum jubatum

Briza maxima

Chasmanthium latifolium • *Hakonechloa macra* 'Aureola' • *Luzula sylvatica* 'Marginata' • *Milium effusum* 'Aureum' •

GOOD COMPANIONS FOR GRASSES

Festuca glauca 'Blaufuchs' (1) (z. 4–8) grouped with *Sedum spectabile* (2) (z. 4–8) will give an interesting textural contrast all summer.

Carex buchananii (3) (z. 7–9) complements orange tulips such as *Tulipa* 'Ballerina' (4) (z. 4–8).

A carpet of the neat *Carex conica* 'Snowline' (5) (z. 7–9) looks good when brought to life by dwarf blue spring bulbs such as *Scilla bifolia* (6) (z. 5–8).

other plants, looking effective when underplanted with richly colored sedges. The dappled shade cast by bamboo clumps is ideal for pulmonarias, heucheras, ivies, and hardy geraniums. Spring-flowering bulbs such as wood anemones, snowdrops, and snowflakes can also be scattered effectively among the underplanting.

From treelike giants to knee-high dwarfs, bamboos come in a vast range of heights. Along with this, the most important consideration when choosing a bamboo is whether it has a clump-forming or a running habit. Needless to say, the clump-forming bamboos are less invasive and will usually be a much better choice for the garden than the running species, particularly where space is limited. Some of the rampant "runners," including most of the sasas, are attractive but they should be reserved for ground cover in large areas or kept in containers where they are unlikely to escape.

The genus *Phyllostachys*, from coastal China, is the one to which most of the medium and large hardy bamboos belong. The black bamboo, **Phyllostachys nigra** (zone 7–10), is a favorite, its slender green culms ripening to glossy, jet black. It forms grace-

BAMBOOS

The reputation of certain bamboos for being rampant and invasive makes some gardeners wary of using them at all, especially in smaller gardens. There is no need for such extreme caution: as with many kinds of plant, there are bamboos adapted to many different situations and many different purposes. These versatile members of the grass family can be attractive and useful, even in confined spaces, one of the main benefits being that they are evergreen. It is worth getting to know the different characteristics of the commonly used types and adding bamboos to the list of possibilities when you are choosing plants for screening, or for ground cover, or for planting as stand-alone specimens.

Bamboos suit many garden styles. They can help to create a "jungly" look when combined with hardy and half-hardy, "tropical" foliage such as tree ferns, fatsias, and phormiums. They lend themselves well to modern and oriental minimalist planting styles—though in this kind of setting, where any untidiness is all too visible, they must be kept especially well groomed. They associate well with many

GROWING BAMBOOS

Bamboos enjoy good living. They like rich, well-drained soil and protection from strong winds, which can make them look untidy and bare. As a general rule, large bamboos are better with at least a few hours of direct sunlight a day, while some of the smaller ones can tolerate quite shady conditions. All bamboos will benefit from a mulch of organic matter: ideally this should be their own sheaths and fallen leaves, which can be left to carpet the ground around the base of the plant

BAMBOOS WITH COLORED CANES *Phyllostachys aurea* (golden) • *Phyllostachys nigra* (green, then black) •

Fargesia murielae

Pseudosasa japonica

(30cm) high. All these are also suitable for planting in containers, where their vigor can be kept firmly under control. *Pseudosasa japonica* (zone 7–9), the Japanese arrow bamboo, can also be invasive (zone 7–10). It makes a good container plant and is often used for hedges and screening, especially in windy or coastal areas.

CANE FACTS

Bamboos differ from other plants in that the diameter of their canes (culms) does not increase after they emerge from the ground. Each season's new culms are usually thicker and taller than the old ones, so the largest canes in the clump tend to be the youngest. To keep bamboos looking smart and healthy, neaten the clumps once a year by removing old and dead canes at the base. The thinnings are always useful in the garden as supports for herbaceous plants, and larger canes can be used to make wigwams or arches for climbing beans, sweet peas, and other twiners and scramblers.

fully arching clumps and grows quite slowly. Though tall, it can be exactly the right bamboo to choose for a bold design effect in a confined area. It also stands well through the winter, which makes it especially deserving of precious space. Black bamboo is much used in contemporary planting and looks stylish in a well-designed container. Different forms are available, including the more compact, smaller-leaved *Phyllostachys nigra* f. *punctata* (zone 7–10).

Fargesia murielae (also known as *Sinarundinaria* or *Arundinaria murielae*) (zone 5–9) was named by the great plant hunter, E.H. Wilson, after his daughter Muriel. This graceful plant, known as the umbrella bamboo, forms weeping clumps of slender canes that change, with age, from bright green to yellow. There are several dwarf cultivars, of which one of the smallest is *Fargesia murielae* 'Harewood'.

Small bamboos can be useful for covering bare ground beneath trees. *Pleioblastus variegatus* (zone 7–8) is slow to establish but is quite vigorous once settled and may need controlling where space is limited. It grows to a height of approximately 3ft. (1m). Its

variegation is attractive even in winter. *Pleioblastus auricomus* (zone 8–9) is taller and has golden foliage. This color will be brighter in a sunny position, especially on the younger stems; prune in late winter to encourage the growth of new stems. *Pleioblastus pygmaeus* (zone 7–8) is one of the very shortest bamboos, rather invasive but only 1ft.

GOOD COMPANIONS FOR BAMBOOS

The golden foliage of *Pleioblastus viridistriatus* (1) (z. 7–8) is flattered by dark-leaved planting at its feet: try *Veronica peduncularis* 'Georgia Blue' (2) (z. 4–8).

The slim, dark canes of *Phyllostachys nigra* (3) (z. 7–10) have a contemporary look that is well complemented by such light-as-air grasses as *Molinia caerulea* (4) (z. 5–9).

Semiarundinaria fastuosa (green, then purple) • *Thamnocalamus crassinodus* 'Kew Beauty' (blue) •

Hostas and ferns

Many people would surely include hostas among their favorite foliage plants. Hardy, tough companions for flowering shrubs and useful for almost any sort of underplanting, they brighten damp, dark corners and are usually very successful in pots. Growing hostas in containers puts their handsome foliage in the spotlight and makes it easier to keep the plants pest-free.

Hosta 'Gold Standard'

Hosta 'June'

Hosta 'Golden Tiara'

HOSTAS

Scarcely a generation ago it would have been a challenge, even for an expert, to list more than 20 or 30 varieties of hosta (zone 4–8). Today, over 1,000 named cultivars and species are commercially available, and many more are known to enthusiasts and specialty collectors. This is due to an insatiable demand from enthusiasts, and to the devotion of breeders and nurserymen, mainly in the United States. Micropropagation now enables salable plants of recently introduced cultivars to be produced more rapidly, and many first-class new hostas are joining old favorites in garden centers and gardens.

From the broad paddles of *Hosta sieboldiana* var. *elegans* to the tiny quills of the aptly named *Hosta* 'Thumb Nail', hosta leaves vary tremendously in size and in many other respects. In texture they can be smooth, ridged, or quilted; in shape they range from long and lancelike to heart-shaped or round. Some are as flat as a board, others are frilled, spoon-shaped or deeply cupped. They can be green, gray, golden, or variegated, or any permutation of these.

The classic conditions for growing hostas are dappled shade, cool, leafy, moisture-retentive soil, and appropriate feeding. However, different kinds do vary in their needs and in their tolerance of sunlight. This means that there is now likely to be a hosta to suit almost any part of your garden. Some of the green forms, such as the night-scented *Hosta* 'Royal Standard', are happy in sun as long as they are not dry at the roots. Like many golden-leaved plants, most hostas with yellow leaves or gold variegation, such as *Hosta* 'August Moon' or the larger *Hosta* 'Gold Standard', actually

---

GOOD COMPANIONS

Asplenium trichomanes (1) (z. 2–6) is on just the right scale for a planting in semi-shade with a small-leaved hosta cultivar such as 'Ginko Craig' (2) (z. 4–8).

Hosta 'Wide Brim' (3) (z. 4–8) is good in difficult, dry shade, where it grows with *Iris foetidissima* (4) (z. 6–9). For early spring, add *Scilla mischtschenkoana* (z. 5–8).

SLUG-RESISTANT ALTERNATIVES TO HOSTAS *Bergenia • Brunnera • Epimedium • Heuchera •*

color better if they receive some sunlight each day (but not so much that their leaves scorch). *Hosta* '**So Sweet**', (zone 4–8) which has fragrant flowers and neat green leaves edged with cream, is fairly sun-tolerant. Blue hostas are much happier in shade, where their beautiful color lasts longer. Two good compact blue cultivars are *Hosta* '**Halcyon**' (zone 4–8) and *Hosta* '**Blue Wedgwood**' (zone 4–8). Variegated blues, such as *Hosta* '**June**' (zone 4–8), develop more contrast in bright light but have prettier, more subtle coloring in the shade. Generally, hostas grown in damp shade will produce larger, lush leaves at the expense of flowers. The same variety grown in sunshine and drier soil will tend to flower more abundantly. Hostas are usually chosen for their leaves, but some cultivars are worth growing for their deep purple flower color too. Compact ones include the white-rimmed *Hosta* '**Ginko Craig**' (zone 4–8) and the gold-edged *Hosta* '**Golden Tiara**' (zone 4–8).

Many gardeners do not think of hostas as potted plants, but life in a container suits most hostas very well.

Some, in fact, are better in pots, though they do demand more frequent watering and repotting when necessary. The extra trouble is worthwhile, because potted hostas are so versatile—either alone or grouped with other container plants—for filling gaps or creating focal points in difficult, shady areas. They can also be kept in optimum shape by moving them around during the growing season to give each one the conditions it likes best. Grow hostas in plastic pots of a suitable size, hiding these inside decorative containers. This makes the plants easier to repot, without the risk of having to painstakingly extract a potbound plant from a prized container.

Hostas with bold, elegantly arching leaves look especially handsome in pots, effective as a stand-alone feature or used in pairs on either side of a doorway or gate. It is usually better to stick to one variety per pot, but other compatible plants such as creeping ivies and compact ferns arranged with a hosta in a larger container will give an attractive tapestry effect of different leaf shapes and textures.

ALTERNATIVE SLUG CONTROL

Every gardener knows that hostas are a favorite of slugs and snails, which can reduce their beautiful leaves to tatters overnight. Keeping these pests at bay is always a priority for those who grow hostas.

Many gardeners prefer not to use chemical slug pellets, and there are various alternative measures. Deterrents include simply making the area around hostas less attractive to slugs and snails. Mulching with grit around the plants will make life uncomfortable for them, and clearing away dying vegetation promptly will give them fewer places to breed. Inspecting the plants with a flashlight on a mild, damp evening will often reveal the culprits, which can then be disposed of. (Don't forget to look underneath the leaves.) Suppliers of biological control products now market a successful biological slug control using pathogenic nematodes. Commercially available copper-impregnated mats and bands are another off-the-shelf deterrent.

Some varieties seem to suffer less slug damage than others: try the large and robust *Hosta* 'Sum and Substance' and the smaller, green-leaved *Hosta* 'Invincible'. There is even a cultivar named 'Silvery Slugproof'. Hostas grown in pots are less likely to suffer slug and snail damage than those in the open ground. As a last resort, instead of hostas, consider growing some of the other leafy ground-cover plants that are less appealing to slugs (see strip at the foot of the page).

Hosta 'Halcyon' is generally acclaimed as one of the best blues. These fine clumps show the impact that hostas can make when they are growing strongly, in the right place, and free from pests.

Luzula sylvatica • *Saxifraga* × *urbium* • *Stachys byzantina* • *Tellima grandiflora* • *Tolmiea menziesii* 'Taff's Gold' •

Dryopteris filix-mas

Polypodium vulgare

FERNS

Fashionable during the Victorian era, hardy ferns then seemed to be out of favor for a long time. The ever-growing interest in naturalistic planting has deservedly brought them back into the limelight, and they are now to be seen bringing a unique grace and delicacy to many a planting scheme. The evergreen types are especially useful for furnishing small gardens with welcome winter foliage that is quite unlike that of any other plant group.

Many ferns are relatively easy to grow but, as with many plants, success depends on your ability to give them conditions close to those they enjoy in their native habitat. For most ferns this means a sheltered, cool position, damp (but not waterlogged) soil, and plenty of humus in the form of compost or leaf mold. Their light requirements vary: filtered sunlight will suit many ferns, but some are happy in dense shade and a few will tolerate full sun. Never let newly planted ferns dry out. A mulch at planting time will help to prevent this.

Some of the hardy ferns grown in gardens are native species, or cultivars derived from these. They are likely to self-sow if they are happy, always an unexpected bonus if they appear in odd places where you may not have thought of planting anything. An easy fern to start with is *Dryopteris filix-mas* (zone 2–7), the male fern. It is one of the least fussy species, tolerating dry as well as damp shade and growing up to 3ft. (1m) high. Although it is not normally evergreen, its fronds last well into early winter, and it is fascinating again from late spring when its fronds begin to unfurl, creating spiral patterns.

For a true evergreen fern, a good choice is *Polystichum setiferum* (zone 7–8). This is the soft shield fern, a European native. It has many garden variants, of different shapes and sizes, with soft, feathery fronds that prefer shade. A good partner is the hart's tongue fern, *Asplenium scolopendrium* (zone 5–9), with undivided, shiny green fronds. This tough and tolerant plant will grow in places that suit few others, reaching 2ft. (60cm) and usually self-sowing generously. It is happy in alkaline soil and sometimes grows on old walls and steps. There are some interesting groups of cultivars available in which the margin is wavy (Undulatum Group) or tightly crimped (Crispum Group). Another wall colonizer that will gradually spread its rhizomes through cracks in stonework or paving is *Polypodium vulgare* (zone 3–6). The fronds are invaluable for their telling tracery of green throughout the winter.

A relative of hart's tongue fern that is completely different but also delightful is the maidenhair spleenwort, *Asplenium trichomanes* (zone 2–6).

FERN WORDS

Fern terminology is a little different from everyday plant vocabulary. The stem on a fern is called the *caudex*; the leaf is a *frond* including the *stipe* (leaf stalk) and the *blade*, which is the expanded portion of a frond. The midrib of a frond is known as the *rachis*. Unlike many other plants, ferns do not make seeds, but *spores*: minute, usually unicellular, asexual reproductive bodies. During late summer and fall many ferns form a crown of up to a dozen tightly coiled young leaves that resemble the neck of a violin and are often called a *fiddlehead* or *crosier*.

MORE FERNS FOR DAMP PLACES: *Athyrium filix-femina • Adiantum venustum • Adiantum aleuticum •*

Adiantum pedatum

Athyrium niponicum var. pictum

Osmunda regalis

This is a compact, small-leaved, and dainty fern that grows in a delicate, tufted star formation.

More often seen as houseplants, the maidenhair ferns include several hardy species. Their beautiful, fragile-looking foliage makes them worthy of a place in any garden where they will grow. *Adiantum pedatum* (zone 3–8), a native of woodland areas, is known as the horseshoe fern because of the distinctive arrangement of its black-stemmed fronds in U-shaped crowns. This is an intriguing deciduous hardy fern for a moist, shady area.

The Latin word *pictum* means painted, and the Japanese painted fern, *Athyrium niponicum* var. *pictum* (zone 4–9), is true to its name, with fronds in a subtle and unusual mixture of silvery gray, wine red, and green. The coloring of the new leaves in spring is especially intense. This is a superb garden fern and makes a fine feature plant in a pot or container. It needs a moist, sheltered, and shady position.

Growing up to some 5ft. (1.5m) in favorable conditions, *Matteuccia struthiopteris* (zone 2–7) is on the large side for small spaces, but its remarkable shuttlecocks of tapering fronds make such a stately feature in late spring that it is worth finding space for it if you can. With plenty of moisture, it can tolerate the dappled sunlight that is so flattering to it. The equally large royal fern, *Osmunda regalis* (zone 2–8), can also tolerate sun, given ample moisture and acidic soil. It looks especially happy in damp ground beside (but not in) water.

GOOD COMPANIONS FOR FERNS

Asplenium scolopendrium Crispum Group (1) (z. 5–9) will brighten a damp, lightly shaded area very effectively with *Lamium maculatum* 'Album' (2) (z. 4–7).

Polystichum setiferum (3) (z. 7–8) will be happy to share a sunless environment with *Fatsia japonica* (4) (z. 8–9), making a carpet of contrasting leaf form.

Matteuccia struthiopteris (5) (z. 2–7) is best surrounded by low planting that will not steal the limelight. Try *Vinca minor* f. *alba* 'Getrude Jekyll' (6) (z. 5–8).

Cystopteris fragilis • Dryopteris affinis • Dryopteris dilatata • Onoclea sensibilis •

HARDY

Into the category of hardy plants come many classic components of the traditional English-style garden. Herbaceous perennials, flowering shrubs, and scented or colorful climbers are the "soft furnishings" that lend richness and depth to structural planting, their impact increasing as they mature from year to year. A well-planned border filled with carefully chosen hardy plants combines the stability and comfortable familiarity of perennial planting with the excitement of constantly changing color and form as the seasons revolve.

RIGHT: Perennial planting edging an informal path

Climbers

Climbing plants are especially valuable in small gardens, where the third dimension is particularly important in offsetting the limitations of ground area. As well as appearing to increase available planting space, climbers are useful for creating privacy, hiding eyesores, muffling sound, and providing shade.

Their scrambling habit and bold, richly colored flowers make clematis good partners for shrubs and other climbers, such as this *Schizophragma*.

When choosing climbers for a small garden it is important to know what to avoid because, once established, many climbing plants become rampant colonizers of space. Keeping them in check is disfiguring for the plants and exhausting for the gardener, so vigorous climbers—such as large rambler roses, *Fallopia baldschuanicum* (Russian vine), *Parthenocissus tricuspidata* (Boston ivy), and *Clematis montana*—should be planted only where there is plenty of room for them to expand. Fortunately, there are many other climbers that are well suited to small gardens or areas where growth must be restricted.

It is also important to select the right plant for the position. Take into account not just the planting conditions—sun or shade, damp or dry—but the type of support: a high wall with trellis; a fence; an arbor, obelisk, or arch. Ensuring that a plant has the right kind of support can be a challenge, but it helps to understand that plants climb in different ways: some adhere, others scramble; some have twining stems, others have curling tendrils or leafstalks.

Provided it is sound and undamaged, a wall is a good support for climbers that adhere by means of either sticky pads or short, stout stem roots. The former include most *Parthenocissus*. The least vigorous and most attractive of these relatives of the grapevine is *Parthenocissus henryana* (zone 8–9), whose silvery-veined palmate leaves turn to russet and red in the fall. Stem-rooting climbers include the ivies (see page 75), *Euonymus fortunei* (see page 45), and *Hydrangea anomala* ssp. *petiolaris* (zone 4–7). This hydrangea is a most useful climber for dull, shady walls. Like other plants that adhere, it is slow to establish and, at first, you will probably need to tie it in to encourage it to cling. However, it will eventually cover even a large surface with greenery enlivened by modest but pretty white flowers in midsummer. *Hydrangea seemannii* (zone 8–9), now becoming more widely available, is similar but has larger, evergreen leaves.

Self-clinging climbers of either type must, of course, be kept away from tiles, drains, and guttering, and they should never be allowed to grow on old, soft-mortared walls or on masonry or stucco that is defective. Stem roots, in particular, will find their way into any cracks or imperfections and make them worse. However, provided these

Shapely, silver-veined leaves, subtle autumn colors, and a more restrained growth habit help make *Parthenocissus henryana* more aristocratic than its rampant relatives, Virginia creeper and Boston ivy.

SHADE-TOLERANT CLIMBERS *Berberidopsis corallina* • *Clematis* 'Nelly Moser' • *Hedera helix* 'Goldchild' •

Solanum laxum 'Album'

Actinidia kolomikta

Yellow blooms of *Jasminum nudiflorum* (1) (z. 6–10) fill the gap between the winter berries (2) and spring flowers (3) of *Cotoneaster horizontalis* (z. 5–7).

Ceanothus 'Concha' (4) (z. 9–10) is a good host for *Clematis* × *durandii* (5) (z. 5–7), providing shade and support.

Cotinus coggygria 'Royal Purple' (6) (z. 4–8) is matched in color and vigor by *Clematis* 'Etoile Rose' (7) (z. 5–9).

Rosa 'Goldfinch' (8) (z. 4–9) and *Clematis tangutica* (9) (z. 6–9): a partnership in summer yellows, with the fluffy clematis seed heads in winter.

Vitis vinifera 'Purpurea' (10) (z. 6–8) is a fine pergola companion for the long-flowering and almost thornless *Rosa* 'Zéphirine Drouhin' (11) (z. 6–11).

Solanum crispum 'Glasnevin'

Akebia quinata

climbers are checked periodically and controlled when necessary, they are unlikely to damage surfaces that are smooth, solid, and well maintained.

Scrambling plants climb with the aid of long, flexible stems that they push up through other vegetation. Some, such as roses (see pages 80–81), have thorns to help them grip neighboring stems; this is how vigorous ramblers manage to hoist themselves far up into the canopy of a tree. These plants are usually well suited to arches and arbors because their pliable young stems can be trained in any direction (although you will need to tie them into position). Other plants in this category include some clematis (see pages 76–77), jasmine (see page 78), *Eccremocarpus scaber* (see page 167), and the semievergreen potato vine *Solanum laxum* (formerly *Solanum jasminoides*) (zone 9–10). This has a long summer season of yellow-centered, lilac blue flowers similar to those of its relative, the potato. The white form, *Solanum laxum* 'Album', is especially beautiful but just as tender. In cold areas

these may need the protection of a warm wall. *Solanum crispum* 'Glasnevin' (zone 8–10), with similar but darker lilac blue flowers, is a little hardier but generally not such an enthusiastic climber.

Climbers with twining stems include beans, honeysuckle (see page 79), and *Ipomoea* (see page 166) The golden hop, *Humulus lupulus* 'Aureus' (zone 5–8), is a good twiner for semi-shade, best against a dark background such as a yew hedge, where its shapely, bright leaves will show up well, especially in spring. It dies down to the ground in winter but will produce new glowing golden shoots early in the next growing season. Another good twining plant with very attractive foliage is *Actinidia kolomikta* (zone 4–8), a relative of the kiwi fruit, which looks stunning on a sunny wall. Each mature leaf tip appears to have been dipped in white and/or rosy pink paint. *Akebia quinata* (chocolate vine) is fascinating too. Look closely at the shapes of its rich, dusky pink, vanilla-scented flowers; male and

Jasminum nudiflorum • *Jasminum officinale* 'Argenteovariegatum' • *Lonicera tragophylla* • *Pileostegia viburnoides* •

GROWING CLIMBERS IN POTS

There are few gardens – even city courtyards and roof terraces – that cannot accommodate at least one climber in a large pot. With regular watering and feeding, carefully chosen climbers will do perfectly well and can grow surprisingly large. Slow-release fertilizer is good for long-term container planting. A mulch of grit or gravel will deter slugs and help retain moisture.

Wherever possible, container-grown climbers should be repotted once a year. For plants that are already in large pots, or those located where repotting would be difficult, replace the top layer of potting medium with fresh planting mix. Loam-based mixes are heavier than most other composts and more satisfactory for climbers that may become top-heavy. Never allow containers to dry out. Apart from depriving the plant, dry medium will make the pot light and unstable.

Climbers grown in pots must be well supported. Trellis and wires will serve a container at the foot of a wall. For free-standing pots, choose a sheltered position and use bamboo canes (more secure if tied together, wigwam-style) or purpose-made pyramids or obelisks. Tendril climbers may prefer tall twiggy sticks or long willow stems, which can be bent and woven into simple shapes and designs.

Don't forget that climbers can grow horizontally as well as vertically. A climber in a pot could be an excellent way to fill a gap in a border or soften a bare area of paving.

Lathyrus latifolius

Passiflora caerulea 'Eden'

female hang side by side. *Aconitum hemsleyanum* (zone 5–8), a twining herbaceous monkshood, also has curious flowers, smoky lilac and hooded, in late summer. Grow it on canes or let it scramble over shrubs in a border.

Various forms of support are suitable for twining climbers. Most twiners will wind around anything they touch: a pole, wires, a wigwam of canes, a trellis, an obelisk or an adjacent branch. They may need tying in to their intended host to begin with, but after that they need no attention other than an occasional check that they have not wandered elsewhere or outgrown their support. Do not let the strongly twining stems of vigorous plants such as wisteria or honeysuckle get out of hand because they can damage trellises, down spouts, and even roofs if left unchecked.

Many climbing plants cling to the support by means of twining leafstalks (for example many kinds of clematis). Others have wiry tendrils: thin, thread-like structures that grow from the plant's stem and reach around in the air until they find something to grasp and cling to. Once contact is made, the tendril coils itself round the support. Most climbers belonging to the pea family have tendrils. These include culinary peas, sweet peas (*Lathyrus odoratus*, see page 131), and the ornamental "everlasting" peas such as *Lathyrus latifolius* (zone 4–7), *Lathyrus grandiflorus* (zone 6–8), and *Lathyrus rotundifolius* (zone 5–10). These scentless perennial climbers

are ideal for clothing a rough sunny bank, fence, or hedge with colorful summer flowers. *Lathyrus latifolius* 'White Pearl' has white flowers that can disguise gaps in borders, where it can be draped over plants whose flowering is over. Other tendril climbers include grapevines. Some of these are rampant, but an excellent one for garden use is the purple-leaved *Vitis vinifera* 'Purpurea' (zone 6–8), a fine partner for roses or clematis on a sunny arbor.

Another tendril climber, *Passiflora* (passion flower) is grown for its intricate, complex flowers whose component parts are said to represent elements of the story of Jesus. There are numerous species and cultivars, varying in color and in their degree of tenderness. The brightly colored types are suitable only for a heated greenhouse or sunroom, but *Passiflora caerulea* (zone 7–10), the most hardy species, with exquisite purple-blue and white flowers, is often found in sheltered gardens. *Passiflora* presents a dilemma in a small garden: the flowers themselves are worthy of precious space, but most plants grow quite large. Compact and hardy, the new cultivar *Passiflora caerulea* 'Eden' has scented pale amethyst-colored blooms.

Climbers with tendrils grow most happily where they can grip something thin such as string, wire, netting, or stems (either their own or those of other plants). They will normally need to be tied to the uprights of a pergola or arbor as they climb.

Ivy (Hedera)

The number of available varieties of ivy runs into the hundreds and offers a wide range of leaf shapes, sizes, and foliage variegations. Yet these versatile evergreens are sometimes regarded as too ordinary for serious consideration in the garden.

Ivies are, at the very least, useful plants for those places where "nothing will grow." They can cope with deep shade and dry, poor soils and will cover the ugliest surfaces in greenery that looks presentable all year round. Given richer living conditions and used imaginatively, ivies can easily take their place in the front rank of valuable garden plants.

As self-clinging climbers, ivies often give rise to concern about the damage they can do to buildings, but carefully managed cultivated ivies are unlikely to cause problems on sound, well-built walls. A less well-known difficulty is that ivy sap can irritate sensitive skin, so take care when handling the plants.

Hedera colchica 'Sulphur Heart' (formerly 'Paddy's Pride') (z. 6–9) is the most familiar cultivar of Persian ivy, a large-leaved, hardy, robust species native to the Caucasus. It tends to need a little initial help to start clinging: splashing walls with water in dry weather may help.

Frilly-edged *Hedera helix* 'Parsley Crested' (z. 4–9) is one of more than 200 garden cultivars of the common English ivy. Many are variegated, such as 'Glacier' (white) and 'Goldchild' (golden), while others—like this one— have leaves that are interestingly shaped or unusual in color.

Hedera canariensis 'Gloire de Marengo' (z. 8–10) is less hardy than the other garden ivies, but it makes such a handsome silver-and-green foliage feature that it is worth risking occasional winter damage to its leaves. The plant itself is unlikely to be killed. Plant it to cover a low fence or a tree stump.

The vigorous *Hedera hibernica* (Irish ivy) (z. 4–9) is very similar to *Hedera helix* but has larger leaves. Its luxuriant, shiny foliage makes good ground cover or an effective backdrop to variegated plants, winter berries, and seed heads, or flowers in pastel colors or white. Note that it can be invasive.

OTHER GOOD IVIES

Hedera colchica 'Dentata Variegata' (z. 6–9) Excellent bright foliage: downturned, leathery, cream-edged leaves in a mixture of green hues.

Hedera helix 'Atropurpurea' (z. 4–9) An attractive bronze-leaved partner for red-berried shrubs, especially good at close range in winter.

Hedera helix 'Buttercup' (z. 4–9) An ivy for sunny sites: the gold foliage turns green in shade.

Hedera helix 'Green Ripple' (z. 4–9) Dynamic leaf shapes make this an interesting ivy for covering a prominent wall.

Clematis

Its unusual velvety red color and contrasting creamy stamens make *Clematis* 'Niobe' a good subject for planting where it is seen close up.

Clematis have few rivals when it comes to bringing color into a garden at eye level and above. Some types are much more vigorous than others: the popular *Clematis montana* (zone 6–9), for example, would soon take over a small space and might be best avoided. But there is a wide choice of more well-mannered clematis for every season and situation.

Like most plants, clematis have a few requirements that need to be met if they are to thrive. These are not the same for all types of clematis, which is perhaps why these climbers are sometimes thought of as difficult to grow. Most people who have grown even a few clematis successfully, however, would eagerly deny that there is any mystique.

Pruning is often seen as a problem with clematis. However, many varieties are straightforward to prune, and these easy ones are also the best for restricted spaces because they tend to produce relatively small, dainty flowers over a long period. Those that flower in winter and spring need no routine pruning. If the plant becomes too large, simply cut out all the shoots that have flowered. Do this immediately after flowering when these shoots are easy to identify. This will give the plant time to recover before the next flowering season.

Clematis that flower after midsummer, such as *Clematis viticella* (zone 5–8) and its hybrids, produce their flowers on new growth. These are the easiest to prune because it is a simple matter of removing all the old growth to make way for new. In late winter, find a strong pair of buds low down on the plant—no more than 3ft. (1m) above ground level and perhaps much less—and cut off everything above these buds.

The large-flowered hybrids that come into flower in early summer need less severe pruning. The ends of the shoots that have flowered die off. Remove all this dead growth in late winter or after flowering, shortening the stems by cutting them back to a good pair of buds.

Another part of the mystique surrounding clematis-growing concerns clematis wilt, a fungal disease that can suddenly strike plants in their prime, making the shoots droop and turn black. The large-flowered hybrids are particularly susceptible, as are young plants. However, wilt will seldom actually kill a clematis plant, and if you plant quite deeply—with about 2in. (5cm) of the stem buried—the plant should be able to produce new shoots from the base to replace any that die.

Many growers find that a much more common cause of clematis failure is simply lack of water. Clematis do need good drainage, but moisture-retentive soil is essential. Add well-rotted organic matter when planting, and water in dry weather, especially plants near walls and fences, where the ground can become very dry.

Clematis roots are best kept out of full sun. They grow very happily among other plants that will shade their roots while allowing their flowering shoots to scramble up into the sunshine. Shrubs can be excellent planting partners for compact clematis varieties, giving them the support and shade they need. If you choose clematis carefully, the flowers will complement foliage shrubs and give flowering shrubs an additional season of interest.

Clematis 'Frances Rivis' (z. 3–9), a well-tried and tested early-flowering clematis, is very hardy and tolerates partial shade. Its beautiful lavender blue flowers blend well with spring colors, and it looks especially good on a partly shaded cream or white wall.

Clematis 'Markham's Pink' (z. 3–9) is a good cottage garden plant, with a strong constitution and mid-pink, semidouble spring flowers. It will thread itself through the bare branches of a deciduous shrub, and it will tolerate a fair amount of shade. It is also good in a container.

With its long season of summer flowers in a lovely shade of moody indigo blue, *Clematis* 'Petit Faucon' (z. 3–9) is excellent for growing in a mixed border. It is not a clinging climber, but it will scramble over and through a shrub such as *Sambucus* (ornamental elder) or an evergreen ceanothus on a sunny wall.

Clematis 'Polish Spirit' (z. 4–9) A favorite newer clematis cultivar. Purple flowers in late summer and into autumn make it a good partner for silver-leaved plants and for verbenas, asters, and perovskia. It tolerates shade and is easy to grow in almost any situation.

Clematis 'Niobe' (z. 4–9) is among the most richly colored clematis, with lovely velvety flowers of deep wine red in midsummer. It is not too vigorous and looks splendid growing with a creamy-colored climbing rose or through a white-variegated shrub.

Clematis 'Huldine', (z. 4–9) with its elegant pearly white flowers, is a good choice for a sunny arbor or arch and perfectly suited to a traditional summer border. The sepals have faint purple stripes on the reverse, developing an attractive luminescence when the sun shines through them.

Clematis tangutica (z. 6–9) is very easy to grow in a sunny place, though its yellow flowers can be difficult to fit into pastel color schemes. Hard pruning may delay flowering enough for it to coincide with the hot colors of late summer. It is worth trying to accommodate it because it has two seasons of interest: after the flowers, the long-lasting fluffy seed heads create a worthwhile display all winter.

A rather special clematis for a sheltered wall is *Clematis cirrhosa* var. *balearica* (z. 7–9). Its scented flowers appear from late winter to early spring, and at that time of year the foliage, green in summer, becomes bronze purple. It also has attractive seed heads. The leaves are finely divided, almost fernlike. This clematis will need fertile, humus-rich, well-drained soil to perform well.

OTHER GOOD CLEMATIS

Clematis 'Abundance' (z. 5–7) Reliable, free-flowering viticella; deep pink flowers.

Clematis 'Alba Luxurians' (z. 5–7) A viticella, with green-tipped white flowers.

Clematis armandii (z. 7–9) Scented white or pale pink flowers in winter. Too vigorous for very small gardens.

Clematis 'Comtesse de Bouchaud' (z. 4–9) Ideal for a container. Shell pink flowers with wavy-edged petals.

Clematis 'Etoile Rose' (z. 5–9) A compact, scrambling clematis with delicate, bell-shaped, deep pink flowers.

Clematis 'Etoile Violette' (z. 5–9) Robust, with abundant rich purple flowers in late summer and into the fall.

Clematis 'Gravetye Beauty' (z. 5–9) Beautiful cherry red flowers shaped like lily-flowered tulips. Compact; needs sun.

Clematis 'Prince Charles' (z. 4–9) One of the newer varieties, raised in New Zealand. A reliable, compact plant, with pale lilac blue flowers.

Clematis 'Purpurea Plena Elegans' (z. 4–9) An old, robust viticella hybrid with abundant, double, mauve flowers.

Jasmine (Jasminum)

The two most familiar jasmines are quite different from each other except in flower form. They are not compact or particularly well-behaved plants, but it is hard to manage without their excellent qualities, even in a fairly small garden. There are good reasons to grow them both.

Jasminum nudiflorum (winter jasmine) (zone 6–10) has cheerful but unscented yellow blossoms on leafless green stems. It tends to scramble rather than climb, making an excellent wall shrub if the long flexible stems are trained onto horizontal wires or a trellis. Add a clematis to scramble through it for color in spring or summer. A neglected winter jasmine soon becomes a tangle of old wood; to prevent this remove the stems that have flowered to make way for new growth.

The other indispensable jasmine is the summer-flowering *Jasminum officinale* (zone 7–10). This luxuriant mass of graceful, ferny foliage, white flowers, and elegant pink-tinged buds is too vigorous for a small wall space, but its scent on summer evenings, particularly in a confined, sheltered area, is so special that you will never regret building an arbor for it to share with climbing roses, honeysuckles, or clematis for all-summer fragrance and color. It also looks lovely when allowed to twine and scramble over a shed or large porch.

Jasminum nudiflorum (z. 6–10) has a crop of sunny, starry flowers on most days all through the winter, even in moderate shade. Use it to brighten an east- or north-facing fence or wall, or to carpet a bank with winter color, pegging the new shoots down. Hard frosts wither the open flowers, but new buds soon break to replace them.

Jasminum officinale f. *affine* (z. 7–10) is a large-flowered form of the summer jasmine, which provides one of the classic scents of summer. This rampant grower is good on a sturdy arbor or arch near the house, where its fragrance can drift through open windows and doors.

The pink-flowered hybrid *Jasminum* × *stephanense* (z. 8–10) does not grow quite as large as its parent, *Jasminum officinale*, but it still needs an arbor or shed to clamber over. It has beautiful fragrant flowers in summer. Plant in full sun.

Although not actually a jasmine, *Trachelospermum jasminoides* (z. 8–9) is a very similar white-flowered, fragrant climber. Slightly tender, it is often seen as a greenhouse plant but also succeeds outdoors in a warm, sunny, sheltered place. Its evergreen leaves take on warm red tones in winter.

OTHER GOOD JASMINES

Jasminum mesnyi (z. 8–9) Similar to winter jasmine but slightly tender, with larger, semi-double flowers in spring.

Jasminum officinale 'Argenteovariegatum' (z. 7–10) Attractively variegated in delicate tones of cream, pale green, and pink.

Jasminum officinale 'Aureum' (z. 7–10) A golden-variegated form grown mainly for its foliage.

Jasminum officinale 'Clotted Cream' (z. 7–10) A new variety with scented, rich cream flowers.

Honeysuckle (Lonicera)

It is said that of the five senses smell is the most evocative. A classic fragrance of the countryside, honeysuckle suggests luxuriant summer hedges and warm, relaxed evenings. The British native honeysuckle or woodbine, *Lonicera periclymenum* (zone 5–8), has developed a number of named cultivars that bring this familiar perfume into gardens. Some other honeysuckle species and cultivars have showier, more colorful flowers, but this is sometimes at the expense of scent, so always check before you buy.

Like many plants, honeysuckles will tend to flower more freely in sunshine, but against this must be set their dislike of excessive dryness at their roots. They generally look healthier, with better resistance to aphids and mildew, if they are in shade for part of the day. Most of them do not need pruning as a matter of course but, if they must be kept to an allotted space, cut them back after flowering, taking care to remove only some of the new stems because these will carry next year's flowers.

Lonicera periclymenum 'Graham Thomas' (z. 5–8) is a popular, long-flowering selection of the British native honeysuckle or woodbine. Its very fragrant flowers age from white to pale yellow, without the pink tones of other cultivars. It flowers better in full sun but likes to have its roots in a shady position, in moisture-retentive soil.

The semievergreen hybrid *Lonicera × brownii* 'Dropmore Scarlet' (z. 4–7), descriptively known as the scarlet-trumpet honeysuckle, is one of the most splendidly colored varieties. It is scentless but it looks exotic and can be grown with other sun-loving plants in hot colors.

Lonicera similis var. *delavayi* (z. 6–9) is a robust, late-summer honeysuckle with fragrant, creamy yellow flowers. Some nurseries recommend it as an alternative to the old favorite *Lonicera japonica* 'Halliana' (z. 4–9), a free-flowering, vigorous variety that became increasingly susceptible to mildew.

Lonicera periclymenum 'Serotina' (z. 5–8) may be thought too vigorous for some gardens, but it is one of the best honeysuckles because it combines good flower color with powerful scent. Its flowering time (over several weeks in late summer) coincides with the period when the weather is likely to be still and balmy and fragrant evenings can be enjoyed outdoors.

OTHER GOOD HONEYSUCKLES

Lonicera caprifolium (z. 5–9) Fragrant, pink-tinged, creamy white flowers in midsummer.

Lonicera japonica 'Aureoreticulata' (z. 4–9) A foliage plant for part shade, with neat, pretty, golden-veined green leaves.

Lonicera periclymenum 'Belgica' (z. 5–8) Early Dutch honeysuckle: an old variety of the romantic wild woodbine, flowering in late spring and early summer.

Lonicera × tellmanniana (z. 5–8) Flowers are a lovely shade of copper-tinted old gold, but not scented. An established hybrid; better in shade.

Climbing roses

Climbing roses might be thought unsuitable for small gardens. Some, it is true, are vigorous, thorny giants that are difficult to manage, and many have a very short flowering season. They are susceptible to all the usual rose pests and diseases, and they will need to be kept in check by regular pruning, which, if too severe, may impair their flowering.

Yet one of the spectacular sights of midsummer is that of roses gloriously covering a wall or arbor, and the fragrance is the very essence of the country garden. Fortunately, there are many climbing roses—and a few ramblers—with a more restrained attitude to growth, and it is these that should be selected for maximum flower power in a limited space.

Disease resistance is especially important in roses that are destined for a small garden because every bug and blight will be only too obvious. Go for a rose that has shining, healthy foliage so that the plant will not be an eyesore when it is not in flower. Look for resistance to mildew and black spot, which can be a particular problem in climbers grown against walls where the air circulation may be poor and the soil dry. Above all, keep the plant well fed and watered, and prune it regularly—though no more than is necessary to keep it to shape and size and encourage it to produce healthy new wood on which to flower in future.

Many of the old roses, undeniably lovely though they are, have too short a season to earn their space in small gardens. There are a few exceptions but, in general, the more recent varieties have been bred to be repeat flowering, so their period as nonflowering "passengers" in the garden is shorter. Many also retain the cottagey qualities of their predecessors, including scent. To compensate for the lack of color during their non-flowering stages, give the roses planting companions, such as sweet peas or a clematis that flowers at a different season.

A carefully placed urn picks up the warm tones of *Rosa* 'Cécile Brünner' to transform a difficult corner in part shade.

Supports for climbing roses in small gardens are likely to be more compact versions of what might be seen in any garden, but they will need to work at least as hard to deserve their space: an arch to frame a view; a small pergola to give shade and scent to a patio; or an arbor to serve as a useful focal point and sitting area. Rope swags or trellis panels double as rose supports and space dividers, and a climbing rose might usefully clothe an unsightly shed. Alternatively, consider fixing a stout pole or obelisk at a focal point in a border, and train a climbing rose up it with a clematis or honeysuckle for company. This is an effective way to put height into a garden while taking up minimal ground space—useful in gardens that may not have room for a tree.

Rosa 'Aloha' (z. 5–9) is a short-growing climber, with large, cupped flowers in two shades of salmon pink. Blooms have a delightful, old-fashioned fragrance and are resistant to rain. 'Aloha' flowers freely from summer through to fall.

As a small-flowered rambler of manageable size, with a very good scent, *Rosa* 'Goldfinch' (z. 4–9) is suitable for arches and arbors, or for training into the branches of a small tree. Its buds open into beautiful semidouble, butter yellow flowers that gradually fade to white.

Rosa 'Crown Princess Margareta' (z. 4–9) is a tall shrub rose with good disease resistance and enough vigor to be trained as a climber. One of the David Austin English roses, it is named after Queen Victoria's granddaughter. Its fragrant, large, peach-colored rosettes look good in a planting scheme with dark bronze foliage.

Rosa 'Emily Gray' (z. 4–9) is a well-scented rambler valued for its large yellow flowers and almost evergreen, shiny foliage. The stems and young foliage are tinged red, and the wood is very thorny. This is not a rose for the impatient gardener because it is at its best only when well established.

One of the best all-round compact yellow roses, *Rosa* 'Golden Showers' (z. 5–11) is suitable for arbors, pillars, arches, and walls, even in shade. It is a good choice for town gardens. The flowering season is long, often extending into late fall.

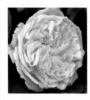

One of the best loved of all climbing roses is the old hybrid *Rosa* 'Gloire de Dijon' (z. 6–11). Its lovely, subtle color, somewhere between pale pink and pale yellow, harmonizes well with old brickwork. This free-flowering and very fragrant rose succeeds on shady walls as well as in sun.

Clusters of rich red, semidouble flowers that have a strong, old-fashioned scent and repeat well make *Rosa* 'Tess of the d'Urbervilles' (z. 4–9) an excellent choice where space is limited. A short and compact climber, it looks particularly striking on a white wall, and it is excellent in a planting scheme of hot colors and bronze foliage.

Rosa 'Snow Goose' (z. 5–10) is a compact, disease-resistant rambler raised by David Austin. This reliable, repeat-flowering alternative to the familiar but huge classic white-flowered ramblers is ideal for an arch or arbor in a tight space. The fragrant, small white blooms fit easily into planting schemes.

Rosa 'Albertine' (above left) (z. 5–9) A classic, very fragrant rambler that is equally suitable for arch, pillar, arbor, or fence.

Rosa 'Compassion' (above right) (z. 5–10) Scented, repeat-flowering climber, with peachy pink flowers and a strong, upright growth habit. The foliage is bronze when young.

Rosa 'Noisette Carnée' (above left) (z. 6–10) Clove-scented, semidouble, lilac pink flowers. Repeats well.

Rosa 'Laura Ford' (above right) (z. 5–9) Miniature amber yellow roses, beautifully shaped, set off by a profusion of glossy, light green foliage. Repeat-flowering.

Rosa 'Madame Isaac Pereire' (above left) (z. 6–10) A Bourbon bush rose that will also climb on a pillar. Very large, very fragrant, deep pink blooms.

Rosa 'Warm Welcome' (above right): (z. 5–9) A useful, long-flowering pillar rose; neat, fragrant, warm orange flowers and copper-tinged foliage.

Perennials

Newcomers to gardening often find their first inspiration in bright seasonal patio displays or spring-blossoming shrubs and trees. Discovering the sustained and repeated pleasures of hardy herbaceous perennials may take a little longer, but selecting and making the most of this invaluable group of plants is the key to creating a garden that is interesting all year.

The themed "colorist" borders at Hadspen Garden in Somerset, England, vividly demonstrate the uses and effects of different flower and foliage color, with lots of ideas that can be adapted to any garden. Here, in the yellow borders, *Lupinus* 'Chandelier' makes a strong, early-summer accent.

"Herbaceous perennial" usually describes a nonwoody plant that dies back each winter and regenerates in spring. (A tongue-in-cheek definition by Henry Beard and Roy McKie in *Gardening: A Gardeners' Dictionary* reads: "Any plant which, had it lived, would have bloomed year after year.") Whether a specific plant is perennial or not may depend on its hardiness in a particular climate. Plants that are reliable perennials in California, for example, may not survive winters in the Midwest.

Perennials encompass an enormous and ever-growing range of plants of different shapes, sizes, colors, and growth habit. Of course, personal taste will to some extent dictate which ones are right for your garden, but it would be very unwise to ignore factors such as the garden's size, soil, aspect, and climate. Choosing suitable plants is one of the best ways to save unnecessary work in a garden: the plants that are naturally happy in the conditions that you can provide are the most able to look after themselves.

In a small garden, each plant has to work very hard to earn its space. If the garden is to be enjoyed all year round, the length of a plant's season of interest should be one of the deciding factors. Flowers will be important in choosing

VALUE-FOR-SPACE PERENNIALS *Arum italicum* ssp. *italicum* 'Marmoratum' • *Sedum* 'Autumn Joy' •

an herbaceous perennial, but consider what "extras" a plant may be able to offer: spring foliage, long-lasting winter seed heads, or a delicious fragrance.

Good use of herbaceous plants is fundamental to successional planting, a method that is especially valuable in gardens where space is limited. For example, when spring bulbs are over, their dying foliage can be masked by a mat-forming perennial such as a hardy geranium. This, having flowered, can be cut to the ground; it will then make a new cushion of foliage, which could receive welcome summer shade from a late-leafing deciduous shrub such as cotinus or a taller perennial such as echinacea. These will look attractive right through until the fall, enlivened in late summer perhaps by the flowering spikes of a crocosmia or the airy heads of *Verbena bonariensis*. All of this plant activity takes up very little space. The trick is to make the most of every bit of ground to ensure that there is always something new and interesting to look at. It is a method that has always been well understood by traditional cottage-style gardeners, but it can be usefully applied in any small-scale garden.

This multilayered planting keeps the ground well covered for much of the year, helping the soil to retain valuable moisture and suppressing weeds, so maintenance during the growing season is restricted mainly to supporting any plants that need it and removing spent flower heads once their contribution is over. An annual overhaul in early spring is a good idea: divide the perennials where necessary, and feed and mulch to ensure that the individual plants get the nourishment they need despite the competition created by dense planting.

PERENNIALS FOR DAPPLED SHADE

Small gardens are often overhung by neighboring trees, but this need not be a problem because, fortunately, many flowering perennials prefer partial shade. Some are native to woodland or woodland-edge habitats, and these are ideal for planting under or around deciduous trees and shrubs. Provided the leaf canopy is not too dense and the soil is not too dry and poor, "difficult" areas like this can become a long-lasting and interesting tapestry of foliage forms and flower color.

Interplant ground-covering, low-maintenance plants, such as suitable hardy geraniums, hostas, and *Tellima grandiflora*, with taller flowering perennials and shade-tolerant bulbs to give structure and seasonal splashes of color. Foxgloves, aconitums, and Japanese anemones are all suitable for a shady spot.

Variegated and golden-leaved plants are also suitable because they are usually better out of strong sunlight, which can scorch their leaves. In early spring they make a fine contrast with emerging primulas, bulbs, and flowering hellebores and, later, with dark aquilegias and violas, *Ajuga reptans*, and ferns.

The showpiece of Hadspen, in England, is the borders around the perimeter of the huge, horseshoe-shaped walled garden. The mellow brickwork provides shelter and a structured backdrop for mixed border planting in a series of color themes.

Penstemon 'Andenken an Friedrich Hahn' • *Veronica peduncularis* 'Georgia Blue' • *Viola* 'Maggie Mott' •

Spring perennials

Bulbs and flowering shrubs are usually considered the stars of the spring garden, completely eclipsing herbaceous plants. However, perennials can be set to work in a valuable supporting role. Their fresh young foliage makes a fine backdrop to dazzling spring colors, expanding most conveniently to hide bulb foliage as it fades and covering bare ground beneath shrubs.

Bergenia 'Abendglut'

Pulmonaria 'Lewis Palmer'

Brunnera macrophylla 'Dawson's White'

Corydalis flexuosa 'China Blue'

Some herbaceous plants, such as peonies, irises, and poppies, produce excellent spring foliage long before they flower, while a number of other worthwhile perennials have spring flowers and good leaves, too. Among these are **pulmonarias** (zone 3–7), which include the earliest-flowering perennials. The warm coral-colored flowers of *Pulmonaria rubra* are a most welcome surprise in late winter, and they are good company for hellebores and snowdrops. The standard pulmonaria color is blue, and the later-flowering *Pulmonaria* 'Lewis Palmer', with its stout spikes of a really deep hue, is one of the best. Like many pulmonarias it has spotted leaves that unfold to make an interesting ground-cover feature in a shady place. *Pulmonaria* 'Excalibur' has leaves of a uniform bright silver with only the margins green. It is less susceptible to the mildew that troubles many pulmonarias later in the season.

Related to pulmonaria, *Brunnera macrophylla* (zone 4–8) is another ground-covering shade lover. Its sprays of tiny, pretty blue flowers and broad, rounded leaves make a very effective weed-suppressing blanket. Variegated forms make this a plant of real distinction. *Brunnera macrophylla* 'Jack Frost' has pearly, silvered leaves with only the veins showing green, while 'Dawson's White' has ivory white leaf margins.

For sheer effectiveness in keeping weeds at bay, **bergenias** (zone 4–8) are difficult to beat. In established clumps, the shiny, round, leathery, evergreen leaves form a seamless mat, which, while unexciting, requires no maintenance year after year. *Bergenia* 'Abendglut' is one of many forms whose leaves turn red in winter. Like many bergenias, its flowers are pink. White-flowered forms include *Bergenia* 'Bressingham White', easier on the eye than pink when planted with spring yellows and blues.

All these rather coarse-leaved plants are useful for their blanketing properties, but they are also valuable as foils for more airy foliage and flower forms. Euphorbias, ferns, and grasses (see pages 86; 68–69; 62–63) offer some good contrasts with more solid-looking plants, and there are other feathery-leaved perennials that can make a worthwhile contribution to the foliage tapestry. *Corydalis flexuosa* (zone 5–8) has finely cut, shimmering leaves and bright blue flowers; *Dicentra formosa* (zone 3–8) is similar in effect but it has pink or white flowers. Both like shade, shelter, and humus-rich soil that does not dry out during the summer. A unique spring-flowering feature plant for a cool, shady garden is *Dicentra spectabilis* (zone 4–7), with elegant, arching branches of dangling, locket-shaped flowers in deep pink or white.

A familiar sight in cottage gardens, **aquilegias** (zone 4–8) begin to form their mounds of distinctive, prettily shaped, gray-green foliage early in the year. These are followed by the familiar "granny's bonnet" flowers in a range of

PERENNIALS WITH VARIEGATED FOLIAGE *Hosta* 'Ginko Craig' • *Houttuynia cordata* 'Flame' •

Dicentra spectabilis 'Alba'

are enthusiasts' plants, for they can be tricky to look after, needing shade and humus-rich soil that never dries out.

Much less fussy (although they prefer shade and humus-rich soil) are the **epimediums** (zone 3–8), which are ground-covering herbaceous relatives of berberis. Their erect, wiry stems carry attractive foliage all year, and a bonus is the beautiful little flowers, which are more likely to be noticed in a small space. There are many colored varieties: pale yellow *Epimedium × versicolor* 'Sulphureum'; mauve *Epimedium grandiflorum* 'Lilafee'; orange *Epimedium × warleyense*; and so on. The flowers show up better if the old leaves are removed in late winter.

colors that has widened considerably with the growing number of cultivated forms that are available. However, the simple charm of the ordinary blue or white columbine, *Aquilegia vulgaris* (zone 4–8), has ensured that it remains a favorite in mixed spring borders.

The same could be said of **primulas**. There are many fancy types and named cultivars, but almost everyone is cheered by the sight of a clump of common primroses (*Primula vulgaris*) (zone 6–7) or cowslips (*Primula veris*) (zone 5–7) on a warm spring day. Cultivated primulas and polyanthus in their variety of bright colors are always useful for early spring borders and containers. Certain types of primula have become collectors' plants. These include *Primula auricula* (zone 3–7), with its hundreds of named varieties. These are ideal for small spaces, where the beauty of the individual plants can be appreciated. Other groups that attract collectors include the exquisite **Gold-laced Group** of polyanthus (zone 6–7), and the double primroses, such as *Primula vulgaris* 'Alba Plena' (zone 6–7) and the sapphire blue *Primula* 'Our Pat' (zone 6–7). These

Primula Gold-laced Group

Epimedium × versicolor 'Sulphureum'

THE BETH CHATTO GARDEN

Beth Chatto has enormous expertise in choosing plants for difficult conditions, and her wonderful garden at Elmstead Market in Essex, England, is full of imaginative and practical planting ideas. The original garden was made from two unpromising sites: a parched gravel slope and a waterlogged valley bottom. Appropriate ground preparation and planting transformed these areas into a Mediterranean garden and a water garden respectively. Since then, a remarkable drought-resistant gravel garden has been created out of a former parking lot, and there is also a richly planted woodland garden.

Iris pallida 'Variegata' • *Lamium maculatum* 'White Nancy' • *Pulmonaria* 'Sissinghurst White' •

Euphorbia

Euphorbias number some 2,000 species and are widely distributed in many parts of the world. They have long been a source of fascination in gardens for their intriguingly constructed flower heads, which often have bright lime green bracts. Many that will grow in temperate gardens are sun-loving and drought-tolerant; few enjoy damp soil in dark corners.

Euphorbias are easy to grow, and most types need little attention. Shrubby euphorbias, such as *Euphorbia characias* (zone 8–9), should have the stems that have flowered cut off when the new stems are coming through and the old ones start to look untidy in early summer. Running species, such as *Euphorbia cyparissias* (zone 4–8) and *Euphorbia griffithii* (zone 5–7), will need curtailing once or twice a year to prevent them from engulfing their neighbors. Always wear gloves when dealing with euphorbias because their milky sap, apart from being extremely sticky, is a common skin irritant.

Euphorbias are natural partners for most sun-loving plants—silver-leaved shrubs, aromatic herbs, sea hollies, thistles, spiky irises, and sisyrinchiums—and they go well with dwarf spring bulbs, such as species tulips, scillas, and anemones. Rich colors—dark red, deep blue, and purple—emphasize their chartreuse coloring. They look good planted in gravel, where they will often self-seed, sometimes with interesting results.

Although the cypress spurge, *Euphorbia cyparissias* (z. 4–8), is sometimes seen as a spreading thug, it is not that hard to control, and it is a useful carpeting plant for dry, poor soil. 'Fens Ruby' (above) has deep bronze shoot tips followed by acid yellow flowers and, later, by an eiderdown of velvety, gray-green, weed-suppressing foliage.

The hybrid *Euphorbia × martini* (z. 7–10) is an effective, small-shrub sized feature from late winter. Its unusual color combination of deep red and yellow-green is a good foil to red tulips and variegated sedges such as *Carex oshimensis* 'Evergold'.

Waxy, succulent leaves help make *Euphorbia myrsinites* (z. 5–9) one of the most drought-tolerant of all hardy garden plants. Grow it in full sun, in gravel, or on top of a retaining wall, to replicate its native Mediterranean rocky habitat.

Euphorbia polychroma (z. 5–8) is a fairly tidy clump former whose dome of bright yellow flower heads in spring looks wonderful with deep blues and purples. Pretty coral tints, which develop with age, often last until the fall.

OTHER GOOD EUPHORBIAS

Euphorbia amygdaloides var. *robbiae* (z. 7–9) Good ground cover for dark, dry shade (see page 46).

Euphorbia 'Humpty Dumpty' (z. 8–9) Compact, shrubby evergreen for all-year structural interest. Ideal for the base of a sunny wall.

Euphorbia characias ssp. *wulfenii* (z. 8–9) Perhaps the best evergreen euphorbia for architectural form, but needs space (see page 41).

Euphorbia 'Chameleon' (z. 5–7) Chocolate colored, with euphorbia yellow highlights. Prone to mildew if dry. Try half-shade.

Euphorbia griffithii 'Fireglow' (z. 5–7) Dashing, tomato red bracts. Tends to run. Likes damper soil than most euphorbias, and full sun.

Hellebore (Helleborus)

Hellebores seem to attract considerable attention from specialty growers. Their breeding, naming, and cultivation are under constant scrutiny by a large following of experts and enthusiasts. Some of the species are rare and difficult to grow, but many new hybrids appear every year, often hailed as darker, spottier, or "more double" than their predecessors. The parentage of some of these specimens is so complicated and uncertain that *Helleborus × hybridus* (zone 6–8) is now considered the only correct way to name them.

It would be a mistake to dismiss hellebores as plants only for connoisseurs, however. Many of them are trouble-free and bring welcome and long-lasting color and interest to the winter and early-spring garden. They enjoy woodland conditions and the company of other shade-loving plants, so they are happy at the back of a border under deciduous shrubs that will shade them in summer. They like humus-rich soil and will benefit from an annual mulch. It is a good idea to remove last season's leaves before the new flowers begin to appear and to cut off spent flowers in the spring to avoid a rash of seedlings. Hellebores hybridize freely, and although you may get some good plants, most seedlings will be inferior to their parents.

Nurseries and private breeders have raised many very good hybrid hellebores. The *Helleborus orientalis* **Hillier Hybrids** (z. 5–8) range includes every color from white to almost black, with pinks, purples, and greens in between. The rare spotted and picotee hellebores are also represented.

Helleborus foetidus (z.6–8) might be considered too dull to merit space in a small garden. However, its developing green flowers, already on the move before the last autumn leaves fall, carry such a promise of spring that it is a welcome sight anywhere. It will tolerate shade at the back of a border and needs no attention besides removing faded flowers in spring.

Helleborus argutifolius (z.6–8), sometimes referred to as *Helleborus corsicus*, has serrated, spreading leaves. It is, like *Helleborus foetidus*, a winter-flowering hellebore with similar pale green flowers, but it is more stately in appearance, and it prefers sun and well-drained soil. It is likely to self-seed.

Helleborus niger (z.4–8) is the true "Christmas rose." This white, large-flowered hellebore blooms in midwinter. It is not easy to grow well, and good forms are always in demand. **'Potter's Wheel'** is an old favorite, with large flowers, although the true cultivar is hard to find. Seeds of the **Blackthorn Group** produce robust plants whose flowers age to pink.

Summer perennials

Summer is the season when perennials really come into their own. With a little careful planning they will provide many weeks of changing color and interest that can last right through the fall as well. No one could claim that herbaceous plants are maintenance-free, but looking after a well-planned border need not involve hours of toil. In any case, working among a rich variety of interesting plant forms and colors can be one of the most enjoyable jobs in the garden early or late on a summer's day.

Easy summer planting uses the contrasting forms of sisyrinchium, tanacetum, and geranium to create a billow of soft perennial color.

While it is possible, with thought and effort, to plan a border in any color scheme for any time of year, certain colors are naturally associated with a particular season: yellows and blues seem to belong to early spring, hot colors to late summer. Early summer is the season when colors are easy to coordinate, a time when borders seem to harmonize effortlessly in soft pinks, lilac, and blues: the colors of roses and hardy geraniums, campanulas, catmint, peonies, and foxgloves. Romantic planting schemes in these colors can be stitched together very simply and effectively by using groups of background plants.

Ideal for background planting are the familiar, easily grown perennials *Stachys byzantina* (lambs' ears) and *Alchemilla mollis*. They are lovely in their own right, but they are especially good for creating a country-garden effect, blending with

other border subjects. Both plants are at their best in early summer. ***Stachys byzantina*** (zone 4–8) makes a silvery white, furry carpet from which glistening flower spikes rise, beautiful in bud. Bees love the flowers but, soon after they open, the spikes begin to lose color and shape, and they should be cut down before they become wan and straggly. The plant then concentrates on making fresh leaves at ground level, and these last well into the fall. Worth looking for is

Stachys byzantina

Alchemilla mollis

the cultivar ***Stachys byzantina* 'Big Ears'**, which has larger leaves that make a more effective contrast with fine-foliaged plants. *Alchemilla mollis* (zone 4–7) slowly builds up to flowering by producing an ever more handsome mound of shapely, pleated leaves that hold silvery droplets of rain or dew. The sprays of tiny lime green flowers complement other flowers for a time, but the plants are best cut to the ground as they fade. This prevents self-seeding and encourages fresh new leaves to grow.

DROUGHT-TOLERANT PERENNIALS *Acanthus spinosus • Centranthus ruber • Eryngium giganteum •*

Another staple of the traditional early-summer border is **nepeta** (catmint), its froth of silvery lilac mixing well with roses, alchemilla, foxgloves, alliums, and any plants with silver foliage. If the classic *Nepeta* 'Six Hills Giant' (zone 4–7) is too large, use compact *Nepeta nervosa* (zone 5–7) or *Nepeta racemosa* 'Walker's Low' (zone 4–7). Cats can damage the new shoots, so cover the crown with chicken wire to protect the plants while they are young.

Iris sibirica

Sisyrinchium striatum

Foamy, small-flowered perennials such as alchemilla and nepeta give planting schemes a relaxed, romantic appeal, but contrasting form and texture is needed to set them off. *Iris sibirica* (zone 4–8) is ideal, rising above the clouds of tiny blossoms with its straplike leaves and distinctively shaped flowers in a wide choice of colors. It dislikes very dry conditions but usually finds the necessary moisture in a border that is kept well covered with ground-level foliage. The bearded irises have stately, sword-

shaped leaves, but they are less well suited to life in a mixed border because their rhizomes need to be exposed to the sun rather than covered by the foliage of adjacent plants. Equally sun-loving but less particular is another vertical plant, *Sisyrinchium striatum* (zone 4–8), whose fans of irislike leaves produce attractive spikes of creamy golden flowers in early summer.

Hemerocallis (daylilies) (zone 4–10) enjoy huge popularity and new varieties continue to appear. Many daylilies are large and spreading, but some excellent and well-established miniatures are ideal for small spaces. *Hemerocallis* 'Corky' has abundant golden yellow flowers that are produced over a long season. *Hemerocallis* 'Mini Pearl' is pale blush pink, while 'Gentle Shepherd' is white, and 'Pardon Me' is a good, compact, long-flowering red.

Hemerocallis 'Corky'

Hemerocallis 'Gentle Shepherd'

GOOD COMPANIONS

The combination of bronze and red always makes a dramatic impact, as in the foliage and flowers of *Dahlia* 'Bishop of Llandaff' (1) (z. 9–11), a comparatively hardy dahlia that may overwinter successfully in sheltered, well-drained gardens. Flowering from summer until the first frosts, it combines well with kniphofias, crocosmias (2), and *Sedum* 'Autumn Joy' (3) (z. 4–8).

For a cool color scheme in late summer, plant *Limonium platyphyllum* (4) (z. 4–8) with *Eryngium giganteum* (5) (z. 4–7) and *Stachys byzantina* 'Big Ears' (6) (z. 4–8).

Euphorbia myrsinites • *Salvia argentea* • *Sedum* 'Autumn Joy' • *Sisyrinchium striatum* • *Stachys byzantina* •

Digitalis grandiflora

Eremurus robustus

Acanthus 'Summer Beauty'

Where space is limited in a garden it is a good idea to take advantage of the many spiky summer perennials that are available. In planting design, spikes and columns are invaluable for giving structure and vertical definition, and they make a very positive contribution to interest and color while taking up little ground space.

Foxgloves (zone 5–8) do this very effectively in early summer. Along with the biennial *Digitalis purpurea*, in its pink or white forms, there are lower-growing perennial kinds such as the delicate ivory-colored *Digitalis lutea*, pale yellow *Digitalis grandiflora*, or dusky pink *Digitalis × mertonensis*.

Veronicas also provide vertical accents, especially cultivars of *Veronica spicata* (zone 5–8), which come in a range of colors from deep blue to deep pink. *Veronicastrum virginicum* (zone 4–8) has similar flowers on a taller plant and is ideal for the back of a border.

A real showstopper of a vertical plant that might (just) be suitable for a well-

drained, sunny spot in a small garden is the foxtail lily, *Eremurus* (zone 5–9). Depending on the species, these can grow up to 8ft. (2.5m) tall, but they can be planted close together, and their long, slender columns of closely packed little flowers in pink, white, or yellow are dramatic. The shoots emerge from the ground in early spring and resemble globe-artichoke buds. After flowering in early summer, the plants die back and later-flowering plants can cover them.

In a cottage-style garden it is hard to do without the charm of **hollyhocks** (*Alcea rosea*) (zone 8–10). Although very tall, they occupy little lateral space, especially if they have a sunny wall for support. The hollyhock's more compact relative **sidalcea** may be better for a very small garden, and it escapes the rust disease that often afflicts hollyhocks, but the color range is limited: there are many pink forms, such as *Sidalcea* 'Elsie Heugh' (zone 5–8).

Another very traditional plant, which has well-cut, glossy foliage as well as

long-lasting architectural flower spikes, is *Acanthus* (bear's breeches). With their spreading leaves and deep, persistent taproots, these are really better kept as specimen plants than grown in a border, where they can be difficult to extricate from other plants. *Acanthus spinosus* (zone 5–8) has the best foliage, but in small spaces the compact form, *Acanthus* 'Summer Beauty' (zone 6–9), may be preferred.

Smaller, violet spikes are to be found on the hardy herbaceous **salvias** (zone 5–8), such as the hybrid *Salvia × superba* and the various cultivars of its parent, *Salvia nemorosa*. The flowering season of these plants is short, but they continue to look respectable after the flowers die off and, if deadheaded, may flower sporadically until the fall. They are good planting partners for the flat heads of yellow or soft red **achilleas** (zone 2–9). For a limited space, gray-leaved *Achillea* 'Moonshine' is probably the best yellow, while *Achillea* 'Summerwine' is a good deep red.

PERENNIALS FOR BEES AND BUTTERFLIES *Aster lateriflorus* 'Horizontalis' • *Centranthus ruber* •

Achillea 'Summerwine'

Verbascum 'Helen Johnson'

Penstemon 'Andenken an Friedrich Hahn'

Taller than salvias, but not dissimilar in habit, are the perennial **verbascums** , or mulleins (zone 6–8). The tough and reliable *Verbascum chaixii* 'Album' has spikes of purple- or pink-tinged white flowers, and there are other forms available in yellow, apricot, or pink. The hybrid verbascums—which have become very popular—are beautiful but short-lived perennials. *Verbascum* 'Helen Johnson' is a stylish, dusky apricot color, while 'Gainsborough' is a shimmering pale yellow. A more enduring mullein, the yellow *Verbascum bombyciferum* 'Arctic Summer' flowers for several weeks in midsummer. Verbascums enjoy well-drained soil and a sunny site.

For prolonged summer color on fairly compact, upright plants, the perennial **penstemons** (zone 7–9) are certainly to be recommended. The many available varieties, in a spectrum of colors, vary considerably. The most hardy and free-flowering is widely acknowledged to be the rich red 'Garnet', a splendid plant, correctly named *Penstemon* 'Andenken an Friedrich Hahn'. If it is deadheaded regularly, it will go on flowering through summer and fall. Other tried and tested color forms include the compact 'Evelyn' (mid-pink), 'Alice Hindley' (mauve), 'Apple Blossom' (pale pink/white), and 'White Bedder'. Penstemons are very easy to propagate from cuttings, which can be taken when the plants are cut back in spring. Be careful not to do this too early: penstemons are slightly tender and they will benefit from the protection the old growth gives to the crown of the plant through the winter.

The herbaceous species of *Phlomis* (zone 7–9) have a unique vertical structure of tiered flower heads on straight stems. The pink-flowered species are generally fairly tender, while the yellow *Phlomis russeliana* is hardier and usually carries its columns of distinctive dome-shaped seed heads right through the winter—they are especially striking when covered in snow or hoarfrost.

GREAT DIXTER

The English fifteenth-century manor house, Great Dixter, near Rye in East Sussex, has been the lifelong home of the respected plantsman and gardening writer Christopher Lloyd. His parents laid out and planted the original garden here, which was designed by Sir Edwin Lutyens. Yew hedging and topiary, the "bones" of the garden, make a formal backdrop to exciting and innovative planting that lasts through summer and well into the fall. From spring to early summer there are flower-filled meadow areas—the subject of one of Christopher Lloyd's many authoritative books. In the borders, hardy perennials combine with each other and with shrubs, bulbs, annuals, and exotics in carefully thought-out ways that bring out the best in each. This is a garden that is always full of experiments, of planting ideas to use in gardens large or small, and, more than anything, of color and form used adventurously and knowledgeably.

Eryngium giganteum • *Limonium platyphyllum* • *Primula veris* • *Sedum spectabile* • *Verbena bonariensis* •

An excellent contrast with vertical perennials is provided by members of the daisy family (Asteraceae). *Anthemis tinctoria* (zone 2–8) is an easy, daisy-bearing plant for summer borders. Young plants perform best and can very easily be produced from cuttings. Pale yellow *Anthemis tinctoria* 'E.C. Buxton' and the taller, paler *Anthemis tinctoria* 'Sauce Hollandaise' will flower repeatedly if the spent flower stems are removed at the base.

As summer progresses, a second generation of daisylike flowers begins to come into bloom, a foretaste of autumn colors to come. **Heleniums** (zone 3–8) are among the first of these. The rich colors of their distinctive blooms, with downturned petals, range from bronze yellow, as in *Helenium* 'Waldtraut', through orange, to the

Helenium 'Moerheim Beauty'

russet red of one of the best forms, *Helenium* 'Moerheim Beauty', which will flower again if deadheaded after its first flowering. Heleniums are soon joined by another native, brassy yellow rudbeckia. Annual and perennial rudbeckias come in all sizes. *Rudbeckia fulgida* var. *sullivantii* 'Goldsturm' (zone 4–8) is a good perennial one of

Rudbeckia fulgida var. sullivantii 'Goldsturm'

Echinacea purpurea 'Kim's Knee High'

manageable size, at about 2ft. (60cm). *Rudbeckia laciniata* 'Goldquelle' (zone 4–9) is taller, with double flowers.

Formerly classified as a rudbeckia, *Echinacea purpurea* (zone 4–8) has similarly shaped flowers but in pink (though there is also a white form). It makes a fine, long-lasting border feature in ground that is not too dry. There is a dwarf cultivar, *Echinacea purpurea* 'Kim's Knee High'. The bronze orange central cone of echinaceas complements many other colors. They are good partners for sedums (see page 100), bronze phormiums (see page 59), and the inestimable *Verbena bonariensis* (zone 8–9). This tall, airy plant is a good partner for a whole variety of late-summer flowers in a sunny border, and does not get in the way even if it sows itself at the front. A light touch of a different kind is given

GOOD COMPANIONS

The pale yellow of *Anthemis tinctoria* 'E.C. Buxton' (1) (z. 2–8) associates well with many other colors. For a contrast of form and color, plant it with *Salvia* × *superba* (2) (z. 5–8) and *Hemerocallis* 'Corky' (3) (z. 4–10).

Erigeron karvinskianus (4) (z. 8–10) is a charming little plant covered all summer in pinkish white daisies. It self-sows into gravel and paving cracks—good for a natural effect in dry places alongside red valerian *Centranthus ruber* (5) (z. 4–8), an even more enthusiastic self-sower. Do not let these plants grow in walls or other masonry where their fleshy roots may cause damage.

92

SEED HEADS FOR FALL AND WINTER *Acanthus spinosus* • *Achillea filipendulina* • *Allium cristophii* •

Verbena bonariensis

Gaura lindheimeri 'Heather's Delight'

Anemone × hybrida 'Honorine Jobert'

Agapanthus Headbourne hybrids

(zone 4–8). Its tiny flowers—delicate but tough—create a pale lavender blue haze that complements adjacent flowers of other colors and also makes an elegant partnership with any strongly shaped silver plants such as eryngiums.

Always fresh-looking and difficult to tire of are the so-called **Japanese anemones**, stalwarts of the late border, even in shade. There are many single and double varieties, both white and pink. The finest white is **Anemone × hybrida** 'Honorine Jobert' (zone 6–8). They are excellent mixers, combining well with everything from yellow daisies to evergreens and variegated grasses. At a height of about 4ft. (1.2m), the mature plants are not small, but they have a long season, looking good both in bud and after the petals drop. The same applies to **agapanthus** (zone 8–9), with the bonus that their spent flower heads dry well to provide material for cut-flower arrangements. White or blue, agapanthus provide drama, without taking up too much border space—only a few are needed to make an impact—and they also do well in large containers. They need plenty of sun. *Agapanthus* 'Jack's Blue' is large and hardy, with good flower color. For more compact plants, choose the strain called **Headbourne hybrids** or the dwarf *Agapanthus* 'New Blue'.

by *Gaura lindheimeri* (zone 6–9), a pretty, late-flowering, white or pink perennial that is increasingly popular with garden designers. It needs plenty of sunshine and well-drained soil.

The late-flowering asters commonly known as **Michaelmas daisies** may be the best known of all fall perennials. There are numerous varieties, although many are unsuitable for a small planting scheme because of their size and invasiveness, their ungainly foliage, and their short season. However, the hybrid *Aster × frikartii* 'Mönch' (zone 5–7) deserves space for its large lavender blue blooms, its long flowering season, and its resistance to the mildew that can plague these daisies.

An easily managed but seldom seen perennial that is good company for the late-summer pinks and mauves is the sea lavender, *Limonium platyphyllum*

PLANTS THAT WEAVE

Some perennials have creeping stems that like to wander among neighboring plants for support and shelter. This habit can be used to good effect for linking different elements in a border to make a harmonious whole. The best weaving plants are those that die back to their original crown in winter, so that the "invasion" does not become permanent.

The tender *Helichrysum petiolare* (z. 8–10) is often used for this purpose in summer containers and can be used temporarily in borders, too, as can the slightly hardier *Senecio viravira* (z. 8–10). Two hardy geraniums with a weaving habit are black-eyed *Geranium* 'Ann Folkard' (z. 5–7), and the plain magenta *Geranium × riversleaianum* 'Russell Prichard' (z. 8). Some of the violas, especially *Viola cornuta* varieties (z. 5–7), like to stray too. For an evergreen wanderer, try the variegated ivy *Hedera helix* 'Glacier' (z. 4–9), but it will need to be restrained or it will root all over the border.

Digitalis lutea • *Dipsacus fullonum* • *Limonium platyphyllum* • *Phlomis russeliana* • *Sedum* 'Autumn Joy' •

Aconitum

Aconitums, or monkshoods, are distinctive border plants that are useful in small gardens because they contribute good color and vertical structure while taking up little ground space. The unusual helmet-shaped flowers are sometimes yellow or white but usually blue. Most aconitums flower in summer, but by choosing a range of varieties it is possible to have them in bloom from late spring until late fall. They are very hardy and easy to grow in almost any good soil, either in sun or part shade, but are slow to settle when newly planted. They should be divided periodically in the fall to keep them uncongested and vigorous.

In both form and color, the deeper blue aconitums complement the yellows of daisy-flowered perennials, such as rudbeckia, heliopsis, and anthemis. They fit into many color schemes, working well as accent plants among pastel colors. Gardeners who find delphiniums difficult should try aconitums as an alternative; unlike delphiniums, monkshoods usually need no staking, and they are also less appealing to slugs and snails.

As their old country name wolfsbane suggests, aconitums are, like many members of the Ranunculaceae family, poisonous. Keep them away from young children and wash your hands after planting or handling them.

A distinctive variety of medium height is *Aconitum* 'Stainless Steel' (z. 4–8) whose deeply cut leaves and grayish blue flowers make its name very apt. It fits well into contemporary planting schemes and looks very effective against a dark background such as an evergreen hedge or dark-stained fence.

A good plant for a shady border or a woodland garden, the species *Aconitum napellus* (z. 4–8) is native to parts of Europe and has been cultivated for centuries. This medium-size aconitum has dark-veined, denim blue flowers from midsummer, but its bright green, ferny foliage contributes to a border from early spring.

The garden hybrid *Aconitum* 'Spark's Variety' (z. 4–8) has been grown for more than 100 years, but it is still one of the best and most widely planted monkshoods. Its flowers on branching stems make pools of intense violet-blue in mid- and late summer, associating well with many traditional herbaceous plants.

Aconitum × *cammarum* 'Bicolor' (z. 5–8) is an unusual old variety with branched spikes of two-tone flowers that are whitish, flushed purple blue. It makes more of an impression in shade than the deeper blue monkshoods and is perfect for adding a subtle touch of color to a white planting scheme.

OTHER GOOD ACONITUMS

Aconitum 'Bressingham Spire' (z. 5–8) Compact, with upright, violet-blue spikes. Widely available.

Aconitum carmichaelii 'Barker's Variety' (z. 4–8) One of several useful tall, late-flowering aconitums, with spikes of pure, deep violet-blue flowers lasting well into the fall.

Aconitum 'Ivorine' (z. 5–8) Ivory white flowers in late spring. A good choice for a cut-flower garden.

Aconitum lycoctonum (z. 5–8) Similar to *Aconitum napellus,* but with pale yellow flowers in midsummer.

Aconitum 'Newry Blue' (z. 5–8) A beautiful, fairly tall strain, with branched spikes of the deepest blue.

Astrantia

This old-fashioned classic deserves to be more widely grown. A member of the Apiaceae family, it has acquired many colorful names, including melancholy gentleman, Hattie's pincushion, and masterwort.

Astrantias are long-lived and fairly easy to grow in any humus-rich, moist but well-drained soil. They form attractive, low-lying clumps of weed-suppressing lobed leaves, and they are good mixers: they fit in almost anywhere and go with everything. They also last well as cut flowers and are easy to dry for indoor arrangements.

The tiny, insignificant flowers are crowded together in a dome-shaped head—like carefully arranged pins on a pincushion—surrounded by a circular parchmentlike bract. This arrangement does not resemble the parsley-like flowerheads of other members of the Apiaceae. In fact, the curious structure of astrantia flowers demands close inspection, and they always intrigue garden visitors seeing them for the first time. The traditional flower color is a combination of soft pink, green, and white, subtle rather than spectacular. The more striking dark red astrantias that have become available are much in demand.

Astrantias are easily raised from seed sown very fresh (they often sow themselves quite freely), but selected named forms should be propagated by division in the fall. Dividing clumps helps to maintain vigor.

One of the most striking dark red forms, and an excellent cut flower, *Astrantia* 'Hadspen Blood' (z. 5–8) flowers freely all summer, with sultry flowers surrounded by very dark bracts. The dark green palmate leaves have almost imperceptible black margins. For the best color, grow this in moist soil in full sun.

Astrantia major ssp. *involucrata* 'Shaggy' (z. 5–8) is named for the distinctive long bracts of its delicate, greenish white flowers. Older plants have the longest bracts, so be patient: it may take three or four years for them to mature, but it is well worth the wait. Make certain you are buying the correct cultivar and not its close relative *Astrantia major* ssp. *involucrata*, whose flowers are less dramatic.

OTHER GOOD ASTRANTIAS

Astrantia major 'Ruby Cloud' (z. 5–8) Compact and late flowering. More of a raspberry color than other red astrantias.

Astrantia major 'Ruby Wedding' (z. 5–8) Brilliant ruby red pincushion flowers, with white at the base of each petal. Flowers all summer.

Astrantia major 'Snow Star' (z. 5–8) Lovely in part shade, with large white flowers and green-tipped bracts.

Astrantia maxima (above) (z. 5–7) A pretty plant with sprightly sprays of small, chalky pink flowers and papery, greenish pink bracts in midsummer.

Astrantia major 'Sunningdale Variegated' (z. 5–8) has boldly splashed cream and yellow foliage in spring and early summer. The variegation becomes less pronounced as summer progresses, but a second flush of bright growth can be encouraged by pruning back existing foliage after flowering. The plant needs some sun to display its unique variegation to best advantage.

Campanula

Classic cottage-garden plants, and a key component of traditional summer borders, campanulas differ widely in plant size and habit. Some are as tall as a man, others hug the ground, but their flowers are usually easily recognizable, even though they vary from open saucers to drooping bells. The classic campanula colors range between blue and mauve, but there are many white forms and also some pink. Named cultivars, which are numerous, have often originated as chance seedlings.

The individual flowers tend to be short-lived, fading once they have been pollinated by bees, but a succession of buds carries on the flowering season. When cut for the house, the flowers often last longer.

Nearly all the campanulas grown in gardens are hardy perennials, but a few are grown as biennials. Most are easy to grow, and unknown varieties are usually worth trying. Campanulas generally prefer moist but well-drained soil, though a few are drought-tolerant and will thrive on neglect. Most will tolerate a fair amount of shade. The white forms look especially attractive in partly shaded borders, and the blues keep their color better if they are not bleached by full sun.

Blue *Campanula persicifolia* (z. 4–8) and its white variant 'Alba' are the most familiar garden bellflowers. They have a simple charm and are easy to grow, resisting drought and most pests and diseases. There are many cultivars, single and double, in blue or white. *Campanula persicifolia* flowers at the same time as most roses, which it partners very well.

Campanula lactiflora 'Prichard's Variety' (z. 5–7) is the best blue cultivar of the milky bellflower. A useful, bushy border plant, it is happy in good soil in part shade, where its color will be deepest.

OTHER GOOD CAMPANULAS

Campanula cochlearifolia 'Elizabeth Oliver' (z. 6–8) A creeping rock-garden form with pale blue double flowers. Likes a well-drained, sunny position.

Campanula 'Kent Belle' (z. 5–9) A good border campanula, with long, shiny, violet blue, tubular flowers.

Campanula glomerata 'Superba' (z. 3–8) Clustered bellflower: a good deep violet blue, but invasive.

Campanula lactiflora 'Loddon Anna' (z. 5–7) Masses of lilac pink bells on a large border plant.

Campanula latiloba 'Hidcote Amethyst' (z. 5–7) Upright columns of wide-open mauve blooms.

Campanula portenschlagiana (z. 4–7) is a pretty, shade-tolerant, carpeting bellflower. It sends trails of quite deep blue flowers among other plants, sometimes clambering up among their stems. It will soften edges and steps, looks good with ferns in shade, and mixes well with low-growing geraniums at the front of a border.

Eryngium

The trend toward warm, drier summers has assured eryngiums of a place in the front rank of border plants. In dry gardens, as other border stalwarts succumb, they go from strength to strength throughout the summer, their silvery bracts complementing almost every other kind of plant. They partner Mediterranean plants and silvery foliage especially well and are highly sought after as cut flowers for fresh or dried arrangements. Bees love them, too.

Eryngiums fall into two groups: the bluish, thistlelike European kinds, which are well suited to ordinary gardens, and the generally larger, strap-leaved kinds from South and Central America, which are harder to grow because they dislike cold, wet winters. Almost all are perennial; one notable exception is the familiar *Eryngium giganteum*, which dies off after flowering.

In sunny, free-draining borders, eryngiums are simplicity itself to grow, requiring only the removal of the spent flower heads once these begin to break up. For drying, they should be gathered in their prime, so it is a good idea to plant some in a separate cutting border to avoid spoiling the display. The plants have taproots, so they can be tricky to establish. The best way is to put in small plants in early spring.

Eryngium giganteum (z. 4–7), also famously known as Miss Willmott's ghost, is a wonderful plant to establish in an informal sunny border. It self-sows generously and, although the seedlings may need thinning, the growing plants look after themselves. When mature, they are an asset to any planting scheme. Site the plant where its architectural, luminous flower heads can be appreciated at dusk.

The beautiful lacy bracts of *Eryngium alpinum* (above) (z. 4–8) vary in color. For a good blue, choose a named form such as *Eryngium alpinum* 'Blue Star'.

Eryngium planum (z. 4–8) has a number of improved cultivars. **'Bethlehem'** is a tall, free-flowering form with smaller flower heads. *Eryngium planum* **'Blue Ribbon'** is perhaps the deepest blue.

OTHER GOOD ERYNGIUMS

Eryngium bourgatii Graham Stuart Thomas's selection (z. 3–8) A small plant with prettily divided, variegated leaves and violet blue flowers.

Eryngium × oliverianum (z. 5–8) The steely blue stems make this a winner for flower arrangements.

Eryngium × tripartitum (z. 5–7) A mass of tiny but typical eryngium flowers on a well-branched plant.

Eryngium variifolium (above) (z. 5–8) White-veined leaves in a glossy evergreen basal rosette, with small, very spiky, bluish flowers.

Geranium

Hardy geraniums (cranesbills) probably constitute the single most useful group of herbaceous plants. Their fine qualities are legion: beautiful flowers in a variety of colors, handsome and shapely weed-suppressing foliage, and a tolerance of harsh conditions from damp shade to sunbaked gravel. Small wonder, then, that the number of available species and cultivars of these paragons of the border is fast approaching four figures. A particularly interesting development is the increasing number of cultivars—across a range of species—that are bred for novel foliage color, resulting in a bewildering array of gold, purple, and variegated forms to choose from.

Most (though not all) hardy geraniums are easy to manage in a restricted space and are especially suitable for small gardens because of their long season of interest, either for flowers or foliage. If foliage looks shabby midseason, a haircut and a good watering will usually produce a clutch of fresh new leaves.

Some popular hybrid geraniums do well in sun or shade, but when choosing species, consider growing conditions: dryish shade suits *Geranium macrorrhizum* (zone 4–8) and *Geranium phaeum* (zone 7–8), while *Geranium sylvaticum* (zone 5–8) prefers damper shade. For a dry, sunny place, choose cultivars of *Geranium cinereum* (zone 5–7) or *Geranium sanguineum* (zone 5–8).

The chocolate-splashed leaves of *Geranium phaeum* var. *phaeum* 'Samobor' (z. 7–8) are best appreciated in close-up, so a shady spot in a small garden is ideal for this stylish plant. Good partners might be *Ophiopogon planiscapus* 'Nigrescens', *Ajuga reptans, Galium odoratum,* or a lacy fern.

Geranium wallichianum 'Buxton's Variety' (z. 7–8) is a well-established cranesbill for the front of a border. Its white-eyed blue flowers keep going all summer and right through to fall, and are good company for mauves, pinks, and whites. It is a well-behaved plant, spreading in habit but not invasive.

Geranium sanguineum var. *striatum* (z. 4–8) is a delightful, pale pink selection of the bloody cranesbill, a European wildflower native to limestone areas. This is another plant deserving close inspection: the flowers have veins delicately penciled in a darker pink, and are set among finely divided, bright green foliage.

OTHER GOOD GERANIUMS

Geranium × antipodeum 'Chocolate Candy' (z. 5–7) A low, carpeting plant with very dark purple leaves.

Geranium cinereum 'Ballerina' (z. 5–7) Exquisite dark-veined, pink flowers borne on a neat and tidy plant. Long flowering season.

Geranium 'Johnson's Blue' (z. 4–8) An old favorite among the hybrids, and still one of the truest blue forms.

Geranium macrorrhizum 'Album' (z. 4–8) Shade-tolerant, weedproof ground cover, with blush white flowers that show up well in a dark corner.

Geranium sanguineum 'Max Frei' (z. 4–8) Improved, compact form of the wild bloody cranesbill. Good for a rock garden or a container.

Geranium sylvaticum 'Album' (z. 5–8) White-flowered form of the British native wood cranesbill.

Heuchera

Look in any pre-1980 plant book or nursery catalog, and you will find scarcely a mention of heucheras. A few gardeners knew them as "coral bells" and grew them more for their little, bright pink flowers than for their small green leaves. Then the first purple-leaved form appeared. Heucheras as foliage plants caught the imagination of plant breeders in the United States, and now there are hundreds of varieties available—with more being introduced all the time—although sometimes the differences between them are very small.

When choosing heucheras, consider leaf color (purple or green, with more or less of a metallic sheen), flower color (ranging from white to bright pinkish red)—important when fitting them into color schemes—and hardiness: some are evergreen, with frost-hardy foliage; some have frost-hardy flowers, too.

Heucheras are not particularly easy to grow well, because they are natural woodlanders from the damp, humus-rich forests of the West Coast. They need moist soil but cannot stand waterlogging; they like some shade, but too much will impair their color. When the base of the plants becomes woody (about every three years), lift them, cut off most of the woody part, and replant the newly trimmed leaf rosettes quite deeply in reconditioned soil. New root systems will develop and plump new foliage should appear.

An old variety, in heuchera terms, *Heuchera cylindrica* 'Greenfinch' (z. 4–8) remains a favorite for its compact, rounded leaves with their attractive silvery marbling. The tall flower spikes are greenish ivory: a graceful and subtle feature in dappled shade, and good for picking.

The dark bronze leaves of *Heuchera* 'Ebony and Ivory' (z. 4–8) make a striking backdrop to the large cream flowers. It suits contemporary "black and white" schemes and can be easier to place than pink-flowered heucheras.

Heuchera 'Plum Pudding' (z. 4–8) is one of the most strongly colored forms, with large, ruffled, silver-mottled leaves on a bold, luxuriant-looking plant. To make the most of its color, this heuchera needs rich soil in full sun.

OTHER GOOD HEUCHERAS

Heuchera 'Amber Waves' (z. 4–8) A most unusual golden amber color. Needs well-drained soil.

Heuchera 'Cherries Jubilee' (z. 4–8) Compact plant with coral red flowers and ruffled bronze foliage. Best in sun.

Heuchera 'Can-Can' (z. 4–8) A larger plant with good, shimmering silver marbling on ruffled leaves. Good with gray-leaved plants.

Heuchera 'Fireworks' (z. 4–8) Well-shaped bronze foliage with a long season of coral pink flowers.

Heuchera 'Green Spice' (z. 4–8) Finely filigreed leaves with a silvery sheen and dark veining; creamy white flowers.

Sedum

Trouble-free and drought-tolerant, the larger sedums are invaluable plants for well-drained, sunny borders. Their neat clumps slowly develop broccoli-like flower heads through the summer, giving unity and form to planting schemes where the profusion of plant growth threatens to become a jumble. Then, as summer turns to fall, the flowers open, creating domes of warm color that change gradually over many weeks into the familiar, long-lasting, russet brown seed heads that are a mainstay of the winter garden.

Given the choice of feast or famine, most sedums are content with the latter. Rich soil and feeding make the clumps top-heavy so that they flop and spoil the display. Too much water or shade can have the same effect. They really do seem to thrive on neglect—although it is a good idea to renew the plants from cuttings every few years because older clumps tend to become open-centered. The spent flower heads should be removed in late winter. Sedums are good plants for gravel.

Some of the newer hybrid sedums have colorful leaves and names to match: 'Stewed Rhubarb Mountain', 'Gooseberry Fool', 'Strawberries and Cream'. These are great fun to experiment with, but if space is precious it may be wise to choose an established variety that is known to perform well.

The creeping alpine sedums are interesting to grow in small gardens, perhaps in gravel or in shallow pots where they can be seen at close range all year. These dwarf, low-maintenance plants are an important component of eco-friendly "green roofs."

The most versatile of the old favorites, *Sedum* 'Herbstfreude' (more commonly called 'Autumn Joy') (z. 4–8) is a robust plant whose large, deep pink, late-summer flower heads last all winter. It complements many other plants: for textural contrast, plant it with *Stachys byzantina*, eryngiums, and feathery, silver artemisias.

The best sedum (and one of the best of all garden plants) for butterflies is *Sedum spectabile* (z. 4–8) , the ice plant. Butterflies flock to its rich nectar on sunny autumn days. More compact than most hybrid sedums, it is good at the front of a border. *Sedum spectabile* 'Brilliant' (above) is an improved, brighter pink cultivar.

Sedum telephium ssp. *maximum* 'Atropurpureum' (z. 3–8) is a favorite with garden designers because of its rich, dark purple foliage. Nurseries have also favored it for breeding, and its qualities have been passed on to some of the modern hybrids.

OTHER GOOD SEDUMS

Sedum 'Bertram Anderson' (z. 4–8) A useful edging plant with purplish leaves and rich red flowers.

Sedum erythrostictum 'Frosty Morn' (z. 4–8) Similar to *Sedum spectabile* but with white-variegated leaves.

Sedum 'Neon' (z. 4–8) A recent hybrid with pink flowers.

Sedum 'Ruby Glow' (z. 4–8) Pinkish red flowers on a compact plant.

Sedum spathulifolium 'Purpureum' (z. 7–10) A hardy, creeping succulent with purple and silver leaves. Good in a shallow container with sempervivums.

Sedum spectabile 'Iceberg' (z. 4–8) White form of the ice plant, with paler green leaves.

Viola

The genus *Viola* contains a number of well-loved garden plants, from the sweet violet of early spring to the highly bred, colorful summer and winter pansies that are grown as annuals or biennials and much used as patio plants. Somewhere in between are the border perennials commonly known simply as garden violets or sweet violets. Especially good in cooler, damper gardens, these charming plants flower on and off for months, usefully filling gaps and weaving their way among other border plants. Many of them also have a wonderful fragrance. Some varieties form neat clumps and are ideal for edging paths and steps.

Violas have long been thought of as enthusiasts' plants. Many rare varieties can be obtained from those nurseries that specialize in them, but the well-known types are widely available. They are not difficult to grow if they are given the right semishaded, moist conditions and never allowed to dry out. To ensure prolonged flowering, cut the plants back quite hard mid-season. Trim them again in late fall.

The 'black' flowers of *Viola* 'Molly Sanderson' (z. 5–8) make it a useful planting partner, although it needs a position that shows it off. Try it with golden-leaved *Lamium maculatum* 'Aureum' or in a "black and white" scheme with *Ophiopogon planiscapus* 'Nigrescens' and carpeting silvery foliage such as that of *Stachys byzantina* or *Lamium maculatum* 'White Nancy'.

Viola 'Maggie Mott' (z. 5–8) is an attractive, old-fashioned viola, a robust plant with very fragrant silvery mauve flowers.

The white form of the "horned violet," *Viola cornuta* Alba Group (z. 5–7) is an excellent, strong-growing border plant, scrambling among other plants and helping to give coherence to a planting scheme, especially when it is used in conjunction with other white or silver plants. It makes good ground cover.

OTHER GOOD VIOLAS

Viola 'Czar' (z. 5–8) Reliable, early flowering variety that has violet blooms.

Viola 'Irish Molly' (above) (z. 5–8) Very unusual gold/khaki flowers with brown centers. A classic old variety.

Viola 'Jackanapes' (above) (z. 5–8) A striking contrast of nearly black and bright yellow. Bred by Gertrude Jekyll.

Viola 'Queen Charlotte' (z. 5–8) This popular variety has dark blue flowers and grows 6–8in. tall.

Flowering shrubs

Because they are part of a garden's permanent framework, shrubs need to be chosen with a respect for their preferences and an understanding of their role in the garden and their relationship with other plants. Like trees, they will increasingly make their presence felt as they mature, so it really is important to ensure that both you and the shrub are happy with the arrangement.

Hardy and compact, the Japanese quinces include white and pink forms as well as the usual red. *Chaenomeles speciosa* 'Moerloosei' is more aptly described by its old cultivar name, 'Apple Blossom'.

The happiness of any plant will largely depend on your success in meeting its individual needs with regard to soil, drainage, aspect, and so on. The right shrub in the right place will reward you by looking healthy and beautiful for many years. Provided the ground is well prepared before planting, there are few places in an average garden where no shrub will grow. Many shrubs will flourish in extreme conditions: shallow, alkaline soil (*Cistus*, zone 8–10), deeply shaded areas (*Ruscus aculeatus*, zone 8), or poorly drained ground (*Viburnum opulus* 'Compactum', zone 3–8). It is just a question of matching the plant to the conditions.

Your own happiness will depend at least partly on being able to relax in the shrub's company, knowing that it will not require constant fuss and worry to

102

Hydrangea paniculata 'Grandiflora' flowers late: keep it to size by hard pruning in early spring.

keep it looking good. In a small space, this means being sure to avoid over-vigorous plants that will require regular battles with pruning shears and saw. This does not mean that you must fill the garden with dwarfs, only that you must make careful choices, for while it is one thing to have to give a shrub an annual haircut to keep it within bounds it is quite another to have to keep hacking it back simply because it is much too vigorous for its position. Furthermore, such pruning will probably ruin its shape or deprive you of the flower display that was the reason for growing it in the first place.

You also need to decide whether to buy a fairly large, mature plant, which will be more expensive but will make an impact from the outset, or to go for a smaller, younger plant and patiently watch it develop. Many gardeners take the view that within a very few years smaller shrubs, being quicker to settle in and start growing, will catch up with—and even overtake—larger specimens.

Having chosen the shrub, consider its position. How will it look with its neighbors in different seasons? Consider whether it will look too prominent when its flowering season is over, and how you might counteract that: can it be pruned back, or could something else be grown over or in front of it to disguise its off-season dullness? Don't forget its needs: does it prefer sun or shade, damp ground or dry?

Container-grown shrubs can be planted at any time of the year, but they will need aftercare. Planting in the fall is ideal as the soil is warm and moist and your new shrub has all winter to establish before growth starts in spring. New shrubs planted in spring and summer will need regular watering throughout their first growing season.

PRUNING FLOWERING SHRUBS

Shrubs do not necessarily have to be pruned; it is the gardener's choice whether to do so or not. In small spaces pruning is desirable not only to contain size but also to maintain a natural, open, airy habit. Indiscriminate trimming will produce dense twiggy plants of inelegant shape and poor flowering performance.

The right time to prune is always after flowering.
Spring- and early summer-flowering shrubs are pruned immediately after flowering. Cut out some of the stems that have flowered, allowing new vigorous shoots to develop. If this is carried out from an early age some of the flowering stems can be cut back annually, almost to ground level. New shoots will then develop from the base of the plant with the whole season to ripen and develop flower buds. Mock orange, deutzias, and weigelas will all form open, graceful plants when pruned in this way.

Late summer- and autumn-flowering shrubs are tidied in the fall and pruned in early spring. They flower on the wood produced during the following spring and summer. As a general rule, prune stems back by two-thirds. This applies in the case of both small shrubs, such as caryopteris and perovskia, and much larger ones, such as buddleia and abutilon.

Flowering evergreen shrubs such as camellias and rhododendrons do not require any pruning, but if you have to prune to reduce size, do this immediately after flowering. Remove branches selectively, preserving the shape and natural grace of the plant.

Hebe 'Youngii' • *Lavandula angustifolia* 'Hidcote' • *Philadelphus microphyllus* • *Sarcococca confusa* •

Winter-flowering shrubs

A surprising number of shrubs thrive in winter conditions, opening their welcome flowers to brighten the garden on the shortest and darkest days of the year and bringing a feeling of spring to the air when so many other flowering plants are dormant. A lot of winter shrubs are fragrant. Whatever the size of your garden, it is well worth finding space for at least one or two.

You may feel that planting for winter is a waste of precious space. However, many winter flowers last for much longer than their spring and summer counterparts, and because they are comparatively few, the pleasure they give is all the greater. It is worth giving

place where you pass every day, such as on a garage wall or in a driveway.

Some compact winter shrubs will flower quite happily without the need for a choice position; in fact, they are most content when tucked away under a deciduous tree or among larger shrubs

the shrubby honeysuckle *Lonicera × purpusii* 'Winter Beauty' (see page 124) and the extremely fragrant winter-flowering daphnes, including *Daphne odora* 'Aureomarginata' (see page 127).

Hamamelis (witch hazel) (zone 5–8) is another fragrant and much admired winter shrub. It will become large in time but it grows slowly, so even in a small garden it is not usually a problem as long as the soil is suitable (many *Hamamelis* are intolerant of alkalinity). The unmistakable spidery flowers appear in late winter in colors that range from yellow to red. The paler forms—notably the popular hybrid *Hamamelis × intermedia* 'Pallida'—show up well against a dark background such as an evergreen hedge.

Chimonanthus praecox

Skimmia japonica 'Rubella'

Skimmia × confusa 'Kew Green'

some thought to where to site them and what to plant with them.

Some winter shrubs, such as the highly fragrant *Chimonanthus praecox* (zone 7–9) and *Abeliophyllum distichum* (see also page 124), are best trained on a wall whose warmth will encourage them to ripen and blossom more freely. They can share their space with a summer- or spring-flowering climber that is pruned hard in winter. A late-flowering clematis would be ideal, or you could use an annual climber such as *Ipomoea* (see page 166). Ideally, plants grown for their winter scent should be placed near the house, where their fragrance can drift in when you open the windows or door, or in a

that will give them shade in summer. Evergreens placed in this way provide useful ground cover, shading out weeds and reducing evaporation of moisture from the soil. **Sarcococcas** (see also page 42) and **skimmias** (zone 7–8) are ideal for this. Both are hardy and trouble-free, although sarcococcas are better in areas with alkaline soil, while skimmias prefer humus-rich, acidic soil. In the case of skimmias, the flowers come later, in spring, but some male clones carry long-lasting, showy buds through the winter. Those of *Skimmia japonica* 'Rubella' are red, while *Skimmia × confusa* 'Kew Green' has greenish white buds. Other natural woodlanders that can be grown in shady places include

Hamamelis × intermedia 'Pallida'

SHRUBS FOR WINTER BERRIES *Callicarpa bodinieri* var. *giraldii* 'Profusion' • *Cotoneaster horizontalis* •

For providing drama in the winter garden, **camellias** really have no equal, their tropical-looking flowers and handsome green foliage never failing to bring cheer to a miserable winter day. However, they ultimately reach quite a size; and they can be tricky to grow well, preferring cool, rich, acidic soil, some overhead shade, and no shortage of water in summer. Choose a sheltered position, and one where early-morning sun will not scorch the buds and flowers after a frosty night. Selecting one from the hundreds of available varieties can be a gamble, and it may be wise to avoid newcomers (which may prove capricious) in favor of one of proven reliability and hardiness. The tall, double red *Camellia japonica* 'Adolphe Audusson' (zone 7–10), an early-flowering variety with an upright growth habit, is an old favorite; and *Camellia × williamsii* hybrids (zone 6–10)—such as the semi-double pink 'Donation' or the single pink 'J.C. Williams'—are worth considering. Provided their requirements are met, camellias are surprisingly successful when grown in large containers

For reliable winter blossom in almost any soil and situation, the **viburnums**

Camellia japonica 'Adolphe Audusson'

Viburnum tinus 'Eve Price'

(see page 109) are a good choice. The evergreen *Viburnum tinus* 'Eve Price' (zone 8–9) or the more common 'Spring Bouquet' (zone 8–9), with lacy blossom and blue-black berries, is fine for the back of a border. *Viburnum × bodnantense* 'Dawn' (zone 6–8) is harder to place. Its fragrant pink flowers are a joy during the winter, but its foliage is rather dull, so put it where it will be hidden when not in flower. Underplant it with hellebores and pulmonarias.

The winter-flowering **mahonias** form an easy-to-please shrub group, generally rewarding mimimal care with a fine display of fragrant yellow blossom that can open well before the end of the fall. They can grow quite large, but their upright habit allows underplanting. The stems can be pruned back after flowering, which prevents the plants from becoming too leggy. The most versatile varieties (hybrids of *Mahonia japonica* and the beautiful but tender *Mahonia lomariifolia*) are *Mahonia × media* 'Charity' (zone 6–9) and the more strongly scented *Mahonia × media* 'Winter Sun' (zone 6–9).

Mahonia × media 'Charity'

Gaultheria mucronata 'Bell's Seedling' • *Myrtus communis* • *Pyracantha coccinea* 'Red Column' • *Ruscus aculeatus* •

Spring-flowering shrubs

Alongside bulbs, flowering shrubs are traditionally the mainstay of the spring garden. There are many wonderful varieties, and yet the number of different shrubs seen in most gardens represents only a tiny percentage of the ones that are available. Exploring the wide range of shrubs is worthwhile because there are plenty of interesting kinds that are suitable for growing in small spaces.

Chaenomeles × superba 'Knap Hill Scarlet'

To earn their space, especially in smaller gardens, shrubs that flower early in the year need to contribute something later as well. The leaves of *Fothergilla major* color richly in autumn.

Everyone wants to make the most of spring in the garden, but, with the rest of the year to plan for, faded spring plants should not take up a disproportionate amount of space. This means using plants that are compact and have more than one season of interest, rather than those that flower for a week or two early in the year and then have little to offer.

An unusual shrub that meets both these criteria admirably is **Fothergilla** *major* (zone 4–8). Although in time it will grow to 6ft. (2m) or so, this woodland-edge native grows slowly. Fragrant, whitish, bottlebrush flowers in spring are followed by hazel-like leaves (fothergillas are related to witch hazels, and share their dislike of alkaline soil). But their best moment comes in the fall, when the foliage is transformed into a rainbow medley of orange, red, and yellow. If you can, site the shrub where its autumn foliage will be set ablaze by late-afternoon sunshine.

The bright red flowers of the most commonly encountered cultivars of the Japanese quince (zone 4–8), such as **Chaenomeles × superba** 'Knap Hill Scarlet', also sing out in late-afternoon light. Like hellebores and daphnes, ornamental quinces look exotic but are hardy enough to sail through the worst of early spring weather. **Chaenomeles speciosa** 'Moerloosei' is beautiful, resembling unseasonal apple blossom on bare branches, while **Chaenomeles speciosa** 'Nivalis' has pure white flowers that look especially good with spring blues and yellows or when planted against red-brick walls. Chaenomeles are good to train on walls and fences, and mature specimens can be made interesting later in the year by letting them play host to a *Clematis viticella* or one of its small-flowered hybrids, which can be pruned hard before the quince flowers.

Another group of early spring "exotics" is the **magnolias**. Most are out of the question for small gardens, but *Magnolia stellata* (zone 4–8) is, fortunately, unusually compact. It is also notable for being reasonably alkaline-

EVERGREEN SPRING-FLOWERING SHRUBS *Choisya* 'Aztec Pearl' • *Prunus laurocerasus* 'Otto Luyken' •

Magnolia stellata

tolerant (although it will struggle in poor, shallow soils). The fragrant, white flowers, produced even on fairly small, young shrubs, are preceded by silvery, silky buds that give a wonderful sense of anticipation as they gradually enlarge in early spring. There are cultivars with larger flowers and with pink flowers, but this is one of those plants that provide no good reason to improve upon the charm of the species itself.

One of the most springlike shrubs is the good old-fashioned *Spiraea* **'Arguta'** (zone 5–8), whose scores of tiny white blossoms are packed densely onto the graceful, arching branches. Although it is seen in many gardens, it does not lose its charm through familiarity. It looks good in part shade, underplanted with pulmonarias and *Euphorbia amygdaloides* var. *robbiae*.

Among the least fussy of shrubs is *Mahonia aquifolium* (zone 6–8), known as the Oregon grape for its blue-black autumn fruits and its place of origin. Though related to the Far Eastern mahonias (see page 105), this low-growing, tough evergreen flowers later and has different garden uses. It is a parent of *Mahonia* × *wagneri*

'Undulata' (zone 6–8), a similar but less easily obtainable shrub with much improved glossy, wavy foliage that looks good all year while providing valuable, weed-suppressing ground cover.

Those who garden on acidic soil may not want to be without **rhododendrons**

Spiraea 'Arguta'

Mahonia × wagneri 'Undulata'

even in a small garden, but so many of the good varieties are just far too large. Garden-worthy, compact varieties that flower profusely include the pale yellow *Rhododendron* **'Patty Bee'** (zone 5–8) and *Rhododendron* **'Shamrock'** (zone 5–7). *Rhododendron* **'Moerheim'** (zone 5–6) is violet blue, while *Rhododendron* **'Rosebud'** (zone 5–6) is pink. All these varieties like sun.

Cytisus (brooms) may be considered for inclusion in the garden because they are tough and undemanding. They come in all sizes, from prostrate dwarfs, such as the knee-high *Cytisus* × *kewensis* (zone 6–7), to the pineapple-scented broom *Cytisus battandieri* (zone 8–9), which will rapidly reach 15ft. (5m) tall. A good, smaller one, which bears a mass of creamy yellow blossom in early spring, is *Cytisus* × *praecox* **'Warminster'** (zone 5–7). It grows into a rounded bush about 4ft. (1.2m) tall. When buying a broom, be sure to ask about size because many of them cannot be pruned very successfully.

Cytisus × praecox 'Warminster'

Osmanthus × *burkwoodii* • *Rhododendron* 'Blue Danube' • *Skimmia japonica* 'Fragrans' •

Flowering currant (Ribes)

Flowering currants are among the classic spring shrubs that are seen in many gardens and recognized by almost everyone. It is tempting to exclude *Ribes sanguineum* (zone 6–7) from small gardens because many of its common varieties are large and coarse— and sometimes with rather nondescript flower color—and they have little to offer during the 50 weeks of the year when they are not in bloom. However, flowering currants are very easy-to-grow, trouble-free shrubs, and the more interesting kinds, planted with carefully chosen companions, can take *Ribes* into an altogether more aristocratic league.

Flowering currants will tolerate indifferent soil and a certain amount of neglect: they are often among the sole survivors in old, long-forgotten gardens. To give of their best, however, they like good, well-drained soil in sun or light shade. Keep the bushes vigorous by pruning out some of the oldest wood each year after flowering.

When choosing companions for pink-flowering currants, strident spring yellows (as in forsythia) are probably best avoided. Blue, cream, and white are better. Silver-leaved pulmonarias, *Vinca minor*, and bergenias are ideal, with the bonus that they provide good ground cover around the shrub as well as contrasting leaf forms.

The Californian native *Ribes speciosum* (z. 6–8) is an intriguing and little-known shrub with pretty foliage and bristly stems that suggest gooseberries rather than currants. It is excellent trained as a wall shrub so that the slim, long-lasting, fuchsialike, red flowers hang from horizontal branches— especially effective on a pale-colored wall.

Ribes sanguineum 'Brocklebankii' (z. 6–7) is a compact, slow-growing plant. Its golden leaves show up well in a shady place, where it will be happier than in full sun. Although its foliage gives it a long season of interest, the combination of yellow foliage and pale pink flowers at blossom time is not to everyone's taste.

Ribes sanguineum 'Koja' (z. 6–7) is a good, compact, flowering currant, with red flowers. A larger alternative is *Ribes sanguineum* 'Elk River Red' (z. 6–7). Underplant with bulbs such as cream *Narcissus*, early white tulips, dark blue hyacinths, pale blue chionodoxas, and *Anemone blanda*.

OTHER GOOD FLOWERING CURRANTS

Ribes sanguineum 'King Edward VII' (z. 6–7) Crimson flowers on a low-growing plant.

Ribes sanguineum 'Pulborough Scarlet' (z. 6–7) Robust and vigorous, with upright growth and dark red flowers.

Ribes sanguineum 'White Icicle' (z. 6–7) Very early, white blossom: better than pink-flowered forms for partnering spring yellows.

Viburnum

Viburnums make up one of the most versatile groups of garden shrubs and are usually among the larger shrub sections in garden centers and nursery catalogs. They encompass many widely differing shrubs—large and small, evergreen and deciduous, winter- and spring-flowering—with an assortment of leaf shapes and flower forms. Some are fragrant; others put on a fine display of autumn berries in black, red, or blue.

In their cultural requirements, viburnums have more in common with each other. All will struggle in really dry, sunny sites, preferring some shade and humus-rich, fertile soil that never dries out. Some, including *Viburnum davidii* (zone 7–9) and *Viburnum tinus* (zone 8–9), are tolerant of drier shade, even when planted in alkaline soil. Others, for example *Viburnum opulus* (commonly known as the European cranberry bush) (zone 3–8), can flourish in permanently damp places. In general, viburnums are easy plants if they are given the right conditions: they suffer from few pests or diseases and do not need routine pruning.

Viburnum opulus 'Compactum' (z. 3–8) is a smaller form of the vigorous European cranberry bush. This useful shrub has something to offer at every season: pretty, white lacecap flowers in spring, attractive maplelike foliage that colors well in the fall before it drops, and shiny, red berries that usually remain on the bush well into winter.

The slow-growing, deciduous **Viburnum × juddii** (z. 4–7) is one of the prettiest viburnums, with clusters of pink buds opening into spicily scented, white flowers. Remove any suckers that appear at the base of the shrub: the plant may have been propagated by grafting onto a rootstock of *Viburnum lantana,* which, given the chance, could take over.

Viburnum plicatum f. **tomentosum 'Summer Snowflake'** (z. 5–8) is a more compact, but less spectacular, version of the widely admired *Viburnum plicatum* f. *tomentosum* 'Mariesii' (z. 5–8), which needs a large amount of room if its beautiful tiers of white blossom are to be displayed to best advantage. 'Summer Snowflake' is easier to accommodate in small spaces but is equally intolerant of soil that dries out in summer.

OTHER GOOD VIBURNUMS

Viburnum × bodnantense 'Dawn' (above) (z. 8–9) A deciduous viburnum with fragrant pink flowers in winter and early spring (see page 105).

Viburnum carlesii 'Aurora' (above) (z. 4–7) A popular, medium-size, deciduous shrub with red buds giving way to fragrant pink flowers.

Viburnum davidii (z. 7–9) Low, evergreen shrub, excellent for ground cover (see page 43).

Viburnum tinus 'Spring Bouquet' (z. 8–9) A very useful, tough evergreen with pinkish flowers in very early spring (see page 105).

Summer-flowering shrubs

A profusion of flowers and fragrance all summer is the aim of many gardeners, but how is this to be achieved in a small garden without letting the planting get out of control? Carefully chosen and thoughtfully managed shrubs will be important in providing the necessary structure and continuity. Judicious and timely pruning is one of the tricks to employ.

Ceanothus 'Puget Blue'

Helianthemum 'Wisley White'

Helianthemum 'Wisley Primrose'

Potentilla fruticosa 'Abbotswood'

you will need a prostrate variety such as *Ceanothus* 'Centennial' (zone 7–10) or the taller, spreading *Ceanothus* 'Italian Skies' (zone 8–10). Choose a sunny site, and use it to support a climber such as a clematis later in the year.

Just as fond of sunshine are the dwarf evergreen rockroses, **helianthemums** (zone 5–8). Trouble-free and tolerant of poor soil, they flower in early summer and are ideal for the top of a retaining wall where they can spill over the edge

A surprising number of summer shrubs are either naturally compact or easy to keep that way by occasional pruning. Others can be welcomed into a small garden only if you choose the right variety from the rows of similar-looking pots in the nursery. The evergreen forms of **ceanothus** are an example of this: everyone admires these beautiful shrubs when they burst into sheets of blue that herald the onset of summer, but some varieties are tremendously vigorous and can quickly take over a garden. *Ceanothus* 'Concha' (zone 9–10) and

Ceanothus 'Puget Blue' (zone 7–10) are medium-size cultivars that, carefully managed on a sunny wall, can be accommodated in a fairly limited space without detriment to their flowering. Keep the shrub securely tied in to the wall, make sure it does not go short of water, and after flowering be certain to trim back the new growth to keep everything close to the wall. Evergreen ceanothus will happily take this treatment but dislike their old wood being cut back hard. Another way to use them is as ground cover, in which case

and make good company for santolina and lavender. Their fragile, papery flowers are short-lived but numerous, and the color range is wide. Good varieties include *Helianthemum* 'Wisley White' (or the easier-to-find alternative, 'St. Mary's'), 'Wisley Primrose' (pale yellow), 'Rhodanthe Carneum' (pale pink), and 'Henfield Brilliant' (brick red). Control helianthemums' tendency to sprawl by trimming them after they finish flowering to leave a neat cushion of gray-green foliage. This may also induce the plant to produce flowers later in the year.

MORE SUMMER-FLOWERING SHRUBS *Abelia* × *grandiflora* • *Ceanothus* × *delileanus* 'Gloire de Versailles' •

A similarly wide color range is one of the many reasons for growing the ultra-reliable shrubby **potentillas** (zone 2–7). These popular, easy little shrubs will flower all summer long, requiring no attention and taking all sorts of adverse conditions in their stride. Good for informal hedging, the compact *Potentilla fruticosa* 'Abbotswood' (with large, white flowers) and *Potentilla fruticosa* 'Hopley's Orange' are both wider than they are tall. *Potentilla fruticosa* 'Primrose Beauty' has silvery leaves and large, pale yellow flowers. Any soil will do, in sun or part shade, although the flowers towards the red end of the color range look better in part shade.

Ozothamnus ledifolius

Escallonia 'Apple Blossom'

Also very tolerant and much used for hedging are the evergreen **escallonias**. Popular in coastal gardens, they are happy in poor soil but need shelter from cold winds. An old favorite is *Escallonia* 'Apple Blossom' (zone 8–10), which grows slowly and has pink flowers.

A small and unusual evergreen shrub that flowers in the summer but looks interesting all year is the sun-loving Tasmanian *Ozothamnus ledifolius* (zone 9–10). Similar to some heathers, it has densely packed, rich green foliage and golden shoot tips all winter. These produce flower buds in glowing orange-

red that open to whitish flowers. By late summer the yellow shoot tips are back, ready to repeat the process.

Early to midsummer is the season for a trio of popular and very traditional flowering shrubs: **weigela, deutzia,** and fragrant **philadelphus**. The many available varieties of each include some very small forms such as *Philadelphus microphyllus* (see page 135) and the

red-flowered *Weigela* 'Nain Rouge' (zone 5–9). The weigelas that are grown for their foliage (see page 54) are also compact. Deutzias have white or pale pink, scented flowers. The slow-growing, upright *Deutzia setchuenensis* var. *corymbiflora* is good for a small garden and has masses of large, star-shaped white flowers. As with the weigela and philadelphus, pruning deutzias should

GOOD COMPANIONS

Deciduous shrubs that flower in early summer are a good support for climbers that can scramble over their branches to flower later. Try *Weigela florida* 'Variegata' (1) (z. 5–9) with the red *Clematis* 'Gravetye Beauty' (2) (z. 5–9).

Plant dwarf tulips around helianthemums—here, *Tulipa* 'Red Riding Hood' (3) (z. 4–8) and *Helianthemum* 'Henfield Brilliant' (4) (z. 5–8). Both like a sunny, well-drained position, and the helianthemum flowers will disguise the tulips' fading foliage in early summer.

Hypericum 'Hidcote' • *Lavandula* • *Philadelphus* • *Syringa meyeri* 'Palibin' • *Weigela florida* 'Variegata' •

Deutzia setchuenensis var. corymbiflora

Carpenteria californica

Nandina domestica 'Fire Power'

best for a tight space. It has slender, bronzed, dark green leaves that deepen to purple in winter, and bright violet flowers in late summer. *Hebe* 'Great Orme' (zone 8–10) makes a larger bush, with bright pink flowers, while the aptly named *Hebe* 'Autumn Glory' (zone 8–10) is more of a dwarf, with smaller, round bronze leaves. It has a rather straggly habit, but if you can keep it tidy it is worth growing because its purple-blue flowers last into late fall. *Hebe* 'Silver Queen' (formerly *Hebe* × *franciscana* 'Variegata') (zone 7–11) is often seen in container, earning its keep in small spaces because it has both purple flowers and attractively variegated leaves.

Purples and blues are very much a theme of late-summer shrubs. The most familiar of these must be the **buddleias**, which are a little on the large side for very small gardens. However, their bulk is temporary because they need to be pruned hard in early spring to encourage good flowers. Most will have reached 6ft. (2m) again by late summer, but they

Hebe 'Mrs Winder'

involve taking out some of the oldest wood from the base after flowering.

In the warmer zones of the United States, *Carpenteria californica* (zone 8–11) will reward you in midsummer with a beautiful display of fragrant, white flowers, each with a central boss of bright golden stamens. It thrives best when trained on a sunny, sheltered wall where its evergreen leaves will be less prone to winter damage.

Another rather special plant for a prominent and sheltered position is *Nandina domestica* (zone 6–9), known as the heavenly bamboo. Unlike carpenteria, it is decorative at all times of the year, with attractive, graceful foliage (similar to that of a bamboo), clusters of small, starry, white flowers in summer, and red berries in warmer

years. *Nandina* is quite compact, but for a really dwarf form, choose *Nandina domestica* 'Fire Power', which grows to only about 18in. (45cm) tall and has foliage that turns rich red in the fall.

Hebes are invaluable evergreen shrubs that vary in hardiness. Some are best suited to mild coastal gardens or a sheltered urban microclimate, but many hebes will succeed in colder gardens. Some of the small-leaved types are grown purely for their evergreen foliage (see page 43), but *Hebe* is a large and varied genus whose species and cultivars include many with beautiful flowers. New forms continue to become available all the time: some are excellent, but do check their hardiness before you buy. Of the established varieties, *Hebe* 'Mrs Winder' (zone 8–10) is one of the

SHRUBS FOR WARM WALLS *Abutilon* • *Aloysia triphylla* • *Carpenteria californica* • *Ceanothus* 'Concha' •

are such a pleasure when covered in butterflies that you forgive them their vigor. Many have rather dull foliage; one exception is *Buddleia* 'Lochinch' (zone 5–9), which has silvery stems and leaves as well as graceful, pale lavender flower spikes. Flower color in buddleias varies from nearly pink (*Buddleia davidii* 'Royal Red', zone 5–9) to nearly blue (*Buddleia davidii* 'Empire Blue', zone 5–9), and there are also white forms including *Buddleia davidii* 'White Profusion' (zone 5–9), though these need prompt deadheading if the brown, spent flower spikes are not to spoil the effect. Deadheading promotes a longer flowering season, which the butterflies enjoy. The shrubs' gawky appearance after flowering can be disguised by planting them at the back of a border, or by allowing them to host a late-flowering clematis or other climber. Buddleias are easy to propagate from hardwood cuttings taken at pruning time.

A smaller shrub—but one that needs similarly drastic pruning treatment—is

Buddleia 'Lochinch'

caryopteris (zone 5–9). This neat and compact late-summer shrub is near perfect for small gardens, with pretty grayish foliage, and flowers in a range of exquisite blues. *Caryopteris × clandonensis* 'Heavenly Blue' is a reliable and well-established variety, but "improved" forms are coming along all the time and include *Caryopteris ×*

clandonensis 'Summer Sorbet', with gold-edged leaves, and *Caryopteris × clandonensis* 'First Choice', which has larger, long-lasting flowers of deep blue. Caryopteris need full sun and well-drained soil, and they are especially happy in alkaline soil. Cuttings root readily and will quickly make new plants to tuck into borders or give away.

GOOD COMPANIONS

Ozothamnus ledifolius (1) (z. 8–10) is a late-spring companion for the orange lily-flowered *Tulipa* 'Ballerina' (2) (z. 4–8), which echoes the shrub's orange flower buds. An amber grass, *Carex buchananii* (3) (z. 7–9) adds textural contrast to the planting.

Unusual partners for late summer, the rich color of *Caryopteris × clandonensis* 'Heavenly Blue' (4) (z. 7–8) contrasts prettily with the pale yellow of *Potentilla fruticosa* 'Primrose Beauty' (5), (z. 2–7) which has foliage of a similar grayish green.

Ceanothus 'Puget Blue' • *Ficus carica* • *Fremontodendron* 'California Glory' • *Myrtus communis* •

A similar blue shrub for a dry, sunny place is *Perovskia* 'Blue Spire' (zone 5–8). Like caryopteris, it is ideal for somewhere near the front of a mixed border and should be cut almost to the ground in early spring—although not so early that its new foliage is likely to be frost-damaged. Its graceful, airy, aromatic foliage and downy, purple calyxes ensure that it continues to look good for some time after the petals have dropped in late summer.

The splendid large-flowered shrub **hibiscus** is by no means compact, but by virtue of its upright growth habit it might just find a place as an accent plant in a small garden border. *Hibiscus syriacus* 'Marina' (zone 5–8) is a good, recent form of an old favorite, with striking, deep violet-blue flowers that can keep up a display for three months or more—and continue into late fall if the weather is favorable. It must have a sunny, well-drained position, but it is otherwise undemanding.

Perovskia 'Blue Spire'

GOOD COMPANIONS

Annual climbers work well with flowering shrubs of many kinds. Let sweet peas (1) scramble up into the sturdy stems of *Buddleia davidii* (2) (z. 5–9), or plant morning glory (*Ipomoea tricolor* 'Heavenly Blue') (3) (z. 10–11 or ann.) where it can twine up and over a white shrub rose such as *Rosa* 'Blanc Double de Coubert' (4) (z. 3–7).

For a contrast of leaf forms in cool, silvery blue colors, choose a well-drained, sunny place to underplant *Perovskia* 'Blue Spire' (5) (z. 5–8) with *Stachys byzantina* (6) (z. 4–8), which will recover from its midsummer doldrums just as the perovskia flowers.

Ceratostigma willmottianum

A small, late-flowering shrub for a sunny border is the hardy plumbago, *Ceratostigma willmottianum* (zone 8). Its starry flowers, of deepest royal blue, are often still blooming as the leaves turn to deep red in late fall. It may die back to the ground in winter, reemerging in spring (when old growth should be cut out). *Ceratostigma* is excellent with other vividly colored plants that glow in autumn sunshine: mix it with fuchsias, sedums, and echinaceas in an end-of-season blast of bright, flamboyant color.

Cistus

A cistus in full bloom, turning its numerous, newly opened, crinkled flowers to the sun early on a summer's morning, is one of those special garden moments. The knowledge that these fragile flowers will have gone by the afternoon no doubt enhances their charm. Cistus—occasionally called sun roses for obvious reasons—are native to the rocky hillsides of the Mediterranean region, so they generally settle well in coastal gardens and do not mind an exposed, windy position. Many of them are surprisingly hardy (zone 8) and long-lived, as long as they have a well-drained, sunny site. They revel in poor soil, to the extent that being fed and watered does not suit them at all.

Cistus come in various sizes: some are naturally compact enough for the smallest garden, while others will need to be trimmed back after flowering each year. They do not respond well to being cut back hard, so an old, woody bush is best replaced with a young specimen. In a very restricted space, helianthemums are a similar but smaller alternative to cistus.

Becoming more widely available, this named hybrid, *Cistus × argenteus* 'Silver Pink' (z. 8–10) started life many years ago as a chance seedling at a nursery. It is a very tough, compact bush with slightly silvery, felted leaves and white-centered, clear, pale pink flowers.

OTHER GOOD CISTUS

Cistus × argenteus 'Peggy Sammons' (z. 8–10) A vigorous but fairly compact, free-flowering hybrid with bright pink flowers.

Cistus × obtusifolius 'Thrive' (above) (z. 8–10) An aptly named hybrid with lots of pure white flowers all summer.

Cistus × purpureus (z. 8–10) Deep pink flowers with a maroon blotch on each petal.

Cistus × hybridus (z. 8–10) is sometimes still listed by its former name, *Cistus × corbariensis*. This compact, low-growing bush has neat, yellow-centered white flowers, with a fresh batch opening from reddish buds every day for several weeks.

Cistus ladanifer (z. 8–10) is an old-established, garden plant whose white petals each have a maroon blotch at the base. Its growth is upright, and in a confined space it can easily be kept to size by trimming back the new growth after flowering each year.

HARDY: FLOWERING SHRUBS

Rose (Rosa)

Many people do not want to be without roses, but in gardens where space is at a premium it can be difficult to use these plants successfully. There are so many roses available, of so many different types, that the potential for choosing the wrong one is huge.

Some roses are simply too large and vigorous for small spaces. Some will not tolerate growing conditions that are anything less than perfect, such as a shady position or poor, alkaline soil. Others are susceptible to the disfiguring diseases that can plague these otherwise lovely plants. Selecting the right varieties is the first step in steering clear of the pitfalls that can make growing roses more of a worry than a pleasure.

Many roses contribute too little to the garden for too much of the year. All have a rather long "off season," which can be hard to ignore in a small space. However, some have ways of compensating—by producing a fine crop of hips in the fall, or by flowering throughout

The outsize vermilion hips of *Rosa* 'Fru Dagmar Hastrup' bring a theatrical touch to the late summer garden.

the summer instead of for only a week or two; some have glossy, semi-evergreen foliage, and some have a pleasing shape. In a small garden, fragrance is also likely to be an important consideration. If you have room for only one or two roses, choosing unscented varieties is a lost opportunity that you may regret on balmy midsummer evenings.

Roses combine very well with other plants, and mixed planting suits them for the purposes of design as well as for more practical reasons (such as providing their bases with ground cover). However, it is important to select appropriate partners. As with climbing roses (see pages 80–81), a clematis can be ideal: it will provide an additional season of flower color and, if you choose a late-flowering variety, it can be pruned in late winter at the same time as the rose. Be sure, however, to choose one that is not so vigorous that it will smother the rose.

Dwarf shrubs can be good partners, too. Roses and lavender are a familiar combination. Other shrubs that can help mask a rose's inelegant legs include santolina, variegated box, dwarf junipers, or the valuable purple-leaved evergreen *Pittosporum* 'Tom Thumb'. Hardy geraniums are very useful rose companions: they help to cover the ground and retain moisture and, if chosen carefully, they provide a long season of very compatible flowers. Spring bulbs such as tulips and anemones, planted at the rose's feet, bring an additional season of interest.

MOTTISFONT ABBEY GARDEN

Extensive grounds surround this former priory on the River Test near Romsey in Hampshire, England. Huge mature trees include planes and a magnificent tulip tree (*Liriodendron tulipifera*). The old walled garden is now the Graham Stuart Thomas Rose Garden. It commemorates the late rose expert and author.

In early summer, the National Collection of old-fashioned roses is in its full glory. There is no better way to get to know these lovely roses than to wander among the fragrant blooms (all labeled) that fill the borders and cascade from arches, walls, and pergolas, so if you travel to England, a visit is a must.

Rosa 'Buff Beauty' (z. 4–9) is an excellent shrub rose that will give pleasure over a long season. It is not for very small spaces, but it is worth making room for it if you can. The copper-toned new growth greens to deep olive, contrasting with the prolific clusters of fragrant flowers, which fade through yellow and buff to creamy white.

Rosa 'Fru Dagmar Hastrup' (z. 4–7) belongs to the rugosas, a group of resilient, easy roses that often succeed in conditions that do not suit other types. Less vigorous than some other rugosas, it has healthy-looking foliage and clear pink, single flowers. The crop of tomatolike hips prolongs its season of interest.

Rosa 'Winchester Cathedral' (z. 5–10) may not be the most compact white rose, but as a well-established English rose with a good fragrance, a bushy habit, and repeated flowers it has few rivals. It can also be grown as a standard. White roses are a good choice for a small space, showing up well against walls, fences, and hedges and causing no color clashes.

OTHER GOOD ROSES

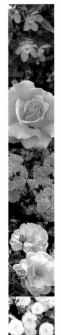

Rosa 'Amber Queen' (z. 4–9) Frilly, scented, golden amber flowers with dark foliage on a low bush.

Rosa 'Arthur Bell' (z. 6–10) Compact and reliable, with scented, semidouble, yellow blooms.

Rosa 'Ballerina' (z. 4–9) Pretty, small, single pink roses throughout summer. Good as a standard.

Rosa 'Blanc Double de Coubert' (z. 3–7) Fine, robust (though quite tall) rugosa with fragrant, double white blooms for a long period.

Rosa 'Crocus Rose' (z. 4–9) Double, fragrant pale apricot flowers fading to cream.

Rosa glauca (z. 2–7) Quite large, but graceful and pretty all season. Gray-green foliage, single pink flowers and red hips.

Rosa 'Just Joey' (z. 5–10) A popular, fragrant, soft orange rose, attractive in bud and with good foliage.

Rosa 'Pink Flower Carpet' (z. 4–9) Bright pink, semi-double flowers on a disease-resistant, ground-hugging bush.

Rosa 'Queen Mother' (z. 4–9) Clear pink, freely flowering patio rose; good in a container.

Rosa 'White Pet' (z. 5–9) Sprays of pink buds open to double white flowers. Long flowering season; compact.

The neat little floribunda *Rosa* 'Trumpeter' (z. 4–9) flowers almost all summer. Shapely, slightly scented, bright scarlet flowers are set off by attractive, healthy, bronzed foliage. This is a good rose to use at the front of a mixed border, as a specimen in a container, or on the edge of a patio.

Fuchsia

Fuchsias are quite unmistakable to almost everyone. Their fresh-looking, hanging bells bring vivid color to late-summer gardens, and they seem to take on a new lease of life in the fall, showing their appreciation of cooler, damper air by flowering even more abundantly until frosts begin. They can be grown as shrubs in mild coastal areas in zone 8 or warmer.

The color range of fuchsias is pink, red, purple, and white, but these colors appear in so many different combinations and variations that the number of available species and named cultivars or hybrids on sale is well over 2,000. Many of these are frost-tender patio or greenhouse plants. More useful for long-term mixed planting are the so-called "hardy" fuchsias.

Although the hardy types die back with winter frosts, they usually regenerate from the base each spring, especially if they are planted slightly more deeply than an average shrub. You can then remove the dead stems. Mulching will help them through the winter, and they will appreciate the improved water retention that a mulch can provide (although they dislike waterlogging). They may not prove so hardy in containers, where their roots are more susceptible to repeated wetting and freezing.

As its name suggests, *Fuchsia* 'Tom Thumb' (z. 7–9) is suitable for even the tiniest garden, reaching a height and spread of no more than 1ft. (30cm). It is never out of flower through late summer and early fall, providing a vivid splash of deep pink and purple just when it is needed. Good with *Verbena bonariensis*.

Fuchsia 'Riccartonii' (z. 6–9) is among the hardiest fuchsias and the most frequently seen. It gives an uninterrupted display of small red flowers with purple sepals from midsummer until the first frosts. A mature plant can make 5–6ft. (1.5–1.8m) of young growth in a season.

The species fuchsias such as *Fuchsia magellanica* (z. 6–9) tend to be hardier and more graceful than the large-flowered hybrids. **Fuchsia magellanica var. gracilis 'Variegata'** is an unusual variegated form. The leaves, edged creamy white and flushed pink, show off small scarlet and purple flowers.

OTHER GOOD FUCHSIAS

Fuchsia magellanica var. *molinae* (right) (z. 6–9) A graceful background plant, with dainty, palest pink flowers.

Fuchsia 'Lady Thumb' (z. 7–9) Dwarf "wife" of 'Tom Thumb' (see above), with paler pink and white flowers.

Fuchsia 'Mrs Popple' (left) (z. 7–9) A fairly compact shrub with large scarlet and violet flowers.

Fuchsia procumbens (z. 7–9) Unusual trailing fuchsia with greenish yellow, tubelike flowers, and magenta fruits.

Hydrangea

Come late summer, gardens can begin to look tired and tattered. This is a good time of year to have, waiting in the wings, a few plants with sufficient "wow factor" to distract attention from others that are past their peak. Hydrangeas fit the bill perfectly and, as a bonus, some of them die off and fade beautifully to leave shapely dried flower heads that endure through the winter.

As with roses and fuchsias, enthusiastic breeders have ensured that there is a bewildering range of varieties available. It is difficult to control the size of most types of hydrangea successfully by hard pruning because their flowering will be impaired, so for a small space it is better to select one of the more compact forms.

Hydrangea color is to some extent dependent on soil: broadly speaking, acidic soil for blue flowers, alkaline for pink. As a result, not all gardeners are able to grow the sea blue hydrangeas that are seen billowing over the walls of gardens in certain areas.

A good blue on acidic soil (pinkish mauve on alkaline), *Hydrangea serrata* 'Bluebird' (z. 5–7) is a pretty, lacecap hydrangea with a compact habit. It flowers early but the blooms are long-lasting, as is its attractive autumn foliage color. It prefers some shade.

The large rosy pink florets of *Hydrangea* 'Preziosa' (z. 5–7) are grouped into small mopheads that mature in fall to purplish red. The foliage colors well, too. This is a fairly compact hydrangea with upright growth, reaching no more than 5ft. (1.5m) in height and spread.

Hydrangea quercifolia 'Sike's Dwarf' (z. 5–9) is a small form of the white-flowered, oak-leaved hydrangea. It flowers rather late in the season, and its attractive lobed foliage usually colors well in suitable fall weather. It benefits from the protection of a wall.

OTHER GOOD HYDRANGEAS

Hydrangea macrophylla 'Lanarth White' (z. 6–9) Dwarf, white-flowered shrub with subtle tints of blue or pink according to soil type.

Hydrangea macrophylla 'Lilacina' (z. 6–9) Attractive, flattish flower heads with a few well-spaced, large, sterile florets at the edge.

Hydrangea macrophylla 'Pia' (z. 6–9) Compact and slow-growing, with persistent red-purple flowers. One of the best hydrangeas for tiny gardens or for containers.

Hydrangea paniculata 'Grandiflora' (z. 3–8) Large, conical panicles of white flowers that age to pink. A hardy plant; can be pruned hard in winter to limit size and encourage larger flower heads.

Hydrangea serrata 'Grayswood' (z. 5–7) Small lacecap with white florets, which in sunshine gradually mature to pink, then deep red.

SENSORY

Small outdoor spaces are an open invitation to explore the rich sensory experiences that the living world can offer, giving wonderful opportunities to get really close to plants. Although we may not be consciously aware of it, the best gardens will appeal to all five of our senses, so when choosing what to plant, plan not only for color and fragrance but also for sounds and textures, not forgetting the satisfying pleasures of growing even a few simple, tasty things to eat.

RIGHT: *Lonicera × purpusii* 'Winter Beauty'

Scent and the senses

Any small, sheltered space—a courtyard garden, or perhaps a secluded arbor tucked away in a corner of a larger plot—will lend itself very well to sensory planting. Scent and sounds will not be whisked away by the wind but can drift into the house through open windows and doors on warm days and balmy evenings: a subtle way to link house and garden that reinforces color, form, and texture, the fundamentals of visual design.

Choosing sensory plants is not as simple as it sounds. All five of our senses are subjective: different scents, tastes, textures, colors, and sounds provoke inexplicable preferences, deep-seated memories, and strong differences of opinion. The best and only advice is to follow your own preferences, choosing plants that appeal to your own senses.

Scent may be the most subjective of all senses: some find the fragrances of myrtle or coriander, of lilies or honeysuckle heavenly, while to others they are sickly or otherwise repellent. Yet the notion of a fragrant garden appeals to almost everyone.

Scent is also notoriously elusive. Few plants are equally free with their fragrance in all circumstances. Scents vary with weather, time of day, and, not least, our own particular perception of them at different times. Sometimes, in a hurry, we fail to notice them at all. At other times, usually when we deliberately seek out a particular fragrance, it can disappoint. Perhaps these are some of the things that make this particular sense so special.

SOUND EFFECTS

Almost everyone enjoys birdsong or the rippling of water in a garden. But don't forget the more subtle soundtrack created by plants themselves. With the crunch of crisp autumn leaves underfoot, the popping or dry rattling of ripe seed pods on a hot day, the swishing of grasses in the wind, or the gentle rustling of bamboos, gardens are seldom silent. See the foot of the page for some sound planting ideas.

A traditional approach to sensory planting: roses and lavender, harmonious classics of the fragrant garden.

PLANTS FOR SOUND *Briza maxima* • *Calamagrostis* × *acutiflora* 'Overdam' • *Cordyline australis* •

Texture

Using plants of differing textures not only enriches the range of sensory experiences that a garden can provide but also helps to achieve visual contrast in planting design. The plant world provides us with an amazing range of textures in the leaves, bark, seeds, fruits, and flowers of many thousands of plants.

Textural planting has a special role in gardens for people with special needs. Like fragrance, it can bring a garden alive for someone with poor eyesight, for example. Young children love the novelty of textural plants. Introduce them to the papery lanterns of *Physalis alkekengi* (zone 4–7) or to *Salvia argentea* (zone 5–8), with its impossibly woolly leaves; the parchmentlike "coins" of honesty seed pods (*Lunaria annua*) (zone 7–9); or a compact snowberry such as *Symphoricarpos* × *doorenbosii* 'White Hedge' (zone 4–7), with its smooth, globular white fruits.

Remember plants at hand- and eye-level as well as those nearer the ground. For example, grow *Garrya elliptica* (zone 8–9) as a wall shrub where its satiny catkins can be brushed against.

The papery, bobbly seed heads of *Allium hollandicum* (zone 5–9) are at just the right height for passing hands. *Clematis tangutica* (zone 6–9) is a good climber, not only for its fluffy seed heads but also for its leathery, bell-shaped flowers that are interesting to touch. So too is tree bark, with its many varied textures.

In tiny gardens, or even on a balcony, **sempervivums** can make a good group of textures. Grasses are always fascinating, from the bristly clumps of *Festuca glauca* (zone 4–8) to the leathery blades of *Luzula sylvatica* (zone 6–8), the fuzzy bottlebrushes of *Pennisetum orientale* (zone 7–9), and the silky hair of *Stipa tenuissima* (zone 8–9)—all compact enough for a limited space.

PLANTS FOR TEXTURE

Fluffy
Pennisetum (above)
Clematis tangutica
Pulsatilla vulgaris

Silky
Cryptomeria japonica 'Elegans Compacta'
Euphorbia cyparissias
Stipa tenuissima (above)

Lacy
Anthriscus sylvestris 'Ravenswing'
Nigella (above)
Polystichum setiferum

Woolly
Helichrysum splendidum
Salvia argentea
Stachys byzantina (above)

Papery
Allium
Lunaria annua
Papaver
Physalis (above)

Spiky
Festuca
Iris
Phormium (above)
Sisyrinchium

Spiny
Dipsacus fullonum
Eryngium
Ilex aquifolium
Ruscus aculeatus (above)

Stiff
Agapanthus
Cotoneaster horizontalis
Kniphofia (above)
Tulipa

Wiry
Briza
Carex buchananii (above)
Triteleia laxa

Bobbly
Ballota
Gaultheria
Phlomis (above)
Santolina

Leathery
Bergenia (above)
Fatsia japonica
Hedera
Limonium platyphyllum

Waxy
Chimonanthus
Helleborus
Hosta (above)
Sedum

Cytisus × *praecox* • *Miscanthus* 'Kleine Silberspinne' • *Nigella damascena* • *Phyllostachys nigra* •

Winter and spring fragrance

Winter scent is one of the great pleasures of the all-year garden, appreciated all the more because it so often catches us unawares. A surprising number of plants can contribute to a garden in this way, releasing their fragrance unexpectedly into the air on mild days and providing deliciously scented sprigs whose perfume will fill a room when they are brought into the house.

Some of the very best winter-scented shrubs are ideal for the small garden. Sarcococcas—for example *Sarcococca confusa* (see page 42) or *Sarcococca hookeriana* var. *digyna* (zone 6–8), with pink-tinged blossom—take up little space, being naturally neat and compact. They provide greenery and ground cover all year, tolerating both shade and poor soil and requiring no attention. Unobtrusive and undemanding almost all year, they suddenly take you by surprise one mild midwinter day, when their mass of fragrant blossom begins to open, scenting the air for some distance around.

Sarcococca confusa

If you have a little more space to devote to winter fragrance, **Lonicera × purpusii 'Winter Beauty'** (zone 5–9) is another midwinter shrub to consider. This is the best of several winter-flowering shrubby honeysuckles, all with the typical sweet smell. Its place in the garden needs to be chosen with care: an open site with some sunshine will help it to bear its white flowers more freely,

Chimonanthus praecox

but its dull summer appearance makes an unobtrusive position advisable. With a height and spread, when mature, up to 6ft. (2m), this shrub is large enough to support a clematis or other summer-flowering climber to give it a second season of interest.

Chimonanthus praecox (zone 7–9) or winter sweet is a true midwinter plant, with small but powerfully scented, pale straw-colored waxy flowers on bare stems for many weeks. It is a shrub for patient gardeners because it is shy to flower as a youngster, but it is worth waiting for. Eventually it will grow quite large but need not become a nuisance if kept trained into a warm wall. *Abeliophyllum distichum* (zone 5–8) also likes wall protection (but not

Abeliophyllum distichum

Iris unguicularis

an east wall, where morning sun could scorch its blossoms after a frost). This unusual forsythia relative, sometimes known as white forsythia, flowers later than winter sweet but has equally fragrant white or pinkish blooms. Prune out the oldest wood after flowering to keep the shrub neat and healthy.

The base of a sunny wall is an ideal site for one of the most exotic-looking of winter flowers, *Iris unguicularis* (zone 7–9). Its foliage becomes untidy in summer, but all is forgiven when one midwinter day, large lilac blue irises begin to unfold. They release a cowslip-like fragrance when brought into the house—best done just before each flower opens. A native of North Africa, this iris must be exposed to plenty of summer sun if it is to flower well the following winter; it must not be grown in rich soil but (to quote Vita Sackville-West) "in contemptible rubbish such as brick-bats and gravel. Starvation is practically all that this iris asks of you."

The many fragrant bulbs include another early-flowering iris for a sunny position in the garden or for growing in pots to bring indoors. The species *Iris reticulata* (zone 5–8) and its cultivars

OTHER FRAGRANT WINTER AND SPRING PLANTS *Hamamelis × intermedia* 'Pallida' • *Hamamelis mollis* •

Hyacinthus orientalis

Galanthus 'S. Arnott'

Narcissus 'Pipit'

Tulipa sylvestris

Tulipa 'Ballerina'

Tulipa 'White Emperor'

bear exquisite little flowers, mostly in shades of blue and purple, very early in spring (see page 176). For scent, the best one to grow is *Iris* 'J.S. Dijt' (zone 5–8), which has reddish purple flowers.

Perhaps the most familiar of scented spring bulbs, traditionally planted in pots indoors, are hyacinths, forms of *Hyacinthus orientalis* (zone 4–8). Their heady fragrance in a room is a very early pointer toward spring when it still seems far ahead. Hyacinths are also surprisingly resilient garden plants, their waxy flowers standing up to severe weather and appearing year after year in early spring. Well-scented varieties include 'Delft Blue', 'Amethyst', and 'Carnegie', a white one.

Snowdrops do not flaunt their scent, but a number of varieties do have a pleasant fragrance when brought into the house. One of the most reliable for scent is the excellent, versatile *Galanthus* 'S. Arnott' (zone 4–8).

Narcissi (zone 4–8) are noted for their perfume, particularly those that belong to the jonquil group. *Narcissus* 'Bell Song', 'Baby Moon', 'Pipit', and 'Sweetness' are fragrant named varieties to look out for. Often seen in floristry, *Narcissus* 'Cheerfulness' is also very pleasantly scented. The less well-known *Narcissus* 'Canaliculatus' has attractive, tiny golden-centered flowers with a rich, fruity aroma. Plant it in a sunny position. Among the last to flower is one of the most fragrant of all, *Narcissus poeticus* var. *recurvus*,

known as pheasant's eye. This is an old-fashioned favorite that is excellent for naturalizing in grass.

An unusual scented flower that is also good for naturalizing is the rare British wild tulip *Tulipa sylvestris* (zone 4–8). It can be tricky to establish but, if you leave it undisturbed in a lightly shaded grassy area, there is a good chance its underground stems will begin to spread to form a colony of

graceful yellow flowers whose scent is similar to that of freesias. The scented tulip species have handed down their fragrance to a few cultivated varieties (zone 4–8). These include the lily-flowered *Tulipa* 'Ballerina' (orange) and 'West Point' (yellow), early-flowering *Tulipa* 'White Emperor' ('Purissima') and the golden yellow 'Bellona', and the very late-flowering, deep orange *Tulipa* 'Dillenburg'.

GOOD COMPANIONS

Wallflowers (z. 7–8) associate well with tulips (1) (z. 4–8): a classic combination that is useful as a temporary filler in a new border. Choose a color scheme that suits the other plants in the border.

Allow sweet peas (2) (ann.) to scramble over the rather dull summer branches of winter-flowering *Lonicera* × *purpusii* 'Winter Beauty' (3) (z. 5–9), to give two seasons of fragrance.

Mahonia 'Winter Sun' • *Osmanthus delavayi* • *Osmanthus* × *burkwoodii* • *Viburnum* × *bodnantense* 'Dawn' •

Viola odorata 'Alba'

Convallaria majalis

Syringa meyeri 'Palibin'

In the front rank of classic springtime scents is that of the sweet violets, **Viola odorata** (zone 5–8). A curious fact about them is that their perfume is fleeting—detectable at the first sniff, but fainter or nonexistent if you try smelling it again a few seconds later. The scent of sweet violets has been bred into a wide range of named violas.

Just as traditional, if more subtle, is the gentle fragrance of the primula tribe. The common primrose, **Primula vulgaris** (zone 6–7), has a pleasant woodland scent that is amplified in some of the cultivated forms, especially the old doubles and the 'hose-in-hose' varieties (where one flower grows out of the center of another). Cowslips (**Primula veris**) (zone 5–7) have a soothing, honeylike scent (see page 85).

No description of garden perfumes would be complete without mentioning wallflowers (**Erysimum**, zone 7–8). They have a warm fragrance all their own and are worth growing specially for cutting, as well as to scent the garden on mild days in spring. They are biennials and can be grown from seed sown in early summer and transplanted to their final position in the fall. Alternatively, buy plants from a nursery in the fall.

A plant with a quite different scent, easy to accommodate anywhere in shade, is lily of the valley, **Convallaria majalis** (zone 4–8). Grow it in pots to bring inside or to scent the patio, or tuck it among ferns and other tough shade lovers at the back of a border. It has a running habit and will need to be kept in check. Lily of the valley dislikes disturbance but appreciates occasional offerings of compost.

Late spring and into summer is the season for another scented classic, the lilac. Lilac bushes tend to be greedy of space, elbowing out other plants and contributing little when they are out of flower. Most of them therefore do not really earn their space in a small garden. However, some newer dwarf forms such as **Syringa meyeri 'Palibin'** (zone 3–8) are ideal. This slow-growing, lavender pink lilac has a dense, compact habit and is unlikely to exceed 5ft. (1.5m) in any direction. Its foliage takes on a bronze tinge in the fall, when it sometimes also bears a few extra flowers. **Syringa 'Red Pixie'** (zone 3–7) is another good dwarf form, with red buds that open to fragrant pink flowers.

GOOD COMPANIONS

A good way to grow certain winter and spring shrubs that flower better on a south-facing wall or fence, such as *Abeliophyllum distichum* (1) (z. 5–8), is to allow them to share the space with a sun-loving, summer-flowering annual climber—perhaps a sweet pea, or *Ipomoea lobata* (2) (z. 9–11).

If you have the room—under a tree not too far from the house—perhaps plant *Sarcococca hookeriana* var. *digyna* (3) (z. 6–8) with early snowdrops (4) (z. 4–8), pink hybrid hellebores (5) (z. 5–8), and *Pulmonaria rubra* (6) (z. 3–7) to create a winter garden that is guaranteed to lift your spirits every time you look at it or catch its fragrance. If space allows, add a daphne or *Viburnum* × *bodnantense* 'Dawn' (z. 6–8).

Daphne

Sweet but never cloying, the fragrance of daphnes is always welcome in the garden, especially in early spring. These delightful compact shrubs have gained a reputation for being difficult to grow. They seem to be among those tantalizing plants that flourish for no apparent reason in some gardens but fail, despite having every attention lavished on them, in others. The only advice can be to have a try, for a successful daphne of whichever variety is a plant to cherish. Every garden has room for at least one.

Daphnes like ground that is well drained but never dries out. Natural woodlanders, they like humus-rich, cool soil, and some prefer light overhead shade in summer. They dislike being pruned, or moved, and tend to be difficult to propagate—probably the main reason why they are so expensive. Daphnes are poisonous, and their sap can irritate skin.

Some daphnes are prone to viral diseases; if one dies for no apparent reason this is often the cause. *Daphne mezereum* has become increasingly susceptible to such disease, to the extent that it is rare now to find a completely healthy specimen of this formerly popular early spring shrub. Try to buy deciduous daphnes when they are in leaf so you can see that the foliage is healthy.

Sun-loving *Daphne tangutica* (z. 6–8) is compact with upright growth, making it suitable for tight spaces. It flowers in mid-spring, often repeating toward the end of summer. Its purple-backed, pale flowers make it a good partner for deep purples: plant it in front of *Sambucus nigra* f. *porphyrophylla* 'Eva' ('Black Lace') (z. 5–7), or with tulips (z. 4–8) such as 'Recreado' or 'Queen of Night'.

One of the taller daphnes, reaching up to 6ft. (2m), *Daphne bholua* 'Jacqueline Postill' (z. 8–9) has a narrow, upright habit and gives good value for space because of its abundant large, sweetly scented flowers over a long midwinter flowering season. Very robust.

Although it is not long-lived, *Daphne odora* 'Aureomarginata' (z. 6–8) is among the more popular daphnes for its early flowers and variegated foliage. Plant it near a door so that you don't miss its wonderful fragrance at flowering time. It is easier to propagate from cuttings than most other daphnes.

Daphne × *burkwoodii* (z. 4–7) is a comparatively reliable, easy hybrid that opens its blooms later than most—in late spring and early summer, when warmer weather will help its fragrance to become airborne. It sometimes flowers a second time in the fall.

OTHER GOOD DAPHNES

Daphne cneorum (z. 4–7) A dwarf, spring-flowering daphne useful for the edge of a border. Can be difficult.

Daphne laureola (z. 7) British native spurge laurel, with fragrant greenish flowers in late winter. Evergreen, useful for wild gardens.

Daphne pontica (z. 8–9) Night-scented daphne, producing green flowers in late spring.

Summer fragrance

There are dozens of plants that can contribute to the special feel of a summer garden through their perfume. Where planting areas are small, it is useful to know a few key plants that will effectively create a wonderfully fragrant garden in this important season without swallowing up too much space. Many of these are traditional cottage-garden favorites.

Temporary plantings such as annuals, biennials, and tender perennials are invaluable for summer scent. They can fill spaces vacated by earlier-flowering plants such as spring bulbs and early-summer perennials. They also tend to have a long season, so there is a greater chance of good "scent weather" during their flowering period: warm, humid days and still, balmy evenings. Night scents are attractive not only to humans but also to moths, while butterflies and bees are drawn by the daytime scent of many nectar-rich plants.

Hesperis matronalis (zone 6–8), sweet rocket, is a self-sowing biennial that is worth establishing in almost any informal garden. Its mauve or white flowers open from spring into summer and release a lovely clovelike perfume, on mild evenings especially. The plants grow quite leafy and large, so plant in an inconspicuous spot, such as among shrubs, where they can be left to self-seed without getting in the way.

Stocks are some of the best annuals for scent. The night-scented stock *Matthiola bicornis* is one of the very easiest annuals to grow: simply scatter seed every few weeks in reasonable soil where you want it to flower. Its daytime appearance is rather dreary, so site it among other plants where it can scent the air unobtrusively. Alternatively, grow one of the improved varieties that have been bred for flower appearance as well as scent. Border stocks for bedding, often called "ten-week" stocks, are grown as half-hardy annuals and produce fragrant, often double, scented blooms. Colors range from purples and pinks to white. The best stock fragrance comes from good strains of the white perennial form of *Matthiola incana* (zone 7–8), a large, woody-based, usually short-lived plant whose shortcomings (it has a certain cabbagelike quality) are forgotten entirely when it bursts into exquisitely scented bloom.

Heliotropium arborescens (zone 10–11), a tender, shrubby perennial, is almost always grown as an annual for bedding and patio tubs. Its rich, jammy aroma is like that of no other plant, exactly reflecting its nickname, cherry pie. Seed strains vary considerably in the strength of their scent; if you find a plant with particularly strong perfume, it is worth keeping it going each year by cuttings. The most widely available seed strain is 'Marine', which has large, rich purple flowers and good bronze foliage but not the most powerful scent.

Petunias and *verbenas* are sold by the thousand in early summer for use as border and patio plants, but their fragrance is not usually made much of. The scent of many of them is indeed unremarkable, but in the case of purple petunias it can be wonderful. If you are choosing verbenas for their scent, go for *Verbena* 'Silver Anne' or 'Pink Parfait'. Another popular bedding plant whose heady, honeylike fragrance is seldom mentioned is *Lobularia maritima*, sweet alyssum. Much used in its dwarf white forms as an edging plant in formal bedding schemes, it is available in different seed strains with taller or cascading flowers, and in a variety of colors; these, in particular, are sometimes highly scented. The common mignonette, *Reseda odorata*, is another hardy annual with clusters of tiny flowers that are usually fragrant—although, as sometimes happens with

Hesperis matronalis

Matthiola incana 'Apple Blossom'

Heliotropium arborescens 'Marine'

FRAGRANT FLOWERS FOR CUTTING *Chimonanthus praecox • Convallaria majalis • Dianthus barbatus •*

Verbena 'Silver Anne'

Cosmos atrosanguineus

Monarda 'Cambridge Scarlet'

fragrance, one individual plant may have more scent than another.

A half-hardy perennial that has increased in popularity is the chocolate cosmos, *Cosmos atrosanguineus* (zone 7–10). Its beautiful, deep velvety red flowers are as unmistakable as its sweet, chocolatey scent. Like dahlias, it will sometimes survive winter in a border if it is well mulched in the fall, but it cannot be relied upon in cool gardens and should be lifted and stored in a dormant state for replanting in late spring. It is a very good patio plant.

Many kinds of *Lilium* (lily; see page 185) are ideal providers of summer scent. They must be chosen with care because not all are scented, nor do they all suit every type of soil.

Only a few of the classic summer border perennials have a really telling fragrance, but *Monarda didyma* (bergamot or bee balm) (zone 3–7) is worth a mention for its strange citrus scent, familiar from the smell of Earl Grey tea, in which it is used as a flavoring. Monardas are not the easiest plants: they dislike light soils and are prone to mildew, but a well-grown clump is valuable not only for scent but also for its splendidly showy flowers in shades of pink and red. Cultivars include the strong red *Monarda* 'Cambridge Scarlet'. For pink, choose *Monarda* 'Croftway Pink' or 'Beauty of Cobham'.

The late-flowering border phloxes, derived from the tall mauve species *Phlox paniculata* (zone 4–8), are another old-fashioned hardy perennial that can be difficult to grow, although sometimes clumps are seen thriving on years of neglect in weedy, forgotten gardens, with no one to appreciate their wonderful airborne fragrance in late summer. There are numerous named cultivars and many more types found in old gardens, with colors ranging from purple through mauve and pink to white. Phloxes are not for the smallest gardens, needing elbow room to spread their luxuriant masses of blossom, but they are a very useful late perennial where space allows. All need rich soil and plenty of water. As with monarda, mildew can be a problem.

CONNOISSEUR'S CHOICE: SHRUBS FOR FRAGRANT FOLIAGE

Aloysia triphylla (lemon verbena) (z. 8–10) A slightly tender, strongly lemon-scented deciduous shrub for a warm wall.

Artemisia abrotanum (southernwood) (z. 5–8) A small, semievergreen, highly aromatic shrub from the Mediterranean, with a very distinctive pungent, sharp, and sour but strangely compelling perfume.

Helichrysum italicum (curry plant) (z. 8–10) A dwarf, silvery gray shrub known for its curious strong smell of curry.

Juniperus communis 'Compressa' (z. 2–7) A dwarf fastigiate evergreen with the typical juniper aroma recognizable in gin (see also page 49).

Laurus nobilis (sweet bay) (z. 8–9) An aromatic broad-leaved evergreen, suitable for small gardens if clipped. (See page 40.)

Myrtus communis (myrtle) (z. 8–9) A bushy, slightly tender evergreen shrub with spicily scented, glossy foliage, whitish flowers in late summer, and aromatic black winter berries. Good for winter decorations.

Prostanthera cuneata (alpine mint bush) (z. 9–10) A dwarf evergreen shrub from Australia, with white flowers and a minty scent.

Rosa rubiginosa (sweet briar) (z. 4–9) A vigorous wild rose with deliciously apple-scented foliage, especially after rain. Where space is tight, prune hard every year. (Can be invasive.)

Erysimum cheiri 'Harpur Crewe' • *Iris unguicularis* • *Lathyrus odoratus* • *Narcissus* 'Bell Song' • *Viola odorata* •

Pinks and carnations (Dianthus)

Classic cottage favorites that have been known in gardens for some five centuries, pinks have such a powerful scent for their size that they are ideal for small spaces. Over the years, specialty breeders and amateur enthusiasts have combined the attributes of various wild dianthus in many ways to produce garden plants that are robust, long-flowering, very pretty with their many colors and patterns, and, above all, well scented.

Pinks love well-drained soil and are happiest in dry, sunny gardens, perhaps partnered by Mediterranean-style planting of dwarf bulbs and small aromatic shrubs. In heavier soils they will suffer in winter but can be grown in pots or raised beds if plenty of grit is added to the soil to aid drainage. Sometimes perennial pinks can last for many years in true cottage-garden tradition, but in most gardens they will do better if new plants are raised from cuttings every few years to replace old stock. Do this any time during the summer, using nonflowering shoots.

Fragrant annual pinks and carnations (which have larger, more patterned flowers, with more petals, than pinks) are easy to grow and flower for longer than the perennial types. They are also useful where the soil is not conducive to overwintering of perennial dianthus.

Dianthus barbatus (sweet William) (z. 3–8), a key cottage-garden plant, is a biennial easily raised from seed. Plant outdoors in late fall to flower in early summer the following year. With their scent and fascinating mixture of colors, sweet Williams are excellent as cut flowers.

Dianthus 'Rainbow Loveliness' (annual) is one of the best annual pinks for fragrance, with a very long season and charming, ragged flowers in shades of pink and white. For best results, sow the seed in late summer, overwinter in small pots under cover, and plant out in spring.

Dianthus 'Mrs Sinkins' (z. 5–10) is the classic old-fashioned perennial pink. Dating from the 1870s, it is widely available and very reliable for scent. As it is white with silvery leaves, it can be fitted into most color schemes. It needs full sun and good soil, which should not be allowed to become bone-dry when the flowers are forming.

OTHER GOOD DIANTHUS

Dianthus 'Brympton Red' (z. 4–9) Intricately patterned in maroon and pink. Introduced by Margery Fish, a British plantswoman devoted to traditional cottage-garden plants such as this one (reputedly discovered in a workhouse garden).

Dianthus 'Dad's Favourite' (z. 3–8) Plant where it can be seen at close range. Frilly double flowers patterned maroon and white.

Dianthus gratianopolitanus (z. 5–8) The wild cheddar pink, a small, very fragrant, mat-forming perennial that is ideal for natural gardens.

Dianthus 'Inchmery' (z. 3–8) A richly clove-scented pink recorded since the eighteenth century, with double, very pale pink flowers.

Dianthus 'London Poppet' (z. 4–9) Frilled semidouble, with a dark maroon eye and whitish petals laced with deep magenta.

Dianthus 'Moulin Rouge' (z. 4–9) A fairly recent hybrid but of the old-fashioned type, with well-scented double, dark-eyed flowers.

Dianthus 'Musgrave's Pink' (z. 3–8) Single, fringed, pure white flowers with a greenish eye.

Dianthus 'Rose de Mai' (z. 3–8) A fairly robust variety with fringed, double lilac pink flowers. Worth trying in dampish gardens as it is less fussy than most.

Sweet pea (Lathyrus odoratus)

Many sweet peas grown today can probably trace their origins far back to the introduction of the wild sweet pea, *Lathyrus odoratus* (annual), into the fragrant gardens built by the Moors in southern Spain some 500 years ago. By the end of the nineteenth century some 300 cultivars were available, and breeders are still producing new varieties all the time. Today's seed companies offer something to suit every grower, from exhibitors to patio gardeners, and even more kinds are available from specialty breeders.

There was a time when the breeders of sweet peas concentrated on size, color, and vigor at the expense of scent, but many of the old varieties are now popular again. They may have smaller flowers than modern hybrids, but they provide the powerful fragrance that many growers of sweet peas seek. To be sure of scent, grow named single varieties that are known to be highly scented or look for packs of "Old-fashioned" and "Heirloom" mixtures.

Sow the seeds in pots in the fall or early spring to plant outdoors later, or simply sow them in spring where they are to grow. Choose a sunny place. Soaking the seed overnight may help germination. Humus-rich soil will help them through dry periods in summer, so dig in compost before planting, but be prepared to water them well in dry weather. Climbing varieties are usually grown up a sturdy wigwam or a row of canes or through tall twiggy sticks. When the flowers appear, they must be picked every day or two in order to keep a succession of new flowers going.

Lathyrus odoratus 'Painted Lady', bicolored in glowing pink and white, is an old-fashioned cultivar recorded as growing in London's Chelsea Physic Garden in 1737. A bushy plant with very fragrant flowers.

Lathyrus odoratus 'Pink Cupid'. Dwarf sweet peas have been available for many years and have their uses in small gardens, as they are suitable for pots, hanging baskets, and tubs as well as borders. 'Pink Cupid' is an old favorite, with flowers bicolored pink and white.

Lathyrus odoratus 'Cupani' is the oldest cultivated sweet pea, now popular again for its rich coloring of deep violet-blue and dark magenta-purple and for its very powerful scent. It is named after the Sicilian monk who originally introduced it to Britain in 1699.

Lavender (Lavandula)

Everyone knows lavender and many people grow it but, despite its popularity, really well-grown lavender plants are less common than one might expect.

Winter rain and cold are the enemies of all Mediterranean shrubs, and lavender is no exception. Give it a really well-drained position, in a raised bed if necessary, with poor soil and plenty of sunshine. Some species are more tolerant of unfavorable conditions, while others, such as *Lavandula viridis* (zone 8–10) and the attractive *Lavandula dentata* (zone 8–10), are decidedly more tender and will require winter protection in all but the warmest gardens.

It is a good idea to prune lavenders every year to prevent the buildup of old wood, which cannot be pruned successfully. Either clip each bush with shears after flowering, or prune harder as the new growth begins in mid-spring, cutting back so as to leave some new shoots at the base of each branch. Woody, old plants are usually best discarded and replaced with younger stock.

Although it is native to southern Europe, *Lavandula angustifolia* is usually known as English lavender. *Lavandula angustifolia* 'Hidcote' (z. 5–8) is the most commonly seen of some 40 cultivars. The true form is a very good compact shrub with silvery leaves and deep purple-blue flowers, but seed-raised plants that may be inferior are sometimes offered for sale.

Lavandula × intermedia (z. 5–9) is a larger hybrid. *Lavandula × intermedia* 'Seal', seen here (right) *Lavandula × intermedia* 'Alba', has light purple flowers. Another cultivar, *Lavandula × intermedia* 'Hidcote Giant', far from being gigantic, is a slow-growing, neat plant, with abundant rich purple flower spikes and good fragrance.

Lavandula stoechas (French lavender) (z. 7–8) is a distinctive lavender species with showy vertical bracts on top of the flower head. There are many similar subspecies and cultivars. One of the most popular is *Lavandula stoechas* ssp. *pedunculata* 'Papillon', grown for its gray-green foliage and early flowers. *Lavandula stoechas* 'Provençal' (left) is a neater, more compact form.

OTHER GOOD LAVENDERS

Lavandula angustifolia 'Loddon Blue' (z. 6–9) Short spikes of deep purple flowers on a neat plant.

Lavandula angustifolia 'Loddon Pink' (z. 6–9) A compact lavender, with flowers of soft pink.

Lavandula angustifolia 'Munstead' (z. 6–9) A mauve dwarf lavender, robust but not such a strong color as 'Hidcote'.

Lavandula angustifolia 'Nana Alba' (z. 6–9) A useful, very dwarf, white-flowered lavender.

Lavandula stoechas 'Rocky Road' (left) (z. 7–8) A compact, upright French lavender, with light pinkish mauve flowers.

Lavandula 'Sawyers' (z. 6–9) A reasonably hardy hybrid between *Lavandula angustifolia* and *Lavandula lanata*, with attractive downy foliage and deep purple-blue flowers.

Tobacco plant (Nicotiana)

Nicotianas are very popular half-hardy bedding plants that most people immediately associate with scent. However, when buying them it pays to be aware that, while the white flowers are usually highly fragrant, those in reds, pinks, or green mostly have very little perfume. Seed specialists tend not make scent a priority, concentrating instead on producing dwarf plants for small borders and tubs, or flowers that look presentable in the daytime: nicotianas naturally droop and look sad during the day, coming to life in the evening.

Nicotianas grow quickly in warm weather and like to have plenty of moisture in the soil. Although they are nearly always grown as annuals, it is sometimes possible, on light soils in mild areas, for the rootstock to withstand a few degrees of frost, allowing the plant to regenerate the following spring.

Nicotiana alata (z. 10–11 or annual) is the popular half-hardy bedding plant, usually grown in mixed colors. Available seed strains vary in size and color mixture. Those with a high proportion of white flowers usually produce the best scent.

Nicotiana sylvestris (z. 8–10 or annual) is the largest and stateliest "tobacco plant" commonly grown in gardens, rapidly reaching about 5ft. (1.5m) tall and soon hung with immensely fragrant tubular white flowers. A good plant for the back of a border in semi-shade, or grown in a large pot to scent a patio or sunroom.

Nicotiana langsdorffii (above) (annual) has become a popular "designer" plant, frequently used in show gardens on account of its distinctive, drooping lime green bellflowers. A variegated form is available: *Nicotiana langsdorffii* 'Cream Splash'.

Scented geranium (Pelargonium)

The scented pelargoniums, or geraniums (zone 9–10), have become widely known in recent years, perhaps partly because they are good sunroom plants, enjoying plenty of light but needing to be kept frost-free and reasonably dry in winter. Like many houseplants, these South African natives benefit from a spell in the garden in summer, and some can grow to quite a size in the open ground. Whether you grow them in a border or in pots, place them in the sun where you will brush against them as you pass, releasing their unique contribution to the medley of summer garden fragrances.

These easy plants are grown primarily for their leaves, which come in a variety of scents from lemon to mint, rose, and spice, and many others that are harder to describe. In Britain in 1996, a Royal Horticultural Society trial of scented pelargoniums attracted an amazing 173 different entries.

The flowers, often dismissed as insignificant, are worth close inspection. Although their charms may be less obvious than those of the mop-headed bedding pelargoniums, the delicate flowers are beautiful, with more variety among the different species and cultivars than may be apparent at first.

Most of these pelargoniums are easy to propagate from summer cuttings, a useful attribute where space for overwintering them is limited. The plants are inclined to become leggy and should be pinched back regularly to keep them bushy.

Pelargonium 'Attar of Roses' (z. 9–10) is the most widely grown of the rose-scented "geraniums," some of which are grown for the perfume industry. The leaves of these and other scented pelargoniums also have a traditional culinary use in flavoring desserts and preserves.

Pelargonium 'Mabel Grey' (z. 9–10) is an excellent "lemon geranium," grown for its refreshing, strong citrus fragrance. This was a favorite of the late Rosemary Verey, whose tip for looking after the plant was to water it with soft rainwater rather than chemically treated tap water.

Pelargonium 'Royal Oak' (z. 9–10) is one of the more decorative types. It is versatile, with a spicy fragrance and slightly sticky, bronze-variegated foliage setting off pink and purple flowers. It has a good tolerance of drought.

OTHER GOOD PELARGONIUMS

Pelargonium 'Chocolate Peppermint' (z. 9–10) Leaves larger than 'Attar of Roses' but similarly blotched.

Pelargonium grossularioides Has small dark red flowers and black-currant-scented leaves.

Pelargonium 'Lady Plymouth' (z. 9–10) A sturdy plant, with finely divided, cream-variegated leaves and a scent that has elements of roses and mint.

Pelargonium 'Prince of Orange' and *Pelargonium* 'Princeanum' (z. 9–10) Both have orange-scented leaves.

Pelargonium tomentosum (z. 9–10) A robust, large species with relatively big, felted leaves and a peppermint fragrance.

Mock orange (Philadelphus)

Philadelphus, with one of the classic scents of the summer garden, are among the most popular of all shrubs. They are sometimes seen as huge, overgrown specimens, but there are several dwarf hybrids and species that lend themselves well to smaller gardens.

Annual pruning is important both to keep the bush to a manageable size and to keep it furnished with branches that will flower. Cut out the oldest wood, with the aim of rejuvenating the whole bush every three or four years. This is usually done after flowering when the flowered wood can be easily identified, but it can just as well be done in winter once you have developed an eye for recognizing the old wood.

Although a philadelphus in full flower is an asset to any garden, the shrub is inclined to look nondescript and gawky during the winter months, so give it a position in a mixed border, perhaps with evergreen neighbors to distract attention.

There is often confusion over everyday names for philadelphus. It is usually called mock orange but often also "syringa," which is a misnomer as *Syringa* is the generic name for lilacs.

Philadelphus microphyllus (z. 6–9) is a naturally dwarf species, dense and twiggy with masses of highly scented single flowers. It is useful in layered, space-saving planting: place it at the foot of a climber and surround it with dwarf early bulbs, such as *Anemone blanda* and chionodoxa, which flower before the philadelphus comes into leaf.

Philadelphus coronarius 'Aureus' (z. 4–8) does double duty in the garden, offering the usual fragrant blossom in summer as well as striking golden foliage. It combines especially well with dark blues in spring. The leaves may scorch in full sun, but you need to get the balance right because too much shade turns them green.

Double-flowered philadelphus are often less fragrant than those with single flowers, but *Philadelphus* 'Manteau d'Hermine' (z. 5–7) is scented and double. It also has more elegant foliage than many philadelphus. It is unlikely to reach much more than 3ft. (1m) in height.

The popular and widely available hybrid *Philadelphus* 'Belle Etoile' (z. 5–7) is reliable and free flowering but is not one of the most compact forms. The flowers, very fragrant, with a hint of pineapple, have a wine red blotch in the center.

135

Herbs

Herbs are wonderful garden plants in so many ways. They have a fascinating history and folklore, serve an everyday practical role in the home, and have fragrant foliage and often attractive flowers, too. However, many herbs look their best for only a short time. Some are rampant spreaders, others profligate seeders. So in small gardens especially, careful selection and planning are needed to fit them in successfully.

Determining what counts as an herb is always rather tricky, but central to any definition is the idea of usefulness. Historically, what made a plant an herb was not its appearance but the fact that it was grown for a practical purpose: for example as a flavoring, a medicine, a dye, a cosmetic, or a fragrance. This encompasses a vast range of plants – as seen in some specialty herb gardens and nurseries. However, the range of herbs grown in small gardens today is most likely to consist of a few popular ones used in the kitchen.

A tapestry of herbs outside the door makes a welcoming and fragrant entrance to a garden.

HERBS WITH SHOWY FLOWERS Borage • Chives • Fennel • Feverfew • Hyssop • Rosemary • Rue • Sage •

HERBS AS GOOD MIXERS

It has become something of a horticultural tradition for herbs to be grown grouped together in an herb garden. This may not be practical in a small space and, in fact, there are several good reasons for growing them among other plants.

The many plants that can be classified as herbs come from a wide variety of habitats and do not all like the same growing conditions. If they are grown among other plants in different parts of the garden, each herb can be given the conditions that suit it best.

Certain herbs attract beneficial insects and/or repel pests, so they can be more widely useful to other plants if they are not grown separately.

Some herbs have a long season of looking dull or overblown, and this can more easily be disguised if they are growing among other plants.

Kitchen essentials such as mint, parsley, and sage, planted in pots, can be fitted into the smallest space. Grow your own favorites.

In even the smallest of spaces it is possible to grow a little collection of kitchen herbs, perhaps in a large pot or tub, a tiny patch of ground, or even a window box or hanging basket. Choose compact herbs that thrive in similar conditions: parsley, chives, and mint, for example, coexist happily for a season in sun or part shade in a good planting mix, provided they are not allowed to dry out. Mediterranean herbs such as thyme, rosemary, and sage can be grown as a separate collection, in a gritty medium and in full sun. You will need to overhaul herb plantings like this once a year, replanting annuals and biennials such as parsley (which will run to seed in its second season), pruning shrubby herbs like rosemary, and dividing perennials such as chives and mint.

Herbs can be accommodated in small gardens in many other ways, according to the space available: in unusual containers, as edging, in a knot garden, or in gravel. Raised beds suit many herbs, especially those needing good drainage. Herbs integrate well with other planting in borders, and there is no need to grow them separately (see below).

GOOD COMPANIONS

For a low-maintenance, neat planting that looks good all year, underplant a standard bay (*Laurus nobilis*; see page 40) (1) in a sunny, well-drained place with a carpet of variegated or golden thyme (z. 7–8). Add dwarf spring bulbs such as crocuses, species tulips, or scillas (2) (z. 5–8), for early color.

Purple sage, *Salvia officinalis* 'Purpurascens' (3) (z. 5–10), is ideal with alliums and euphorbias, enjoying the same sunny, sharply drained position. It also looks good as a young plant next to its handsome, variegated, golden-leaved counterpart *Salvia officinalis* 'Icterina' (4) (z. 5–10). Newly rooted cuttings of either or both, planted in groups, are effective as a foliage backdrop to summer bedding plants.

Use golden feverfew, *Tanacetum parthenium* 'Aureum' (5) (z. 4–9), to brighten gloomy corners with its bold yellow, ferny foliage from early spring. Grow it with other plants that tolerate dry shade, such as *Euphorbia amygdaloides* var. *robbiae* (6) (z. 7–9) and *Iris foetidissima* (z. 6–9).

HERBS FOR INFUSIONS Chamomile • Dill • Fennel • Feverfew • Lemon balm • Lemon verbena • Mint •

Growing herbs

Fresh herbs are now sold in supermarkets, but they cannot compare with a bunch of basil picked in the sunshine from a pot on the patio, or the first chives of the new season snipped from just outside your own back door. Even the smallest garden can accommodate some herbs, so find space, first, for the ones you like to use regularly. Having the best fresh herbs conveniently available makes all the difference in the kitchen.

Once you have found room for your favorites, think in terms of value for space for other herbs. Shrubby herbs, particularly evergreens such as **rosemary** (zone 8–10) and **sweet bay** (*Laurus nobilis*) (zone 8–9), may take up space but, unlike many herbs, they contribute structure and interest to the garden every day of the year. Both can be clipped to keep them compact. Bay works well as a standard (see page 40) or clipped into a cone or pyramid.

Another woody herb to consider is **sage** (zone 5–10). This low, velvety-leaved evergreen shrub has cultivars with colored foliage, which earn their space in an ornamental border. *Salvia officinalis* 'Purpurascens' has grayish purple leaves, while those of *Salvia officinalis* 'Icterina' (which seldom flowers) are variegated in yellow and green. A third ornamental sage, slightly more tender, has even fancier leaves, variegated in grayish green, white, and pink. This one has the fitting name *Salvia officinalis* 'Tricolor'. All three can be used in the kitchen in exactly the same way as ordinary common sage. The plants are inclined to become leggy and sprawling if not pruned annually. Do this either in early spring or after flowering, cutting back to the new shoots around the base of each branch. Fresh growth will quickly develop.

Hyssop (*Hyssopus officinalis*) (zone 3–8) is a lovely shrubby herb that gives a late summer lift to any dry, sunny border—perhaps planted with sages, to prolong flowering after the sage blooms fade in midsummer. Its slender flower spikes are deepest cool blue. This beautiful color late in the season is the plant's chief asset, making the ordinary blue form a much better garden feature than the white or pink forms that are also available. To keep hyssop neat and free-flowering, prune it in the spring, cutting out the flowered shoots from the previous year almost to their base.

If space permits, consider **angelica** (zone 4–8), a fine—if temporary—ornamental herb for a damp garden. The ordinary green kind, *Angelica archangelica*, is a stately biennial that grows to 6ft. (2m). This is a good accent plant for a moisture-retentive border. The leaf stalks of angelica are candied and used to decorate cakes and desserts, while the roots and seeds are used medicinally. It is attractive to bees. For use in a planting scheme with other rich, deep colors, try *Angelica gigas*. This has similar umbelliferous flower heads, but in a deep claret color, carried on tall, stiff tubular stems.

An ornamental potager: a practical and attractive way to grow herbs and vegetables in a limited space.

DROUGHT-TOLERANT HERBS Bay • Borage • Fennel • Marjoram • Rosemary • Sage • Summer savory • Thyme •

Herbs with differing leaf forms and colors create a visually satisfying small-scale planting scheme.

A good alternative for a similarly bold, late-summer structure in a dry, sunny border is **fennel**. For ornamental use, *Foeniculum vulgare* 'Purpureum' (zone 5–8) is the variety most usually chosen because of its lovely, strongly aniseed-scented, bronze filigree foliage. The yellow flower heads that eventually develop are attractive to beneficial insects such as hover flies. Fennel can be cut down at any stage if it becomes too tall, and it is certainly better not to allow it to drop its abundant seed crop in the wrong place, because the resulting seedlings soon put down taproots and become difficult to remove. Bronze fennel can be used in salads and for flavoring fish and Mediterranean dishes, exactly like the ordinary green fennel *Foeniculum vulgare*. (The tender vegetable Florence fennel has a similar flavor but is a different plant, with a fleshy base.)

Like fennel and sage, **lemon balm**, *Melissa officinalis* (zone 6–8), has plain and decorative forms that in both culinary and medicinal respects are the same. The "colored" forms of lemon balm are plain gold (*Melissa officinalis* 'All Gold') and gold-variegated (*Melissa officinalis* 'Aurea'). All have the same crinkled leaves and share a pungent, lemony fragrance when crushed: nice just to sniff, or to add to a bath or to cold drinks on a warm day.

The golden-leaved forms are useful shade plants that look very cheerful in spring. Like many herbs, they lose this springlike freshness as they approach flowering time, but they then become a magnet for bees. As with fennel, it is advisable to cut down the plants before they seed, not least because the abundant seedlings of all varieties except 'All Gold' will be plain green.

Another attractive, freely seeding, gold-leaved herb is golden **feverfew**, *Tanacetum parthenium* 'Aureum' (zone 4–9). The garden forms of Feverfew are both single- and double-flowered, with either golden or green leaves that have a pungent, rather musty scent. It is a medicinal rather than a culinary herb, well known for treating migraine. The golden forms are ideal for dry shade in an informal garden. Although it is a perennial, young plants perform best, so pull up older plants once it has established itself by seeding. Unlike those of fennel, unwanted seedlings are easy to weed out.

Related to feverfew but with finer foliage is **chamomile**, *Chamaemelum nobile* (zone 5–8). The daisylike flowers, similar to those of feverfew, are used to make a soothing infusion—chamomile tea—and for cosmetic purposes. The creeping, nonflowering *Chamaemelum nobile* 'Treneague' is the form that is used for chamomile

HERBS IN FOLKLORE

Herbs have always had a special significance in folklore and are surrounded by stories and superstitions. Here are a few of them.

Parsley grows well only where a woman is in charge of the household. (This is said of several other herbs.) It is also said that transplanting parsley, or giving it away, will bring bad luck. Parsley germinates slowly and is said to go down to the devil seven times before it comes up. To prevent this, sow it on Good Friday.

Rosemary placed under the bed will protect against bad dreams.

On the Eve of St. Agnes (January 20), unmarried women should place a sprig of rosemary in one shoe and a sprig of thyme in the other, in order to see a vision of their future husband.

"He who would live for aye, must eat sage in May."

A dying bay tree is a bad omen. Before the death of the Roman emperor Nero, all the bay trees in Rome are said to have withered.

Angelica (below), dill, and vervain are a few of the many herbs said to give protection against witches.

SHADE-TOLERANT HERBS Angelica • Balm • Lovage • Mint • Parsley • Pennyroyal • Tarragon • Winter savory •

Allium schoenoprasum

Anthriscus cerefolium

Anethum graveolens

lawns and seats. When well grown and maintained, chamomile can be a delight, releasing an appealing applelike fragrance when the foliage is walked over or sat on. A small garden is in some ways an ideal place to use a substitute for grass, but bear in mind that a chamomile lawn requires regular maintenance to keep it healthy looking and free from the weeds that seem to find their way all too easily into any gaps between plants.

Chives, *Allium schoenoprasum* (zone 4–10), are a handy perennial herb to grow close to the kitchen for culinary purposes. They are one of the very first "crops" in early spring. With a little maintenance, the plants can remain decorative enough all season to grow in a flower border. If you cut them to the ground as soon as they begin to look untidy after flowering, a new crop will soon appear. Divide the clumps from time to time to keep them vigorous. The purple flowers of chives are edible and can be used to decorate salads. A white-flowered form, which may fit better into particular color schemes in the garden, is available from herb specialists. **Chinese chives**, *Allium tuberosum* (zone 3–8),

also have white flowers, on larger plants. They do not come into flower until late summer but, like some other alliums, they retain their seed heads into winter.

One of the most essential herbs in the kitchen is fortunately one of the most decorative: **parsley**, *Petroselinum crispum* (zone 5–8). It never looks out of place in a flower border. It is difficult to germinate successfully, but fresh seed seems to avoid this problem: if you leave a plant or two to run to seed in its second year (it is a biennial), you will have parsley plants every year—as long as you take care not to weed them out when small. They are easy to recognize, even when tiny. *Petroselinum crispum* var. *neapolitanum* is the flat-leaved or French parsley. It is less decorative but usually hardier, with a stronger flavor. Parsley does best in a fairly moisture-retentive soil in either sun or part shade.

Chervil, *Anthriscus cerefolium* (annual), looks a bit like parsley but has more delicate foliage and a unique fresh, slightly aniseed flavor. It is invaluable in early spring, for the plants are active early in the year and usually run to seed by early summer. Like parsley, it can easily be encouraged to self-seed.

Another similar umbellifer, with white flowers and a most distinctive sour, spicy smell that most people either love or loathe, is **coriander**, *Coriandrum sativum* (annual). It is grown both for its leaves and for the aromatic dried seeds, which are a staple flavoring in curries. Similar again is **dill**, *Anethum graveolens* (annual), fast-growing from seed and pleasant to eat with fish or in a cucumber salad. Gather the aniseed-flavored seeds and use them in cucumber pickles and relishes, or as an infusion to aid digestion, keeping back a few to sow next year if necessary.

A very subtle aniseed flavor is found in a quite different plant, **tarragon**. Its Latin name is *Artemisia dracunculus* (zone 3–7) and it is closely related to the ornamental artemisias familiar to many gardeners for their excellent silvery foliage, for example the beautiful *Artemisia ludoviciana* 'Valerie Finnis' and *Artemisia* 'Powis Castle'. Tarragon has little in common with these, but it has a lovely delicate flavor. For this, do not grow Russian tarragon, which is coarse and flavorless, but French tarragon. This does not set seed so it has to be bought as a plant or grown from cuttings.

HERBS FOR SALADS Basil • Chervil • Chives • Coriander • Lovage • Mint • Parsley • Tarragon •

Ocimum basilicum var. purpurascens 'Purple Ruffles'

Borago officinalis

Just as tarragon is associated with classic French cookery, so **sweet basil** *(Ocimum basilicum,* zone 9–11, annual) seems to belong naturally in Italian dishes. It is a classic partner for tomatoes—both like sunny conditions. Keep a plant or two indoors on a sunny windowsill, both in case of failure in the garden due to bad weather and to prolong the picking season for this lovely summer herb. Sow seeds in spring and keep the plants warm, pinching out the tips to use in the kitchen and keep the plants bushy. Over twenty kinds of basil are available as seed, including the deep purple-leaved cultivar *Ocimum basilicum* **var. purpurascens 'Purple Ruffles'** (which looks good grown with summer flowers in patio containers); **lemon basil,** *Ocimum* × *citriodorum*; and the spicily scented **Thai basil,** *Ocimum basilicum* 'Horapha'.

Another herb that spells summer is **borage** *(Borago officinalis)*, a strong, hairy annual plant. It overwinters as seed and very often sows itself on light soils to provide a supply every summer. Its pretty blue flowers are a traditional and delightful decoration for summer drinks and desserts.

GOOD COMPANIONS

The bronze fennel *Foeniculum vulgare* 'Purpureum' (1) (z. 5–8) is a good companion for too many plants to list. In spring its mound of fine bronze foliage complements fresh greens, or orange and red tulips. As it grows bigger, the effect is misty and translucent, good with phormiums (2) (z. 8–10), oriental poppies, and purple-leaved shrubs.

The beautifully colored flowers of *Hyssopus officinalis* (hyssop) (3) (z. 3–8) make it a good partner for silver-leaved plants, many of which seem to come to life in late summer when the hyssop is blooming. Choose plants with contrasting foliage form, such as the feathery *Artemisia* 'Powis Castle' (4) (z. 6–10), waxy *Euphorbia myrsinites* (z. 5–9), or, for a startling color contrast, the horned-poppy *Glaucium corniculatum* (5) (z. 6–9), which has deep orange flowers and unusual wavy-edged gray leaves. All these will be happy in a well-drained, sunny border.

HERBS FOR THE POT Basil • Marjoram • Parsley • Rosemary • Sage • Savory • Thyme •

Mint (Mentha)

Mint is one of the most familiar herbs, known by every cook and grown in many gardens. When it comes to a cooling herb for hot weather, there is no substitute. Brush against it and sniff it in the garden; put sprigs into cold drinks along with a slice of lime; or use it in a refreshing cucumber salad or with fruit in desserts.

Growing mint in a small garden can be a problem because it is so invasive, sending out runners that creep through neighboring plants with alarming speed. A good solution is to grow it in a pot. It will be happy in a tucked-away corner, and provided it never goes short of water, it will produce leaves over a long season, from early spring to late summer. Cut it back from time to time for a fresh crop of young leaves, and repot cuttings in gritty potting mix every year in the fall or early spring so the plant does not become overcrowded and starved. Use the variegated, curly, and small-leaved mints to create a collection of three or four pots, each containing a different mint. This transforms a potential thug plant into an attractive and useful garden feature for a shady spot.

Of the eighty or so available types of mint, the best for most kitchen uses is *Mentha spicata* or spearmint (above) (z. 4–10). The scent is variable, but spearmint usually lacks the pungency of peppermint (*Mentha × piperita*), a hybrid that has spearmint as one of its parents.

The gold and green foliage of a thriving specimen of *Mentha × gracilis* 'Variegata' (ginger mint) (z. 3–8) looks most attractive until it runs up to flower, when red stems and lilac flower heads tend to spoil the effect. Its scent (not very gingery) is akin to spearmint.

Plant the tiny-leaved, ground-hugging *Mentha requienii* (Corsican mint) (z. 7–9) where it can eventually spread to form a sizable mat and be walked on to release its very strong, cooling peppermint aroma—it smells just like toothpaste. It will not tolerate drying out and is happy in part shade. It has tiny, pretty mauve flowers.

Most variegated plants are less vigorous than their green-leaved counterparts and *Mentha suaveolens* 'Variegata' (variegated apple mint or pineapple mint) (z. 7–10) is no exception, so it is unlikely to take over a border. As its name suggests, it has a fruity fragrance.

OTHER GOOD MINTS

Mentha aquatica var. *crispa* (curly water mint) (z. 4–10) A very decorative mint with bright green ruffled leaves. Good for growing in a container. Cut back often to encourage bushy growth.

Mentha × piperita (peppermint) (z. 4–8) The essential oil derived from this mint contains a high proportion of menthol, a strong aromatic widely used in pharmaceuticals, toothpaste, and candies.

Mentha × piperita f. *citrata* (z. 4–8) Differing cultivars of this form of peppermint are eau de cologne mint, bergamot mint, chocolate mint, lemon mint, basil mint, and orange mint.

Mentha pulegium (pennyroyal) (z. 6–10) A prostrate creeping mint with small oval leaves and mauve flowers. A good carpeter for shady, reputed to drive ants away.

Marjoram (Origanum)

The genus *Origanum* includes a considerable variety of aromatic plants, both hardy and tender. The flowers of all of them are very attractive to bees and butterflies. The wild marjoram, *origanum vulgare* (zone 5–8), occurs naturally on chalk and limestone grassland in many parts of Europe, and cultivated origanums also do best in well-drained, alkaline soil.

Some origanums are particularly suited to kitchen use; others are more ornamental. These include some very glamorous plants introduced by breeders in recent years, often with large, showy colored bracts. Several of these are compact enough for the smallest gardens, but most tend to be fussy and will thrive only in a sunny, well-drained border.

Origanum vulgare 'Aureum' (golden marjoram) (z. 5–8) is an easy, slow-growing plant, perfect for the edge of a border in part shade, and for underplanting deciduous shrubs. It looks its best in spring, combining well with the deep blue flowers and bronze leaves of *Veronica peduncularis* 'Georgia Blue'. Trim the plant back after flowering to encourage a second flush of golden leaves.

Origanum majorana (sweet marjoram) (z. 8–9) is a tender, very fragrant kitchen herb with delicate soft, grayish green leaves and tiny white flowers. It is delicious sprinkled on top of pizzas and used in marinades. Give it a sunny spot in the garden in summer and a warm windowsill indoors in winter. Sow fresh seed each spring.

Origanum laevigatum 'Herrenhausen' (z. 5–8) is a useful ornamental marjoram for all-year interest, with purple-flushed winter foliage and abundant pink flowers in late summer. It combines well with some of the silver-leaved plants that are at their best in late summer and into the fall.

OTHER GOOD MARJORAMS

Origanum amanum (z. 8–10) A very decorative little marjoram with slender, tubular pink flowers.

Origanum 'Barbara Tingey' (z. 7–10) Another small ornamental cultivar, in shades of purple and pink.

Origanum 'Kent Beauty' (z. 7–9) A compact plant with pink and green bracts. Needs a sunny, well-drained site.

Origanum onites (pot marjoram) (z. 8–9) A medicinal and kitchen herb, with a fairly mild flavor. Attracts bees.

Origanum vulgare (wild marjoram) (z. 5–8) An easy plant for a wild corner. Attracts butterflies and bees but invasive.

Origanum vulgare 'Gold Tip' (z. 5–8) A spreading plant, with curly, yellow-tipped leaves.

Rosemary (Rosmarinus)

Rosemary has been an herb of significance throughout civilization. It is still used for cosmetic and medicinal purposes as well as in the kitchen, where it is a favorite barbecue herb and a particularly good partner for lamb. It is also a traditional symbol of remembrance and friendship.

Perhaps more than any other herb, rosemary is able to capture the atmosphere of its native Mediterranean hillsides, even on a miserable winter day. It associates well with other sun-loving, aromatic shrubs such as lavender, salvia, and cistus, all united in their dislike of winter wet and cold and happiest in a sunny, sheltered spot on free-draining sandy or alkaline soils.

The hardier types of rosemary may tolerate conditions that are less than ideal: growing them in a raised bed and/or incorporating grit into the soil may help.

Rosemary flowers encouragingly early in spring, with flowers ranging from pale and silvery to a deep shade of blue. Pink- and white-flowered forms are available, but these are less hardy than most blue cultivars.

Keep rosemary compact by clipping back the shoot tips every spring after flowering. Old, woody bushes do not usually respond well to being cut back hard, and eventually it will be time to grow a replacement, either from layered branches or from cuttings taken in early fall.

Rosmarinus officinalis var. *angustissimus* 'Benenden Blue' (sometimes known as 'Collingwood Ingram') (z. 8–10) is often chosen for its lovely deep blue flowers. As its Latin name suggests (*angustissimus* means "very narrow"), it has slender needles and is a little more tender than varieties with stouter, more leathery foliage.

Rosmarinus officinalis Prostratus Group (z. 8–10) comprises several cultivars, all with low, arching growth no more than about 2ft. (60cm) high. They are less hardy than many rosemaries and need a warm, well-drained, and sheltered site such as the top of a south-facing retaining wall.

With a fastigiate habit that makes it ideal for the back of a sunny border in a small garden, *Rosmarinus officinalis* 'Miss Jessopp's Upright' (z. 8–10) takes up less lateral space but grows taller than most rosemaries, to a height of about 6ft. (2m). Its flowers are pale blue with darker flecks.

OTHER GOOD ROSEMARIES

Rosmarinus officinalis 'Gorizia' (z. 8–10) A vigorous, new variety of rosemary, with upright-growing shoots and very large blue flowers.

Rosmarinus officinalis 'Severn Sea' (z. 8–10) A well-established cultivar that grows to about 3ft. (1m), with mid-blue flowers on arching branches.

Thyme (Thymus)

Like rosemary, most thymes are native to southern Europe, but they will happily grow in more northerly gardens if given a sunny position on well-drained soil. They are very well suited to sandy and limestone soils; in fact, *Thymus serpyllum* (zone 4–10) grows wild on dry grasslands, dunes, and heaths in Britain.

Even the smallest garden can accommodate a few thyme plants provided there is enough sun. The ground-hugging creeping thymes are ideal for planting in paving cracks or gravel, because they are reasonably tolerant of being walked on, which releases their fragrance. These compact evergreens can also be planted in the top of a low retaining wall to make a fragrant seat cushion—but do keep a watch out for bees when the thyme is in flower.

Thymes growing in gravel or used as edging make good partners for low-growing euphorbias and dwarf spring bulbs such as chionodoxa and scilla. By the time the thyme is ready to be cut back in summer after flowering, the bulbs' foliage will have died off.

Ordinary *Thymus vulgaris* (z. 7–8) is the best culinary thyme, with a savory aroma that adds a southern European flavor to soups, marinades, and sauces. Place whole sprigs in a dish during cooking and remove them before serving. Makes a low, small-leaved bush, with palest lilac flowers.

Thymus 'Doone Valley' (z. 5–8) is a neat and compact hybrid thyme with very decorative foliage. Its dark green leaves are lightly flecked and spangled with gold. The flower buds are an attractive red color.

Thymus × *citriodorus* 'Silver Queen' (z. 5–8) is a compact, bushy shrub, combining a pleasant lemony fragrance with attractive, minutely variegated foliage that provides valuable winter interest. Use the herb for barbecues and Mediterranean-style fish dishes.

The appropriately named *Thymus serpyllum* 'Minimalist' (z. 4–10) is the smallest thyme of all, with tiny leaves perfectly in scale and small, very fragrant, pinkish mauve flowers. It is ideal for an interestingly shaped (and well-drained) container in a sunny place, or for a trough or a small area of gravel.

OTHER GOOD THYMES

Thymus pulegioides 'Aureus' (golden broad-leaved thyme) (z. 5–8) Larger leaves than common thyme and more decorative but with a similar flavor.

Thymus × *citriodorus* 'Bertram Anderson' (z. 5–8) A prostrate, lemon-scented thyme, with yellow-flushed foliage that creates an attractive lime green effect from a distance.

Thymus herba-barona (caraway thyme) (z. 9–10) A compact, wiry, cushion-forming thyme, with a spicy scent and pale pink flowers. Good for paving cracks or gravel.

SEASONAL

Small spaces, especially near the house, should always invite attention with something fresh and stimulating to look at. Once a basic planting scheme is in place you can embellish it with seasonal highlights, choosing container plants, annuals, and bulbs for short-term impact and color at different times of the year. The rules for permanent planting are overturned: experiment; make changes from year to year; choose plants on impulse. Don't worry about making mistakes: they will not be the expensive kind, and you will not have to live with them for long.

RIGHT: Early bulbs in a classic spring planting

Plants for containers

When it comes to transforming a small garden space, plants in containers have almost limitless potential. With proper care, a huge range of plants can be grown in pots. Of the many advantages to growing plants in this way, the chief one is perhaps mobility: plants can be moved and rearranged for the best effects throughout the year. In addition, you can grow plants that may not tolerate certain conditions in the garden, such as an alkaline soil.

Almost any garden, of any size, will benefit from the addition of a few containers. A well-chosen, imaginatively planted pot can act as a focal point or brighten a shady corner. Container planting can open up all kinds of possibilities in areas where there is no soil, poor soil, or unsuitable soil. Plants in pots may need more attentive watering and feeding, but looking after them is seldom physically demanding. In many ways, they are ideal for gardeners with little time, or for those with a disability, because their demands never become overwhelming in quite the same way as an overgrown border.

Grouped containers look best if they have something in common. Here, this is achieved by color harmony in blues and purples.

A variety of products is now available to help with container maintenance: controlled-release fertilizers; water-retaining granules or matting; container composts; wheeled pot platforms for easy mobility; watering wands that enable the gardener to reach high containers; and self-watering planters, plus a range of other watering aids, from drip-feed gadgets for individual pots to complete irrigation systems. All these make the job of looking after potted plants easier than it used to be.

THE CONTAINER

The choice of containers is now wider than ever—glazed or unglazed terra-cotta pots, hypertufa troughs for alpines, streamlined modern planters of shiny steel, elegant leadwork cisterns, or the many lightweight plastic containers that are designed to resemble lead, stone, wood, or pottery. In most cases, the type of container used will not affect the plant's ability to thrive, provided it is the right size and has provision for drainage. Matching the plant visually to the pot is one of the skills of container planting, and it is an easy one to acquire.

As a rule, modern formal plantings of spiky subjects or geometric topiary will suit a stylish contemporary container, and patterned pots look better with very simple planting. Groups of pots make an interesting and attractive display, but they look best if most of the containers have a style element in common—for example,

148

ALL-YEAR-ROUND CONTAINER PLANTS *Buxus sempervirens* 'Elegantissima' • *Carex buchananii* • *Festuca glauca* 'Elijah Blue' or *Festuca glauca* 'Blaufuchs' • *Hebe* 'Red Edge' • *Ophiopogon planiscapus* 'Nigrescens' •

Plant of the moment: a simple terra-cotta pot in the right place puts a choice, gold-laced primula in the spotlight.

a collection of brightly painted, old oil cans, or a cluster of terra-cotta urns of various shapes and sizes. Wide, shallow clay pots tend to suit low-growing plants such as sempervivums or echeverias, while vertical plants are accented by planting them in tall containers. Consider color as well as style when choosing a container. Silver- or golden-leaved plants suit dark pots, perhaps in a deep shade of blue or a dark metallic gray.

GOOD COMPANIONS

Buy young plants of sun-loving, spiky-leaved perennials, such as yuccas and phormiums (1), to combine in container displays with summer foliage plants such as *Helichrysum petiolare* 'Variegatum' (2) (z. 8–10). This foliage framework will serve as a summer-long backdrop to complement colorful pelargoniums, gazanias, and salvias. For winter, partner the "spikies" with a fluffy grass such as *Stipa tenuissima* (3) (z. 8–9) and small-leaved evergreens like *Lonicera nitida* 'Baggesen's Gold' (z. 7–9).

Senecio cineraria 'Silver Dust' (4) (z. 8–10) with deep purple petunias (5) is a classic, fragrant, sun-loving plant partnership that will look good all summer. For variety, add *Brachycome* Outback series and a lilac verbena.

The easy-to-grow pimpernel *Anagallis monellii* ssp. *linifolia* (6) (z. 7–9) has jewellike, starry, blue flowers. They combine well, in a sunny spot, with many other colors. Plant with orange nasturtiums (7) and the blood red *Dahlia* 'Bishop of Llandaff' (8) (z. 9–11) or the yellow *Argyranthemum* 'Jamaica Primrose' (z. 9–11, ann.).

For the best effects, it is also necessary to choose a container to suit the setting. Highly contemporary pots are unlikely to do themselves justice in an old-style property, and a reproduction classical urn would be lost in a rustic cottage garden or on a modern roof terrace. Mixtures of plants, and more elaborate containers, look best against a plain wall or with a simple backdrop of a lawn or hedge. For an accent in a busy flower border, a single, well-structured plant in a simple pot is likely to work better.

In mixed plantings, consider the cultivation requirements of individual plants, as well as the more obvious factors such as color, texture, shape, and season of interest. Groups of plants that share a native habitat, for example drought-tolerant silver-leaved subjects or woodland foliage plants, will tend to look good together and be happy sharing a container.

149

• *Osmanthus heterophyllus* 'Goshiki' • *Phormium* 'Bronze Baby' • *Polypodium vulgare* • *Polystichum setiferum* • *Sempervivum* • *Stipa tenuissima* • *Yucca filamentosa* 'Bright Edge' •

Containers for restricted spaces

Container planting offers some ingenious solutions to the three-dimensional challenge of small-space gardening. Make the most of special containers such as window boxes and hanging baskets to improve the appearance of a drab building. Use large pots and tubs to accommodate valuable height-giving climbers, or a trough for alpines to pack intensive plant interest into a tiny area. Ideas like this will make all the difference to the feel of your small space.

Choose hanging-basket plants for the context: silver and gold are ideal for a dark background.

WINDOW BOXES

Window boxes are good for linking indoors and out. Their planting is under constant scrutiny from both sides of the window, so they must always look interesting and be well groomed. There is plenty of scope for originality, in both choice of container and planting. Check the ultimate height of the plants you choose and avoid anything likely to keep out light or block the view. Fragrant plants are good to include in a window box that will be warmed by the sun, helping the scent to drift in through open windows. Herbs such as **thymes** and compact **lavenders**, or **pinks** and purple **petunias**, will all suit a sunny windowsill. Use a free-draining potting mix.

HANGING BASKETS

Hanging baskets are good for fitting dense planting into small spaces and, if properly looked after, can be very effective at brightening a dull building. Either choose a really stylish hanging container, or plant traditional wire or plastic baskets generously in such a way that the container disappears beneath a mass of planting. Flowering baskets need sunshine, which quickly dries out the potting mix and makes daily watering and deadheading essential.

For any planting that is to be mounted on a building, choose colors with the walls in mind. Against red brick, blue, purple, and white flowers are better than hectic pink or orange. Interesting foliage shapes and red flowers show up well against white walls, while natural stonework is flattering to most plants. Use plenty of greenery to soften the effect.

For a shady space, or for winter, do not overlook the great potential of a mixed foliage display. Combine tender ferns with foliage houseplants, such as begonias and trailing tradescantias, for unusual, luxuriant summer schemes. For winter, try evergreen **sedges**, **ivies**, and small rooted cuttings of interesting evergreens such as **box** or **sage**. Window boxes and hanging baskets are an ideal first home for many newly propagated plants like this, which can be planted outdoors in garden borders after their first season.

Don't forget that both window boxes and hanging baskets can be very heavy when filled with plants and damp potting mix, so choose sturdy containers and fixings, and attach them securely. When positioning a container, you also need to think about what is underneath, because there is likely to be some runoff after watering though a suitably planted container beneath may enjoy the drips.

CLIMBERS

Many climbing plants grow well in containers (see page 74). The extra attention they will need is easily offset by all the design advantages of having climbers where they could otherwise not grow. This might apply in many situations: a roof garden or courtyard; a place where an arch or trellis is wanted

TRAILING PLANTS FOR WINDOW BOXES AND BASKETS *Bidens ferulifolia* • *Chlorophytum comosum* 'Variegatum'
• *Dichondra micrantha* 'Silver Falls' • *Hedera* • *Helichrysum microphyllum* 'Silver Mist' •

but there is no planting bed at its foot; or simply a place where a tall plant is needed as an accent or for screening in areas of hard landscaping.

Always choose a large container and a climber that will not be too vigorous. Sun-loving annuals including **sweet peas**, *Ipomoea tricolor* **'Heavenly Blue'** (morning glory), or *Rhodochiton atrosanguineus* (see pages 166–67) are ideal, quick fillers for a sunny position. For something more permanent, most compact long-flowering varieties of clematis, such as the double white-flowered *Clematis florida* var. *sieboldiana* (zone 6–9) or the lavender-blue *Clematis* **'Prince Charles'** (zone 4–9) suit sheltered sites that are not too hot. Choose forms that need hard pruning in late winter, and pinch out growing tips to keep the plants bushy. Brighten shady areas with a golden hop (Humulus lupulus 'Aureus') (zone 5–8) or a **variegated ivy** (see page 75).

Annual climbers in pots are useful short-term fillers in restricted spaces: here, *Ipomoea lobata* at RHS Garden Rosemoor in Devon, England.

AN ALPINE TROUGH OR SINK GARDEN

Planting a miniature garden of jewellike alpine plants in a container is a rewarding way to pack maximum plant interest into a tiny space. You may be lucky enough to find an old stone sink or trough, or you can use any large, shallow ceramic container. There are some excellent reproductions available in stone and plastic, or you can make your own alpine sink from a mixture of sand, cement, and potting mix. The main requirements are good drainage, shelter, and sunshine. Use a gritty potting mix, and choose reliable, easy plants to begin with. Aim for a mixture of different plant forms: rosettes, tufts, and cushions, perhaps with a few small spring bulbs. Some plants to try are: *Arenaria montana* (z. 4–8), *Androsace sempervivoides* (z. 5–7), *Armeria juniperifolia* (z. 4–8), *Azorella trifurcata* (z. 5–9), *Dianthus alpinus* (z. 3–7), *Draba aizoides* (z. 4–8), *Raoulia australis* (z. 8–9), *Saponaria* × *olivana* (z. 3–8), *Saxifraga* × *irvingii* 'Jenkinsiae' (z. 6–8), and *Silene hookeri* (z. 3–7).

GOOD COMPANIONS

The aptly named tender foliage plant *Helichrysum petiolare* 'Limelight' (1) (z. 8–10) tends to scorch in bright sunshine but has a refreshingly cool look in shade, where it is a good partner for bronze-leaved *Impatiens* (2) (ann.). Choose one with small flowers of a rich, deep red.

Try a spring grouping of potted foliage plants such as hostas and ferns in a shady spot (3); see page 69 for some ideas, and choose containers of different sizes that harmonize well to hold the collection together.

Helichrysum petiolare • *Lobelia erinus* (trailing types) • *Lysimachia nummularia* 'Aurea' • *Pelargonium* (ivy-leaved types) • *Petunia* (Surfina types) • *Sanvitalia* • *Thunbergia alata* • *Tropaeolum* • *Vinca minor* 'Argenteovariegata' •

Container plants for winter

In all but the coldest zones (1–5), planting in pots, tubs, window boxes, and hanging baskets is an easy and effective way to bring color and interest to the garden in winter. A colorful winter display provides a cheerful welcome, and carefully positioned containers also ensure that there is something interesting to look at from the windows—an uplifting sight on gloomy winter days.

Alone or with other plants, skimmias are among the best berrying plants for winter pots.

A standard holly will not be cheap, but it will give pleasure in every season for many years. Patient gardeners can train their own.

choose the attractive dwarf silver fir *Abies concolor* 'Compacta' (zone 4–7) for its neat conical shape, sturdy branches, and blue-gray waxy needles.

Topiary will bring a formal, strong architectural element to a garden. Simply clipped evergreens can look very striking in low winter sunshine or when covered in hoarfrost. Especially where space is limited, their clean lines provide a seasonal contrast of mood after the crowded profusion of summer planting. Pot up small specimens of *Buxus sempervirens* (box, zone 6–9), or *Laurus nobilis* (bay, zone 8–9) and clip them into simple cones or pyramids. The pots can be relocated for different effects and will earn their space all year.

Evergreens with berries—perhaps varieties of *Skimmia japonica* (zone 7–8), or *Ilex* (holly; see Good Companions, opposite)—will give a few years' winter value in containers if they are repotted regularly. Remember that you may need to grow male and female varieties together to ensure fruiting. In some cases, you can save space by choosing hermaphrodite or self-pollinating varieties, such as the holly *Ilex* 'J.C. van Tol' (zone 6–9).

Winter interest comes in many forms. Woody plants grown in containers give a sense of permanence and structure to small spaces: choose slow-growing ones that will not outgrow the pot too soon. Evergreens are an obvious way of furnishing the garden in winter, and this is true of plants in containers just as much as in borders. Dwarf conifers in well-chosen pots add valuable winter structure. A miniature form of the Irish juniper, *Juniperus communis* 'Compressa' (zone 2–7), has dark green, silver-backed, needlelike leaves. For a touch of elegance at Christmas,

---

POT PRACTICALITIES

Early fall is the best time to prepare winter containers and baskets. This is the tail end of the growing season, so the plants will grow and become established before really cold weather sets in.

Drainage is critical to the success of winter containers. Few plants will tolerate too much water in winter, especially in very cold weather. Remember to put a layer of broken crocks in the base of each pot to assist drainage, and add coarse grit to the potting mixture. This will also prolong the life of clay pots. Do ensure that any such pots you plan to leave outdoors over winter are frost-proof, and preferably keep them in a sheltered place.

Many winter potted plants can be planted out in the garden after their season is over. Others can be left in their containers as permanent features; remember to repot these when necessary. Feed the plants at the start of the growing season, and don't under any circumstances let them dry out in summer.

OTHER IDEAS FOR WINTER CONTAINERS *Carex comans* 'Frosted Curls' • *Cotoneaster dammeri* • • *Fatsia japonica* • *Lamium maculatum* 'Aureum' • *Osmanthus heterophyllus* 'Variegatus' • *Polystichum setiferum* •

GOOD COMPANIONS

For winter, plant small evergreen shrubs such as skimmias, hollies (1), and fragrant sarcococcas in attractive containers and underplant them with colorful winter pansies (2). Trim the shrub's lower branches if necessary, and remember to deadhead the pansies for a succession of flowers.

The dark-leaved succulent *Aeonium* 'Zwartkop' (3) (z. 9–11) is a plant to treasure. Enjoy it in a frost-free conservatory in winter, and in summer move it out to bask in the company of scarlet pelargoniums (4).

Naturally compact evergreen shrubs that are useful for winter containers include some hebes (see page 43) and winter-flowering heathers (see page 47). Varieties of *Erica carnea* (zone 5–7) and *Erica* × *darleyensis* (zone 4–7) are excellent for seasonal decoration or even as longer-term residents in pots.

Winter fragrance is a bonus offered by certain small shrubs, including *Sarcococca confusa* (zone 6–8) and *Sarcococca hookeriana* var. *digyna* (zone 6–8), both of which thrive in shade (see pages 42 and 124). For a splash of sunshine, plant the easy, golden-leaved evergreen shrub *Lonicera nitida* 'Baggesen's Gold' (zone 7–9), which can be kept clipped to shape or allowed to straggle.

Variegated evergreen leaves are a great winter asset, especially useful in small gardens when they belong to easy plants that look good all year. One such example is *Euonymus fortunei* (zone 5–8) and its numerous cultivars. A good compact one is *Euonymus fortunei* 'Emerald Gaiety', with leaves that flush pink in winter. The variegated box *Buxus sempervirens* 'Elegantissima' (zone 6–9) is also valuable for its neat habit and slow growth.

Also worth considering for winter containers are trailing evergreens, useful for hanging baskets, for softening the edges of window boxes and tall pots, and for balancing the height of tall spring bulbs. Variegated ivies (*Hedera*, see page 75) will enliven the gloomiest corner with their bright leaves, while the periwinkles (*Vinca*) have trailing shoots studded with blue, purple, or white flowers. Variegated forms, such as *Vinca minor* 'Argenteovariegata' (zone 5–8), are especially useful for winter.

From early fall, a wide array of pot-grown winter bedding plants becomes available. These plants offer an inexpensive way of adding splashes of instant color to the winter garden and are good either on their own or as underplanting for other shrubs or trees in containers. The favorites generally tend to be richly colored **primulas** and **cyclamens**, and the **winter pansies.** *Primula* 'Wanda' (zone 3–7) is an old favorite, with its purple-flushed stems and jewellike flowers. Winter pansies need plenty of light if they are to bloom well. The flowers are produced intermittently through the winter with the main flush appearing in the spring.

A different sort of winter bedding, especially suitable for containers, are the **ornamental cabbages** and **kales** (zone 3–9), with their pink, green, and white ruffled leaves. The foliage begins to color attractively with the cooler nights of early fall.

Bulbs that flower at winter's end are extremely valuable, guaranteed to lift spirits with an early burst of color. Most bulbs grow happily in containers for a season. Plant them thickly but not touching each other in pots, and after flowering plant them out in the garden, where they are never too greedy of space. Particularly good early bulbs include the dwarf irises, hyacinths, early crocus, narcissi, and species tulips.

The easiest of window boxes: cyclamen and winter-flowering heather are both readily available and will provide instant color. Uncomplicated containers are usually the most effective, allowing a good planting combination to speak for itself.

Ruscus aculeatus • *Thymus* • *Tolmiea menziesii* 'Taff's Gold' • *Viburnum davidii*

Container plants for summer

There is virtually no limit to the range of flowering plants that can be grown in outdoor containers in summer, and with plant breeders launching more new patio plants every year it can be hard to know where to start. But this is one area of gardening where mistakes are short-lived and impulse buying is ideal. To brighten your patio for a few months, abandon caution, head off to a garden center, and choose just whatever tempts you.

Bold-leaved plants such as cannas take container planting into another dimension, here providing a valuable foil for summer petunias.

SEASONAL FLOWERS

Summer containers are an opportunity to go all out for seasonal color, so it is not surprising that the most popular patio plants are those that flower flamboyantly and without interruption all summer. Fashions come and go, but it is hard to outdo the reliable and free-flowering favorites. Many of the most durable new plants from breeders are simply improved versions of plants we have known and grown for many years. There are good reasons for their popularity, and many of them get better and more varied all the time. This is why verbenas, petunias, impatiens, pelargoniums, lobelias, argyranthemums, and their ilk are still the plants that fill patio tubs and hanging baskets in most summer gardens. They are all frost tender, so either keep them under cover (or cover them up on cold nights) until after the last frosts of spring, or delay buying until the weather is warm enough.

Argyranthemums (z. 9–11, annual) are an excellent example of plants that combine the very best of old and new. These slightly tender patio shrubs produce daisies uncomplainingly from the last frosts of spring to the first ones of fall. Old favorites include the pretty marguerite daisy, *Argyranthemum frutescens*, with its simple, charming white daisies on a compact, ferny-leaved bush. With patience, it can be trained as a standard. *Argyranthemum* 'Jamaica Primrose' is a delicate, pale yellow variety. New developments include the free-flowering **Daisy Crazy** series and **Madeira** series. The latter consists of 11 different compact varieties in an extended range of colors from white to carmine, each named after a town on the Portuguese island of Madeira.

Verbenas (zone 7–11, annual) tell a similar story: traditional bedding plants boosted by expert breeding to produce, for example, the successful **Tapien** and

CONTAINER PLANTS FOR FULL SUN *Aeonium* • *Agapanthus* • *Agave* • *Aloe* • *Anagallis monellii* subsp. *linifolia* • *Astelia chathamica* • *Brugmansia suaveolens* • *Calibrachoa* Million Bells series • *Canna* 'Lucifer' •

Temari series—fast-growing, weather-tolerant plants with dense flower heads in purples, pinks, and white. The semi-trailing **Aztec** series verbenas have been bred for resistance to mildew.

Petunias (zone 5–9, annual) also remain firm favorites, with new colors appearing every year: red and blue, in the case of the **Wave** series, which boasts earlier flowers and superior all-season performance. Trailing petunias include the well-established **Surfina** hybrids and the many-colored **Supercascade** hybrids. When choosing petunias, remember that the purple ones usually offer the bonus of a summer-evening fragrance not unlike that of old-fashioned garden pinks (*Dianthus*) (see page 130). The deep purples combine well with scarlet **pelargoniums** and silver- or golden-foliage plants.

Blue lobelias (cultivars of *Lobelia erinus* zone 4–8, annual) are classic companion plants. At one time their regimented partnership with red pelargoniums and white alyssum (*Lobularia maritima*, annual) in formal bedding schemes was a ubiquitous set piece of town parks and suburban gardens. As with many overused combinations, this did work, and lobelia is still popular for its ability to combine well with large, bright flowers. The dark blue forms, whether trailing or bushy, do this best, their masses of small, long-lasting flowers emphasizing the form and color of more strongly structured companions. Other plants that create a similar effect are the perennial *Nemesia caerulea* (zone 9–10) and diascias (zone 8–11), particularly *Diascia barberae* 'Blackthorn Apricot' and *Diascia* 'Lilac Belle'. A useful partner for part shade is *Sutera cordata* 'Snowflake' (formerly *Bacopa* 'Snowflake') (zone 9–11). This tender perennial has small white starry flowers and combines well with shade-tolerant flowering plants such as impatiens (see page 170)

Carefully chosen: the geranium and honeysuckle flatter both their setting and each other.

Patios are for basking, and there are no better plants to bask alongside you than the many subtropical daisies that are grown as tender annuals. **Gazanias** (see page 164) and **zinnias** come from climates where hot sunshine is taken for granted, and they must have a sunny position to perform well. The same is true of **osteospermums** (zone 9–10), some of which (for example *Osteospermum jucundum*) may survive a touch of winter frost if planted in a well-drained pot positioned in a sheltered site. The popular *Osteospermum* 'Whirlygig', with unusual, spoon-shaped ray florets, and the primrose-yellow *Osteospermum* 'Buttermilk' are a little more tender but may still survive mild winters.

A delightful and unusual, surprisingly hardy daisy for hanging baskets is the Mexican creeping zinnia, *Sanvitalia* (annual), with trailing stems of irrepressibly cheerful little sunflower lookalikes in yellow or orange with contrasting black centers. Also from Mexico is another easy, long-flowering trailer, *Bidens ferulifolia* (8–9), with ferny foliage and starry, yellow flowers; 'Golden Star' is a compact variety.

Brachycome (Swan river daisies) are compact annuals that have found a niche as patio plants, producing flowers a little like those of Michaelmas daisies (perennial asters) in shades of blue, purple, pink, and white. For the most intense color and extended flowering, look out for the **Outback** series.

Fuchsias (see also page 118) are a long-standing patio favorite, especially the tender varieties, which have larger, showier flowers. Choose from the many available forms: bush or trailing, with single or double flowers in various colors. Recent breeding successes have included the large-flowered **Southern Belles** collection (zone 7–9) and the well-colored **Buds of May** (zone 7–9). Tender fuchsias need regular watering and feeding in the growing season and will repay you by flowering exuberantly well into the fall. When frosts threaten, cut them back and bring them into a well-lit, frost-free place, keeping them only slightly damp through the winter.

The same winter care routine applies to **pelargoniums** (zone 9–10), usually known as geraniums (correctly applied only to the related hardy genus). There are several types, including the regal, zonal, and ivy- and scented-leaved kinds (see also page 134). Pelargoniums are constantly being improved: look out for the 'Maverick' and 'Designer' varieties for strong, large-flowered plants. Pelargoniums range from red and purple to pink and white, with double or single flowers. They look especially good grown in simple pots against a plain background of pale stonework or a white wall.

Celosia argentea • *Convolvulus sabatius* • *Cordyline australis* • *Cuphea* • *Echeveria* • *Felicia amelloides* • *Ficus carica* • *Pennisetum setaceum* 'Rubrum' • *Lilium* • *Lobelia richardsonii* • *Melianthus major* •

Pruned hard each spring, ornamental elders make surprisingly good container plants. Here *Sambucus nigra* f. *porphyrophylla* 'Gerda' ('Black Beauty') partners *Vinca* 'Illumination'.

FOLIAGE PLANTS

While brightly colored flowers are often seen as the classic summer patio plants, foliage too has an important role to play. Courtyards, roof gardens, and other urban small spaces may be dominated by hard landscaping and will benefit greatly from the softening effect of massed foliage. Shady areas will be unsuitable for many flowers, and so alternative planting ideas must be sought. Situations like these are the cue for foliage to step forward into the limelight.

There is a whole world of foliage to be explored for original container planting ideas. Foliage plants tend to have a longer season than many of their flowering counterparts and, while there are few that come close to being maintenance-free, most require less attention on a regular basis to keep them looking smart.

In a very small space or to create a focal point—beside a doorway or a gate, for example—arrange a collection of foliage plants in a single container. If space permits, group them, each in its individual container, to create a visually satisfying planting scheme. This way, each plant can be treated individually as regards pot size, moisture requirements, and so on, and plants can be replaced easily when they are past their best. Tender plants can be moved under cover as winter begins, replacing them perhaps with frost-hardy stalwarts. Attractive containers may form an integral part of the display, or if you have used ordinary plastic pots, they can be disguised beneath the foliage.

Among the familiar foliage plants often sold with summer bedding are several cultivars of *Senecio cineraria* (zone 8–10), with felted, shining-white leaves. They include *Senecio cineraria* 'Silver Dust' and *Senecio cineraria* 'White Diamond', which are both compact and lacy. Similar but less well known is the attractive scrambler *Senecio viravira* (zone 8–10). The trailing *Helichrysum petiolare* (zone 8–10) is seen everywhere and is more tender. Its round, silvery, felted leaves on long stems are good mixers with brightly colored flowers in hanging baskets and raised beds. For a similar effect on a smaller scale, use *Helichrysum microphyllum* (zone 8–10); look for its new seed-raised cultivar 'Silver Mist'. All these silvery plants are excellent foliage companions for linking spiky grasses, sedges, and succulents such as agaves, and all thrive in sunshine. In less sunny areas use the pale yellow-leaved *Helichrysum petiolare* 'Limelight', which prefers part shade and brightens gloomy corners very effectively.

A newer, less familiar trailing plant, grown for its cascades of small, rounded silver leaves, is the drought-resistant *Dichondra micrantha* 'Silver Falls' (zone 9–11). The silver luster intensifies with age and in sun, and it is striking tumbling from a hanging basket or window box. Other ideas for trailing summer foliage include the variegated ground ivy *Glechoma hederacea* 'Variegata' (zone 3–9) and the common household spider-plant, the stripey-leaved *Chlorophytum comosum* 'Variegatum' (zone 9–11), which shines in this context.

156

CONTAINER FOLIAGE PLANTS FOR SHADE *Buxus sempervirens* 'Elegantissima' • *Fatsia japonica* •

Variegated plants hold a special fascination, and a number of tender ones are suitable for summer foliage containers, although they should be used sparingly or their effect is lost. *Plectranthus madagascariensis* **'Variegated Mintleaf'** (zone 9–11) is a vigorous spreader, happiest in shade. Its strong scent is unpleasant to some. The coprosmas are tender foliage shrubs mainly from the Southern Hemisphere, reminiscent of evergreen euonymus. *Coprosma × kirkii* **'Kirkii Variegata'** (zone 8–10) is the most common.

King of the variegated leaf is *Solenostemon* (coleus, zone 10–11 or annual). Flowers are superfluous with this hectic foliage, splashed with red, purple, yellow, and green. Grow coleus from seed, which germinates like cress, or buy named varieties. Feed and water well for the most vigorous leaves. They will be happy in a reasonable amount of sun. For striking foliage effects in shade, turn to the **begonias** (zone 10–11 or annual). Their leaves come in different shapes, sizes, and interesting patterns and textures. The rhizomatous forms, especially, include some intriguing compact varieties, such as *Begonia* **'Munchkin'** and *Begonia* **'Tiger Paws'**.

Some tender flowering plants have varieties with added leaf interest, such as variegated *Felicia amelloides* (zone 10–11 or annual), with its long-lasting, yellow-centered blue daisies. Many pelargoniums have interesting variegations, including some of the scented ones (see page 134), and there are also variegated fuchsias, such as the compact *Fuchsia* **'Tom West'** Meillez (zone 7–9) or the special **Goldrush** collection (zone 7–9), with golden foliage.

Bronze and orange are natural partners, complemented here by a dark container.

Variegated foliage contrasts well with big, dark leaves. A star here is *Colocasia esculenta* **'Black Magic'** (zone 8–10), a tender tropical exotic with huge, elephant-ear leaves of almost jet black. It needs shelter and ample water. Dark-leaved **phormiums** and **cordylines**, young **Japanese maples**—*Acer palmatum* **'Bloodgood'** (zone 6–8) for example—and rooted cuttings of purple *Sambucus* (elders), *Physocarpus*, and *Cotinus* (see pages 52 and 54) all contribute valuable bronze and purple elements. Smaller, purple-leaved annuals include *Perilla frutescens* var. *purpurascens* and **purple basil**.

Grasses should be included for their textural contribution (see pages 62–63). The unusual ice blue grass *Elymus arenarius* (zone 6–8) is invasive but is safe when restricted to a pot. *Festuca glauca* **'Elijah Blue'** (zone 4–8) and **'Blaufuchs'** (zone 4–8) in the same color range but are more compact. Novelties such as *Carex comans* **'Frosted Curls'** (zone 4–9), with its tightly curled tips, and the red grass *Imperata cylindrica* **'Rubra'** (zone 6–9) are also useful.

A MINI POTAGER

The ornamental vegetable garden, or potager, is a long-respected garden tradition, seen most famously, on a vast scale, at the Château de Villandry in the Loire Valley in France. The idea of growing vegetables for beauty as well as taste also works very well where space is short, and the ultimate space-saving potager is one made in a container. Choose a large tub, fill it with humus-rich planting mix and plant it with ornamental leafy salads and herbs for an original and useful patio feature. Buy some of the young plants that are now sold in large garden centers, or grow your own from seed. Try purple basil (*Ocimum basilicum* var. *purpurascens* 'Purple Ruffles') with parsley, chives, and one or two red lettuce varieties such as 'Lollo Rosso' (above left) and 'Cocarde'. You can also include plants with edible flowers such as calendula (see page 162) and borage (see page 141). For early spring and fall, choose a mixture of hardier chicories and endives, growing them as "cut-and-come-again" crops and perhaps including one of the colored Swiss chards (above right) such as 'Bright Lights'. Herb specialists often sell unusual varieties with interesting foliage such as the variegated land cress, with boldly cream-splashed dark green leaves, or the variegated marjoram *Origanum vulgare* 'Country Cream'.

Hedera helix 'Oro di Bogliasco' • *Hosta* 'Ginko Craig' • *Lamium maculatum* 'Aureum' • *Tolmiea menziesii* 'Taff's Gold' •

Annuals and biennials

If there were such a thing as an instant garden, it would be created with annuals. Like a firework display, it would be a short-lived but brilliant affair: these are plants that live fast and die fast, coming and going in the space of a few months or even weeks. Biennials are slightly more sedate, being slower to reach maturity, but they, too, have only one good season of flowering, so while their impact may be dramatic it is only ever temporary.

Annuals and biennials are both grown from seed, but biennials normally need two growing seasons in order to mature and flower. Wallflowers, Canterbury bells (*Campanula medium*), and forget-me-nots (*Myosotis*) are all biennials. Seed is sown in late spring or early summer, and the plants will flower the following year. Some, if they are started early enough, may flower in their first year, although they make better plants and flower more profusely in their second. Some will even survive for another season, although their flowering ability often dwindles. Some hardy annuals, particularly sweet peas, can be sown in the fall to make stronger, earlier-flowering plants the following year.

Annuals and biennials are by nature short-lived, but they are invaluable in all gardens, large or small, new or established. They offer a wide variety of form, color, and habit, bringing another dimension to the summer garden and enabling gardeners to experiment with new ideas without committing to long-term schemes. There are those that climb (see pages 166–67), others that creep; some form huge, soft sprays of foliage and flowers, while others are short plants tightly packed with blooms. The color range of annuals is unsurpassed, but an even greater asset

Seed suppliers often market annual seed mixtures that, in the right place, can give a fast-maturing display of summer color that is second to none. Most such mixtures include easy-to-grow flowers such as poppies, marigolds, and cornflowers.

ANNUALS AND BIENNIALS FOR CUTTING *Consolida ajacis* • *Cosmos* • *Dianthus chinensis* • *Lathyrus odoratus* •

is that many of them will flower only a few weeks after planting, so they are perfect for disguising gaps in established borders—after early-summer perennials are over and before midsummer ones come into flower—or for achieving color quickly in new beds. When you create a new border or clear an old one, fill it with annuals for the first growing season. This will help eliminate persistent weeds before you make long-term plantings (when weeds are far more difficult to eradicate). The following year, plant annuals and biennials among the new permanent residents to prevent more weeds from taking hold and to fill short-term gaps into which perennial plants will eventually grow.

Most annuals and biennials are easy to cultivate as long as they are given moderately fertile soil that drains well but is not too dry, and plenty of sun. Many are do-it-yourself experts: plant them one year and they will self-seed and come up again the next (see Useful Self-seeders, right). All you then need to do is remove or transplant those that have appeared in inappropriate places. Alternatively, cut off the seed heads just before they shed their seed, and scatter the contents in areas where you want them to grow next year; or save them in paper envelopes in a cool, dry place and scatter them the following spring.

Over the years, breeders have created so many varieties of some annuals and biennials that it can be difficult to decide which ones to grow. When making a choice, consider the three ways in which cultivars most commonly differ from each other: color range, plant height, and disease resistance. New varieties are often disease-resistant, but some older cultivars remain popular because their color is particularly good. One of the great pleasures in choosing annuals or biennials is knowing that, whatever your requirements, you will find some to suit you.

USEFUL SELF-SEEDERS

Papaver rhoeas (Shirley poppy), single or double and in a range of colors, is useful for dry soils.

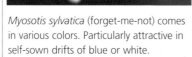

Meconopsis cambrica (Welsh poppy) seeds as readily as any poppy but is more shade-tolerant

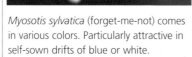

Myosotis sylvatica (forget-me-not) comes in various colors. Particularly attractive in self-sown drifts of blue or white.

Many annuals and biennials (as well as perennials) will sow themselves if left to their own devices after flowering. Self-seeders can play a very useful role in holding a border design together. They often have the knack of seeding in just the right place, and those that get it wrong are easily weeded out. Seedlings of the most enthusiastic self-seeders are likely to need judicious thinning, but otherwise you can just sit back and wait for them to perform.

OTHER GOOD SELF-SEEDERS

Alchemilla mollis

Atriplex hortensis var. *purpurea*

Digitalis purpurea

Eschscholzia californica

Euphorbia (some)

Galactites tomentosa

Geranium robertianum 'Celtic White'

Helleborus (some)

Iberis umbellata

Limnanthes douglasii

Lunaria annua

Lychnis coronaria

Nigella damascena

Papaver somniferum

Salvia viridis var. *comata* (*Salvia horminum*)

Sisyrinchium striatum

Tropaeolum majus

Verbascum (some)

Nicandra physalodes (shoo-fly plant) should be better known for its big blue flowers and long-lasting "lantern" seed heads.

Silybum marianum is grown mainly for its variegated leaves, which are larger when it is grown in good soil.

Molucella laevis • *Nigella damascena* • *Salvia viridis* var. *comata* (*Salvia horminum*) • *Tropaeolum majus* •

Using annuals and biennials

Among many gardeners, annuals have something of a reputation for being unsubtle and flashy, but this is not always deserved. While there are those that like to make an impact—and this characteristic can be very useful—there are also many that make a more subtle contribution to the garden. These are easily slipped into gaps in beds full of perennials or are used for edging, and all are excellent for extending the season of interest.

One such little beauty is the corncockle, **Agrostemma githago**, perhaps best known in the form **'Milas'**, named after its Turkish home. This delicate plant has open-faced pale pink (dark pink in 'Milas') summer flowers on spindly gray-green stems. In an exposed site it needs some support, but this is easily provided by other plants. **'Milas Cerise'** ('Purple Queen') has flowers that are even darker pink than 'Milas', while those of **'Ocean Pearl'** are pure white with black speckling. Use staggered groups of a single cultivar (or all three) to provide gentle punctuation in a mixed border.

Nemophila menziesii

Agrostemma githago

Nemophilas are also low-key annuals that look good at the front of flower beds or perhaps in the shade along with cool-colored impatiens (see page 170) and violets. *Nemophila menziesii* is a delightful little plant with bright blue flowers and toothed, bright green leaves, while *Nemophila maculata* (probably better known) has white flowers with a blue spot on each petal and sometimes blue veining. Both like a reasonable amount of moisture in the soil.

If you like blue then the *Ageratum houstonianum* (floss flower) cultivars have a lot to offer. They produce their unusual, powder-puff flower heads in blues, pinks, or whites and are available in mixtures or single colors. **'Blue Mink'** is a standard soft blue cultivar, and **Hawaii series** is available

Ageratum houstonianum 'Blue Mink'

as a blue, pink, and white mix and in single colors. Floss flowers are effective at the edges of beds, although they prefer sun, and look attractive with other low-growing bedding plants such as petunias and verbenas.

The open, filigree foliage and airy, lacework umbels of the white flowers produced by *Ammi majus* ensure that this annual is subtle enough to be included almost anywhere—despite being quite tall, up to 4ft. (1.2m). If you have the space, it is at its best when growing en masse—sow the seed where you want it to grow. Equally tall but more statuesque is the dependable foxglove *Digitalis purpurea* (zone 5–8). Its spires of purple-pink flowers are part of early summer. Grow it for the bees, if for no other reason. The **Foxy Group** hybrids have flowers in white, dark pink, or creamy yellow, all with distinctive dark spotting, while **'Sutton's Apricot'** is a warm shade of pink, good for color associations with clematis, roses, and dark foliage shrubs.

Although they have large flowers, the two best-known cultivars of *Lavatera trimestris*, **'Silver Cup'** and **'Mont Blanc'**, are not overly dominant. They are not very tall—'Silver Cup', the larger

ANNUALS AND BIENNIALS FOR BEES *Borago officinalis • Digitalis purpurea • Helianthus annuus •*

Digitalis purpurea 'Sutton's Apricot'

Lavatera trimestris

Clarkia unguiculata (Clarkia elegans)

Scabiosa atropurpurea 'Ace of Spades'

Scabiosa stellata

of the two, is only 30in. (75cm)—and the satin delicacy of the flowers (rose pink in 'Silver Cup' and ice white in 'Mont Blanc') lends the plant a special subtlety. These are wonderful cottage-garden plants, ideal for growing among nigellas and larger-flowered poppies, and are also able to hold their own among small shrubs. Try 'Mont Blanc' with foliage plants, such as hostas, and 'Silver Cup' with larkspur, **Consolida ajacis**, an annual with feathery leaves and elegant spires of flowers in shades of pink or blue.

Of the same ilk, but perhaps slightly more attention seeking, is **Clarkia unguiculata** (*Clarkia elegans*), whose early-summer, single or double flowers in candy colors (including pink and rich maroon) are complemented perfectly by the taller, more genteel larkspur. With a little imagination, this combination could be used as the basis of a pleasing, sophisticated meadow-flower mix: include **Centaurea cyanus** (cornflower), **Convolvulus tricolor** (annual bindweed), and scabious to complete the effect. The cornflower is available as mixed or single colors, and the larger varieties can be up to 3ft. (90cm) tall. The bindweed, which is much more refined than its wild cousin, spreads rather than climbs and so makes a fine edging plant. It has rich, royal blue flowers of the typical *Convolvulus* open funnel shape. **Scabiosa atropurpurea**, with its pale blue, pincushion flowers, is the best-known scabious; but for a little more refinement try the rich red, almost black, **Scabiosa atropurpurea** 'Ace of Spades'. Add **Scabiosa stellata** for its rounded, papery seed heads, which are attractive in dried flower arrangements. Scabious prefer neutral to alkaline soil.

One of the plants most frequently cultivated for the purposes of picking and drying is **Limonium sinuatum** (statice). This bushy plant has stiff,

---

GROWING ANNUALS FROM SEED

In theory, hardy annuals and many biennials can be sown directly into the soil where they are to flower, but this does not always result in success. Reliable self-seeders will grow happily when treated in this way, but you cannot always be sure which ones are going to be good self-seeders in your garden. Some of the more choosy varieties are best raised in seed trays or individual pots and then planted in the ground when they have reached a reasonable size. This also gives them a head start against pests such as slugs and snails, which like nothing better than newly emerging seedling leaves. An easy guide to whether a plant is choosy or not is the number of seeds in the packet. If there are very few then this is a choice plant and may be difficult; if there are more than 40 or so, you should be pretty safe in experimenting to see whether they will survive direct sowing in the open garden.

Limnanthes douglasii • Reseda odorata • Salvia viridis var. comata (Salvia horminum) • Tropaeolum majus •

winged green stems at the top of which are produced clusters of tiny, funnel-shaped flowers. The large number of colors—blue, lavender, purple, white, yellow, apricot, pink, red—are available as mixtures or single shades. 'Soft Pastel Mixed' is a tall blend, while 'Forever' is shorter but has stronger colors. For fresh arrangements, pick the flowers at the first sign of color; if they are required for drying, wait until most of the cluster is colored.

For a plant that really stands out from the crowd, choose *Amaranthus caudatus*. Better known as love-lies-bleeding, this huge, bushy annual, which can reach 5ft. (1.5m), has light green leaves and long, pendent tassels of rich crimson flowers. *Amaranthus caudatus* var. *viridis* has bright green tassels, while those of 'Pony Tails' are green and crimson. This is not a plant to hide. Give it plenty of space and provide it with some strong competition in the form of other tall, brightly colored flowers, such as *Dahlia* 'Bishop of Llandaff', yellow perennial rudbeckias, or

Amaranthus caudatus

some of the larger grasses (see pages 62–63). In *Amaranthus tricolor* 'Joseph's Coat', a smaller relative of love-lies-bleeding at 2ft. (60cm), all the color is in the plant's foliage—bright crimson-scarlet and gold in the upper part of the plant and chocolate, yellow, and green in the lower. It can be used in containers or for focal points among lower bedding plants. Amaranthus need sympathetic feeding and watering if they are to do well.

For impact without size, opt for the ever-popular *Begonia*. Begonias are a widely differing group, each with its own merits. Like amaranthus, they benefit from regular feeding. The fibrous-rooted semperflorens types make short upright plants with succulent leaves, often bronze, and small, brightly colored flowers. Hybrids such as 'Devon Gems', 'Lotto Mixed', and 'Peek a Boo' vary mostly in their color mixes and height, but all are guaranteed to produce flowers in abundance throughout the summer. Grow them in borders, or in pots and window boxes, with other bedding plants such as salvias, petunias, and verbenas. Tuberous begonias (*Begonia* × *tuberhybrida*) are well known for their big blowzy flowers produced amid lush, attractive foliage on short bushy plants.

Begonia 'Nonstop'

Begonia × *tuberhybrida*

Although they have a reputation for being temperamental, the modern hybrids are excellent performers and are comparatively disease-resistant. The popular 'Nonstop' varieties make compact plants with upward-facing flowers in a choice of bright, strong colors. The blooms of 'Show Angels' are softer pastels and are produced on pendent stems. Because of their slightly lax habit, they are best in hanging baskets, where their flowers can be enjoyed at eye level. Other useful tuberous begonias include the variety 'Devil', which are tidy, weather-resistant plants with shiny, bronze foliage, and the spectacular 'Pin-Up' hybrids.

Like begonias, the marigolds are long-standing favorites. Few annuals are easier to grow than the humble pot marigold, *Calendula officinalis*, which has orange daisy flowers and rich, pale green foliage. Once in flower, deadhead the plants regularly and they will go on blooming with immense generosity until early fall. There are many cultivars—all in yellow, cream, or orange and red

Calendula 'Art Shades Mixed'

Calendula 'Radio'

ANNUALS FOR FOLIAGE *Atriplex hortensis* var. *rubra* • *Brassica oleracea* (ornamental cabbages) • *Kochia scoparia* •

African and French marigolds (*Tagetes*) come in all sizes and are justifiably popular for their cheerful flowers, which last for weeks and withstand bad weather.

Tagetes patula

Mimulus luteus 'Viva'

similar color to its own. At the other end of the scale, *Tagetes erecta* 'Vanilla' is prized for its large, creamy white double flowers, which can be used in borders of quieter colors.

Commonly called monkey-flower, the unusual *Mimulus* is another bright annual. Aside from being colorful with a long succession of blooms, it is valued by gardeners for the fact that it relishes damp spots in sun or dappled shade. It produces masses of wide-faced flowers on compact plants. Grow a mixture for a brilliant show or choose a cultivar with limited colors, such as 'Royal Velvet' (deep maroon with a yellow throat) or 'Yellow Velvet' (yellow splashed with red), for a more refined effect.

Among the wide range of annuals are

shades—and most have inherited the flowering ability of the species. 'Art Shades Mixed' has frilled flowers in apricot, orange, and cream, while those of 'Radio' are rounded and deep orange, with quilled petals. Both of these are ideal for providing patches of color near the front of a border. The taller variety 'Indian Prince', with deep orange, mahogany-backed petals, shows up better among other plants. Calendulas look good with flowers in other strong colors, such as purple verbenas and petunias. For an interesting effect, try them in small numbers among lavender, especially *Lavandula stoechas* (see page 132), or other gray-leaved shrubs. In *Calendula* 'Touch of Red' the yellow, orange, and cream flowers are etched with red. This will soften their impact and make them easier to use in a bed of quieter colors.

Pot marigolds are hardy annuals, while what are commonly called African

marigolds (*Tagetes erecta* cultivars) and French marigolds (*Tagetes patula* cultivars) are half-hardy annuals. African marigolds have large, pom-pom flowers; French marigolds have almost pom-pom flowers, usually on smaller plants. Further hybridization has resulted in the Afro-French marigolds, which tend to have numerous single or double flowers. The colors of all are in the red, orange, and yellow range. None of these plants are out of place in a cottage-style garden or in more formal bedding schemes, as their colorful flowers are useful in both situations. However, they are more of a challenge if subtle combinations are sought, partly because the plants are generally quite stiff in habit. *Tagetes patula* 'Striped Marvel', a French marigold that has flowers striped in bright yellow and rich red, is elegant enough to be used among softer-colored annuals such as taller nigellas and cornflowers, or with flowers of a

ANNUALS FOR CHILDREN TO GROW

Children love annuals for their bright colors and quick results. Give them space to grow their own plants in the border or provide attractive pots.

Bellis perennis (common daisy) Double forms in shades of pink and white are usually grown as biennials.

Bracteantha bracteata (*Helichrysum*) (everlasting flower) Papery multipetaled flowers in many colors . Good for dried-flower arrangements.

Calendula officinalis (see page 162)

Eschscholzia californica (Californian poppy) Sun-loving, drought-tolerant and easy. Grow in generous drifts.

Gourds (ornamental) Available in a variety of shapes and sizes; make interesting indoor decorations.

Helianthus annuus The ever-popular annual sunflower, unfailingly cheerful and often nurturing a competitive spirit.

Limnanthes douglasii (see page 164)

Papaver commutatum (see page 172)

Ocimum basilicum var. *purpurascens* 'Purple Ruffles' • *Solenostemon* (coleus) • *Tropaeolum majus* 'Alaska' •

Phlox drummondii

Coreopsis grandiflora 'Early Sunrise'

Limnanthes douglasii

Tropaeolum majus 'Empress of India'

Gaillardia pulchella 'Kobold'

numerous cottage-garden favorites, including the annual phlox (*Phlox drummondii*). It is very similar to its perennial relative but perhaps more exuberant in every way, with more flowers on smaller plants and in brighter colors over a longer period. *Phlox drummondii* is available in a wide range of mixtures and single colors. Try '**African Sunset**' for flowers in shades of red on plants of only about 4in. (10cm) tall and '**Chanal**' for double flowers in an attractive, deep shade of cotton-candy pink.

Two more cottage-garden stalwarts are *Limnanthes douglasii* (meadowfoam) and *Tropaeolum majus* (nasturtium). *Limnanthes*, a keen self-seeder, has neat, ferny green leaves on a short plant that disappears under a mass of saucer-shaped, white-edged yellow flowers. It is an effective ground-cover and edging plant. Try interplanting it with dwarf French marigolds or blue love-in-a-mist. While meadowfoam spreads quickly, it is nothing compared to

the nasturtium (see also page 167). This vigorous climber or scrambler has long, trailing stems clothed with umbrella-shaped, usually blue-green leaves, and flowers in shades of orange, red, yellow and cream. Although comparatively late to get going, it is excellent as ground cover, and its flowers never offend no matter where they pop up. Dwarf hybrids derived from *Tropaeolum majus* are also available in single or mixed colors: '**Peach Melba**' has stems only 12in. (30cm) long and soft yellow flowers with red markings; '**Empress of India**', similar in size, is rich, velvety red. Both of these are best in containers.

Some of the best-value plants available to gardeners are those that belong to the daisy family. Many of the perennials are grown as annuals and produce their flowers over long periods, some into early or mid-fall. Colors range from bright to pastel, and the plants vary from small to huge. The early flowering *Coreopsis grandiflora* '**Early Sunrise**' has double, rich yellow daisies on

medium-height plants from late spring into summer. Combine it with glowing orange calendulas and eschscholzias in a sunny corner, or with deep purples and blues to create eye-catching contrast. *Coreopsis tinctoria* cultivars have a wider color range, including reds and mixtures; flowering begins in summer. '**Mahogany Midget**' is aptly named and makes an excellent edging or container plant. Try it with the annual quaking grass, *Briza maxima* (see page 63). *Gaillardia pulchella* (blanket flower) has yellow daisies edged with red from summer to fall. Cultivars include '**Red Plume**', which has entirely red, double flowers, and '**Goblin**', a dwarf variety in which red is edged with yellow.

For low-growing plants smothered in large daisy flowers from early to late summer, **gazanias** are hard to beat. Above gray-green, often hairy foliage, these stocky plants produce wide-rayed flowers with wide centers. Gazanias come from tropical Africa, and their one drawback is that they hide their faces

SCENTED ANNUALS AND BIENNIALS *Dianthus chinensis* • *Dianthus barbatus* • *Heliotropium arborescens* •

Gazania

Rudbeckia hirta 'Irish Eyes'

Rudbeckia hirta 'Marmalade'

Callistephus chinensis

Another member of the daisy family, but with quite a different color palette, is the annual China aster (*Callistephus chinensis*). If it likes the conditions in your garden (neutral to alkaline soil and no early frosts), it will flower from late summer until late fall, producing blooms like those of chrysanthemums in pink, blue, cream, and a variety of shades in between. The large size of the flowers and their fresh appearance, at a time when other plants are beginning to go into their quiet season, can make China asters somewhat difficult to integrate into bedding schemes. Like bedding chrysanthemums, they are probably best planted in drifts of a reasonable size, or grown on their own in containers. Choice varieties to look for include the dwarf **Milady** series, which is wilt-resistant, and the intermediate **Duchesse** series.

when the sun goes in, although the multiflowered **Kiss** series is less likely to do this. The *Gazania* **Daybreak** series has very short stems and comes into flower early. Plant gazanias en masse or among similarly bright flowers in the warmest border in the garden, or use them in containers on a sunny patio.

A deservedly popular late-summer bedding plant, in all its varieties, is *Rudbeckia hirta* 'Marmalade', some 18in. (45cm) tall and very bushy, reliably producing large flowers of orange-yellow with brown centers; these are sensational with blue-flowered annuals. A popular cultivar is **'Indian Summer'**, taller at 2ft. (60cm), with large flowers in golden yellow. Again it looks good with blues and can be used to soften the impact of pure yellow flowers. For something daisylike but elegant, choose *Rudbeckia hirta* **'Irish Eyes' ('Green Eyes')**. This has yellow flowers with olive green central cones. At a height of up to 30in. (75cm), it is a good mid-border plant and, like all rudbeckias, it is excellent for cutting.

ANNUALS FOR FALL COLOR

The fall is often rather unpredictable in terms of weather, but if frosts and heavy rain hold off, it can be the most colorful and beautiful time of the whole year. Bold, richly

colored annuals, having at last got into their stride in late summer, will go from strength to strength, continuing to grow and looking wonderful in clear, low sunshine against a backdrop of slowly mellowing leaf color—appreciated all the more, of course, because each good day is a bonus and could be the last of the season. The following annuals will make a really powerful impression in a good fall:

Calendula officinalis
Callistephus chinensis
Cosmos bipinnatus
Lavatera trimestris
Rudbeckia hirta
Tithonia rotundifolia
Zinnia

Lobularia maritima • Lathyrus odoratus • Matthiola bicornis • Matthiola incana • Nicotiana • Reseda odorata •

Annual climbers

With the possible exception of sweet peas, annual climbers are a much undervalued group of plants that deserve more attention. Small gardens especially can benefit from the new interest and color they bring to permanent borders: from just a few packets of seeds, you can provide changes each season with different planting on fences, trellis, and obelisks. Annual climbers are also invaluable while you wait for permanent climbers to reach their potential.

Ipomoea lobata

Cobaea scandens

Ipomoea tricolor 'Heavenly Blue'

Eccremocarpus scaber

As temporary fillers, annual climbers can bring a furnished look to a new garden in its first season, quickly softening the starkness of bare walls or a recently erected shed or arbor, while the permanent plantings are becoming established. In older gardens, an annual can replace a perennial climber that may have died or been removed, filling its space while you decide on its permanent replacement.

Some of the climbers that we grow as annuals from seed every year are in fact tender perennials: given a series of warm winters, they could go on from year to year. One such is **Cobaea scandens**, known as the cup-and-saucer vine. This vigorous tropical climber from Mexico is probably the best choice if you are aiming to cover a new arch or arbor with greenery and color in a single season. It may seem slow to begin with, but in a warm and sunny summer it will grow prodigiously and will have no

trouble reaching 15ft. (5m). Its bell-shaped flowers are similar to those of Canterbury bells (*Campanula medium*), but they develop from pale green to purple, so that at any given time the plant will carry flowers in a range of colors. An elegant white-flowered form is also available. Warm summer weather and a mild early fall should ensure a succession of flowers for many weeks until the plant is eventually killed by frost. In very mild winters the root system may survive to throw up new shoots in the spring.

Much less vigorous—partly because it detests cold weather—is **Ipomoea tricolor** (morning glory) (zone 10–11 or annual). In late summer, the seed strain **'Heavenly Blue'** produces flowers that stop passersby in their tracks. Perfect trumpets of pure, sky blue open, like unfurling umbrellas, after sunrise but last only a few hours before rolling inward from the rim and eventually withering.

Morning glory is easily grown from seed, but it should not be planted out until warm weather arrives, when it needs a sunny, sheltered spot with support at hand—perhaps an obelisk or a wigwam of canes—for its twining stems. It can be successfully grown in a large, heavy pot, provided it has something to climb up and is kept well watered. The flowering period of a container-grown plant can be extended by keeping it in the greenhouse or sunroom early and late in the season.

Morning glory is just one of a number of blue, purple, and red convolvulus lookalikes that are valuable for summer color. However, *Ipomoea* is a varied genus: it includes the sweet potato (*Ipomoea batatas*) and another highly ornamental climber, **Ipomoea lobata** (also known as *Mina lobata* and *Quamoclit lobata*) (zone 9–11 or annual). A useful component of a hot color scheme, *Ipomoea lobata* produces unusual, one-sided racemes of flowers

TALL ANNUALS AND BIENNIALS *Cleome spinosa • Consolida ajacis • Cosmos bipinnatus • Digitalis purpurea •*

CLIMBERS TO EAT

When choosing ornamental climbers to fill space quickly, don't overlook vegetables. Runner beans, a type of pole bean, were originally grown not for food but for their scarlet flowers. The 1855 variety 'Painted Lady', which has bicolored flowers in red and white, is still available. Climbing French beans can be equally ornamental, with pods of deep purple ('Blauhilde'), red ('Lingua di Fuoco'), or golden yellow ('Corona d'Oro'). Peas with purple flowers (and sometimes purple pods, too) are also available: try the excellent snow pea variety 'Carouby de Mausanne'.

Many of the edible squashes grow too large and heavy to climb successfully, but given appropriate support some smaller types can be grown to great effect as climbers. These include the bright orange 'Jack Be Little', the yellow patty pan squash 'Sunburst', and the curious, curved, bell-ended zucchini 'Tromboncino'.

that mature from scarlet to white. Different again is *Ipomoea alba* (moonflower) (zone 8–11 or annual), which is grown for the large, scented, tubular white flowers that open at night.

Another exotic-looking climber that adds height to late summer borders is ***Eccremocarpus scaber***, the Chilean glory flower. It is usually treated as an annual, although it may survive the winter in mild zones. Its tubular flowers are abundant all summer. The usual color is orange-red, but seed strains are available in yellow and red, or mixed colors. The plant is vigorous enough to cover an arbor or arch in a season, and it will sometimes self-seed.

A familiar ornamental climber is ***Lablab purpureus*** (hyacinth bean). Its fast-growing, twining, red-tinged stems produce fragrant pink or purple flowers followed by purplish pods that contain edible seeds. The variety **'Ruby Moon'** has the best color.

Rhodochiton atrosanguineus (zone 10 or annual) is also a purple-flowered climber, but its blooms are unusual and most intriguing. The actual flowers are almost black, each one suspended from a deep, pinkish red calyx. Maroon-tinged, heart-shaped leaves complete the picture, making a very stylish plant for a sunroom or a sheltered, sunny spot in the garden. Combine it with a silvery shrub such as *Elaeagnus* 'Quicksilver' or the tender, white-felted scrambler *Senecio viravira*.

Many varieties of nasturtium (see also page 164) have a climbing habit; those that have been bred as dwarf plants do not, so make sure you choose the right seeds. For a true climber, try the Canary creeper, ***Tropaeolum peregrinum*** (zone 10 or annual), which has lobed, gray-green leaves and bright yellow, fringed flowers.

Yellow and orange annual climbers also include ***Thunbergia alata*** (zone 10–11 or annual), the familiar black-eyed Susan. This twining perennial from tropical Africa has yellow, orange, or cream flowers, which often feature in window boxes and hanging baskets. Given a sheltered place and favorable conditions, it will wind its way up its support to a height of 8ft. (2.5m).

An annual climber grown mainly for its dizzyingly fragrant flowers (the more you pick the more you get) is the sweet pea, ***Lathyrus odoratus***, described in full on page 131.

Lablab purpureus

Rhodochiton atrosanguineus

Tropaeolum peregrinum

Thunbergia alata

Dipsacus fullonum • Helianthus annuus 'Velvet Queen' • Nicandra physalodes • Nicotiana sylvestris •

Snapdragon (Antirrhinum)

Most of the snapdragons in cultivation are derived from *Antirrhinum majus* (zone 6–10), a short-lived perennial species, but the cultivars are usually grown as half-hardy annuals or biennials. Most have been bred to produce more or less tubular flowers, tightly arranged in upright spikes in a huge range of bright colors—reddish purple, crimson, red, pink, lilac, white, yellow, bronze, orange, and bicolors. They are popular with children because their "mouths" open and snap closed when the flower is squeezed and released from behind, hence the common name. Doubles and more open-faced flowers are also available.

Annual snapdragons are not subtle or delicate, but they do have several big attractions: they flower from summer to fall in cooler climates with little attention, they come in a range of heights from 1ft. (30cm) to 3ft.

(1m), and most of them do not require staking, although the taller kinds benefit from the protection of other plants. A few have a gently spicy fragrance.

Because of their bright colors, snapdragons can be tricky to place in a small garden, especially as most of the readily available seed strains are marketed as mixtures of different colors—a design challenge that applies to many popular annuals. Snapdragons look best among other brightly colored flowers. Tall and intermediate forms are useful for providing vertical accents and, if planted in small repeating groups, will not be too imposing. Use the dwarf kinds for edging and in pots.

Sow seed from late winter to mid-spring on a windowsill or with other protection. When you plant snapdragons out in the garden, choose sites in full sun or light shade with good drainage.

A snapdragon for the discerning gardener, *Antirrhinum* 'Night & Day' is a particularly striking plant with dark leaves and mid-height spikes of rich crimson red flowers, each with a silvery white mouth.

True to its name, *Antirrhinum* 'Miniature Magic Carpet' is a low-growing selection that reaches only 6in. (15cm). It has a slightly trailing habit and flowers in a variety of colors.

Antirrhinum majus 'Appleblossom' is tall with spikes of white flowers that have delicate soft pink markings in the throat. Its subtle coloring means it is relatively easy to place, while its height makes it an ideal candidate for creating accents.

Antirrhinum Sonnet series can be relied on for flowers of good quality from early in the season. Produced on bushy plants of medium height, the flower spikes range from red to white and yellow, including shades of burgundy and bronze.

OTHER GOOD ANTIRRHINUMS

Antirrhinum 'Brazilian Carnival' Cherry, orange, carmine, white, and combinations of these, are some of the colors produced by this tall variety.

Antirrhinum 'Jamaican Mist' Soft pastel flower colors on plants of medium height.

Antirrhinum 'Sawyers Old-Fashioned Snapdragons' A comparatively hardy, medium-height antirrhinum, sold as a colorful mixture.

Cosmos

The two species of annual cosmos in cultivation have soft, threadlike, rich green foliage—like that of fennel or dill—and large, round, daisylike flower heads; both foliage and flowers are good for cutting. *Cosmos bipinnatus*, or Mexican aster, is half hardy and among the tallest of annuals, capable of reaching about 5ft. (1.5m) when in flower. *Cosmos sulphureus* is only slightly shorter and is frost-tender. Because they are so tall, cosmos are perfect for infilling toward the back of perennial borders. You do need to be careful, however, because their large flowers have quite an impact and could dwarf other occupants, especially in a small area. Avoid this by giving each plant plenty of space and ensuring that its immediate neighbors are quite large, with contrasting form and color. Good choices include the ethereal *Verbena bonariensis* (see page 92) and dark foliage shrubs such as some elders or *Physocarpus opulifolius* 'Diabolo' (see page 52). Their height also makes cosmos candidates for more experimental use. For example, they make good short-lived hedges. Disguise their stems by planting shorter companions at their feet.

Cosmos grow quickly from seed so can be sown quite late: mid- or even late spring will be early enough. Sow them indoors in seed trays, or *in situ* in late spring. They prefer well-drained soil in full sun.

Cosmos bipinnatus 'Purity' is a choice old variety. There is something hugely satisfying in seeing its large, clean white flowers against the backdrop of fine, feathery green foliage. With its stately habit and long flowering season, this is a useful annual for mixed borders.

For those who like something showy, *Cosmos bipinnatus* 'Picotée' is the cosmos of choice. This selection from the **Sensation** series has pure white flowers edged with rose red. Flowers in the Sensation series (above) are white, pink, or red and particularly large.

The various shades of *Cosmos bipinnatus* 'Sea Shells' mixed—white, crimson and shell pink—make it awkward to fit into some color schemes, but the flowers are worth having for their distinctive petals, each rolled into a cone.

OTHER GOOD COSMOS

Cosmos sulphureus 'Cosmic Yellow' Plenty of bright yellow flowers on short, multibranched plants. 'Cosmic Orange' is also available.

Cosmos bipinnatus 'Gazebo Mixed' At 2ft. (60cm), this is another comparatively short cosmos, ideal for pots or near the front of borders. Flowers in shades of pink and white.

Cosmos bipinnatus Sonata series A worthy dwarf variety, with seed available in pure white (left) or a mixture of pink, red, and white.

Impatiens

The modern impatiens is one of those plants that cottage gardeners of old would have loved to grow. It comes in a wide range of colors, endures all sorts of conditions although it is happiest with a little shade, and just flowers and flowers.

Most of the many kinds of impatiens that we grow today are descendants of the tender perennial *Impatiens walleriana*. Rarely more than 10–12in. (25–30cm) high and usually smaller, they are perfect for the front of beds and for combining with other annuals in pots. The New Guinea-type hybrids are bigger, often with bronzy foliage as well as bright flowers, while the *Impatiens balsamina* cultivars, which are less widely grown, can be even taller but are less extrovert in their flowering.

Single-colored varieties of impatiens are more successful than mixtures when used with other plants. Try them in partial shade with foliage plants such as the trailing, yellow-green, hanging-basket favorite *Helichrysum petiolare* 'Limelight' or the variegated *Plectranthus madagascariensis* 'Variegated Mintleaf'.

Impatiens can be grown from seed (sown in a warm place in early spring), but young plants are so widely available that it hardly seems worthwhile. They will collapse if frosted, so plant them outdoors only when the danger of extreme cold is past. If the plants get leggy in the middle of the season, cut them down to about 3in. (7cm) above soil level. They will soon be flowering profusely again.

The well-established *Impatiens* **Expo** series gives us a reliable, versatile range of impatiens, happier than some in sunshine but content in part shade too. The plants are tightly branched and quite robust, with large, bright flowers in a good range of colors from early summer until the frosts.

Impatiens balsamina (right) grows up to 30in. (75cm) tall and produces its wide-lipped, spurred flowers in the leaf axils. This impatiens looks good with diascias in complementary colors or surrounded by contrasting verbenas.

An ideal choice for small hanging baskets, window boxes, and pots is the compact but fast-growing *Impatiens* **Mini Pixie**. It is packed with colorful flowers, but its blooms are petite and dainty, in scale with the plant. It can quickly be deadheaded by overhead watering—though not in full sun.

One of the attractions of *Impatiens* **Fanfare** is its growth habit: strong, mounded, and trailing branches are covered with flowers in fuchsia, lavender, or orange colors. This makes it a good choice for a hanging basket or tall pot. Grow it on its own or combine it with small-flowered petunias in similar colors.

Love-in-a-mist (Nigella)

There are several annual species in this genus, but *Nigella damascena* and its cultivars are by far the most commonly grown. Above delicate, dill-like foliage, its dainty flowers (pale blue in the species) on thin stalks are supported by a spiky green ruff. The seed pods that follow are puffed out, somewhat like miniature hot-air balloons, and usually have purple-brown markings. Both flowers and pods are good for cutting.

Nigellas are deservedly one of the most popular hardy annuals. They look good with many other plants including hot orange annuals, such as eschscholzias and calendulas, the warm reds and peachy pinks of poppies and dianthus, and any of the pink-flowered hardy geraniums. Their delicate form makes them perfect for softening the impact of more solid, stiff plants like irises and sisyrinchiums but also enables them to mingle easily with other such loose-stemmed plants as the hardy geraniums. Gentle self-seeders, they are ideal for creating a cottage-garden ambience.

Sow love-in-a-mist seed in situ in spring or fall. The best plants come from a fall sowing; they may reach 2ft. (60cm) and make compact bushes. Love-in-a-mist prefers a fertile, sunny site but it is a tolerant plant and will grow in poorer soil, too.

No doubt its supremely talented namesake would have loved *Nigella damascena* 'Miss Jekyll', which has semidouble cornflower blue flowers. This lovely color is perfect for combining with pale, soft yellows such as the spikes of the tree lupin (*Lupinus arboreus*).

The flowers of *Nigella damascena* **'Mulberry Rose'** open creamy pink and darken to deep rose pink. A large group is effective, with flowers at different stages of blushing. Try it with a soft-colored partner such as *Penstemon* 'Apple Blossom' or 'Stapleford Gem'.

All the various love-in-a-mist colors are combined in *Nigella damascena* **Persian Jewels** series. This selection has flowers in shades of blue, lavender, pink, white, and carmine, making eye-catching color associations difficult but enabling it to blend with many different plants in the garden.

A very dwarf variety at only 6in. (15cm), *Nigella damascena* **'Shorty Blue'** grows quickly and rewards careful cultivation with a profusion of dark violet blue flowers. Its tiny size makes it excellent for bedding and containers.

OTHER GOOD LOVE-IN-A-MIST

Nigella damascena 'Flore Pleno' The fully double flowers of this tall strain are in mixed shades of white, pink, and blue.

Nigella damascena 'Oxford Blue' A useful single-colored cultivar of medium height, with double dark blue flowers and dark seed pods.

Nigella damascena 'Miss Jekyll White' The best white seed strain, lovely in part shade, with other pale flowers, or with silver foliage plants.

Nigella papillosa 'Midnight' Unusual dark purple seed pods follow large purplish blue flowers.

Poppy (Papaver)

The brilliant red field poppy, *Papaver rhoeas*, must be among the most familiar of all plants, having as it does such a strong association with both the countryside and with cultivated cornfields as well as the bloodshed of World War I. Although it is a common sight in meadows and on roadsides, the field poppy is not easily coaxed into gardens. However, its relatives do make good garden plants. Easy to grow and quick to bloom, the annual poppies have brightly colored but delicate flowers, ideal for creating splashes of color wherever they are wanted. All produce pepperlike seed pods. The pods of the opium poppies, *Papaver somniferum*, are the most attractive, decorating the garden after the flowers are finished and remaining intact for a long time in dried-flower arrangements. Opium poppies can reach about 3ft. (1m), while most of the other annuals are smaller, but none will be too dominant, even in the smallest of spaces.

Annual poppies are best sown where they are to flower. The seeds are tiny, but you usually get plenty. To ensure even sowing, mix them with some sand and scatter this carefully. Well-drained, fertile soil in a sunny site suits most poppies; they self-seed if they are happy but seldom reproduce their parents exactly.

Among the most popular of the annual poppies, *Papaver rhoeas* Shirley Group is available in a mix of single and double flowers in a lovely range of colors from pink and crimson to orange and white. Unlike their wild ancestor, they do not have a black blotch at the base of the petals.

A voluptuously dark poppy that grows up to 3ft. (90cm) tall, *Papaver somniferum* 'Black Paeony' has frilly, fully double flowers of the deepest purple red. The seed heads are an attractive blue-green.

Papaver commutatum has single, shining crimson blooms with a bold black blotch at the base of each petal. It is widely available as the selection 'Ladybird'.

Papaver somniferum 'Hen and Chickens' has attractive large, pale pink-lilac flowers, but its real value is in its seed pods. Several little seed pods are produced around the base of each pepperlike main seed pod: hence the cultivar name.

OTHER GOOD POPPIES

Papaver rhoeas Angels' Choir Group A delectable mix of double-flowered poppies in a range of soft colors.

Papaver rhoeas 'Mother of Pearl' Group A delightful selection, with flowers in mother-of-pearl shades and bicolors, including gray and gray-white, soft blues and reds, lilac, and peach.

Papaver rhoeas 'Picotée' A development of 'Angels' Choir', selected for their picotee-edged petals and bicoloring.

Papaver somniferum var. *paeoniflorum* Opium poppies with fully double flowers, in mixed colors or single color selections.

Papaver somniferum 'Seriously Scarlet' Truly scarlet, the flowers have dark purple centers and very ruffled petal edges.

Salvia

Perhaps best known for culinary sage, *Salvia officinalis* (see page 138), the genus *Salvia* contains another species that is also extensively planted, if not always recognized as a sage: *Salvia splendens* (zone 5–9). Because it flowers so reliably for such a long period, this little plant is probably the most widely grown of all bedding annuals. People who think they do not like bedding plants may well have this one in mind. It is best known in its ubiquitous short-growing, bright red-flowered form. Other species grown as annuals are more discreet in their displays: the elegant *Salvia patens* (zone 8–10) and *Salvia farinacea* (zone 8–10), for instance, and the rather more down-to-earth but nonetheless very attractive *Salvia viridis* var. *comata* (zone 8–10, annual).

Salvia splendens is best used as intended, for bedding or in pots. *Salvia patens* is superb in a terra-cotta pot, which shows off its flowers perfectly; it can be lost in a bed of bright annuals but is good among airy, gray-leaved plants such as perovskia, artemisia, santolina, and smaller echinops. These also make effective partners for *Salvia farinacea* and *Salvia viridis* var. *comata*, though the latter could hold its own among brighter companions.

Salvia splendens (z. 5–9) is an indefatigable performer, producing flowers in a range of colors, depending on the selection, including the well-known brilliant red, but also rich, dark purple, pale peach, salmon, and bicolors. Generally under 12in. (30cm), this hardworking plant can look wonderful with gray-leaved or white-flowered companions; single-color cultivars are good in color-themed plantings.

The decorative part of *Salvia viridis* var. *comata* (*Salvia horminum* or annual clary) (z. 8–10, ann.) is the showy bracts that grow on the spikes above the tiny flowers. These may be blue-purple, pink, or white and often have darker veining; they last into the fall. The plant itself is fairly short and upright—good for the front of the border.

Salvia patens (z. 8–10) looks like a delicate rarity yet is easily raised from seed and flowers reliably. The flowers are an eye-catching royal blue—giving the plant its common name, gentian sage. The flowers open over a long period but in modest numbers, which adds to their charm. **'Cambridge Blue'** is pale blue, lovely but not quite as special.

Salvia farinacea 'Victoria' (above) (z. 8–10) bears flowers and bracts in a deep shade of blue on purple stems. The overall effect is very distinctive. Other *Salvia farinacea* cultivars include **'Cirrus'**, which is white, and **'Strata'**, with blue flowers and gray-white stems.

OTHER GOOD SALVIAS

Salvia coccinea 'Coral Nymph' (z. 4–10) An intriguing color blend of pale pink with a coral pink lower lip.

Salvia coccinea 'Lady in Red' (z. 4–10) Bright red flowers set off by rich, glossy dark green foliage, like a classy version of *Salvia splendens*.

Bulbs, corms, and tubers

Even in a very small garden, it somehow always seems to be possible to find room for a few more bulbs. Most bulbous plants occupy little lateral space and, performing for only a limited time, they are particularly easy to fit in beside, underneath, or behind other plants. Many of them will come up year after year and, for only a minimal investment, can be relied upon to bring good cheer to any garden.

Container-grown hyacinths and tulips inject a dash of instant color into an early-spring border. Strongly structured *Fritillaria imperialis* 'Rubra' makes an exotic-looking focal point.

Bulbs, corms, and tubers are extremely important elements in a successful mixed garden. They may not contribute permanent structure, but they are invaluable for seasonal color and for an instant effect in new plantings. It is not necessary to wait patiently for them to mature: many bulbs will give of their best in their very first season. Others go from strength to strength, multiplying happily and looking more and more comfortable every year.

Bulbs are remarkably good value for money and many become permanent residents in borders. For use in pots and containers, bulbs are cheap enough to be considered a disposable commodity: allow yourself the indulgence of choosing new bulbs each year and don't be afraid to experiment with different colors and varieties.

CHOOSING BULBS

Bear in mind that for every "old favorite" that is available year after year there are dozens more species and cultivars that are just as easy to grow but are not as well known.

When buying species bulbs, check their environmental credentials. Buy only those that have been grown in the nursery from reputable cultivated stock and not harvested from the wild. Always buy more than you think you need, and select healthy specimens— that is, bulbs that are firm to the touch,

BULBS FOR GRAVEL *Allium caeruleum* • *Allium karataviense* • *Anemone* × *fulgens* • *Chionodoxa sardensis* •

show no signs of mold, and have not begun to sprout.

As with all plants, choosing the right bulb for the right place is important. This means considering the bulb's requirements during its dormant season as well as when it is in flower. For example, some bulbs need to be baked by the summer sun after flowering, while others cannot tolerate drying out so will benefit from deep planting in the shade of deciduous shrubs that will shield them from hot sunshine. Many spring bulbs suffer if a period of dry weather coincides with the time when they are replenishing their reserves after flowering, so they may need watering if rain is scarce. Few bulbs thrive in continuous deep shade.

PLANTING BULBS

Having purchased your bulbs, plant them as soon as possible. Bulbs deteriorate in storage, developing molds and rotting in a damp atmosphere, or drying out if their environment is too warm or too dry. Select a planting position carefully,

Many bulbs flower best with some sun. *Cyclamen hederifolium*, on the other hand, is shade-tolerant and thrives in the company of woodland ferns.

> ### BULBS AND NONBULBS
>
> All plants that have an underground storage organ are loosely called bulbs, but, botanically speaking, not all of them are true bulbs. Some (crocuses and crocosmias) are corms: round, lumpy underground stems that completely renew themselves every year. Others (dahlias and cyclamen) are tubers: solid, potato-like swollen roots or underground stems. Certain irises, as well as other plants, have rhizomes, which are thickened, horizontally spreading stems that usually form roots on their underside. True bulbs, such as those of the lily, tulip, and narcissus, have layers of roughly concentric fleshy scales like an onion.

considering not only the bulb's needs as to soil, moisture, and light but also a suitable planting design (see page 183). Plant them in generous groups for the best effect. An often-quoted rule of thumb is to plant bulbs in twice or three times their own depth of soil; in free-draining soils they can be planted a little deeper. Most appreciate a little slow-acting fertilizer to sustain them in future seasons. In heavy soils, add grit to improve drainage as many bulbs will simply rot if they are planted in waterlogged ground.

After flowering, it is important to allow bulbs to die off naturally and not to remove the foliage while it is still green. Bulbs, corms, and tubers are underground storage organs that need to be fed if the plant is to live on. This happens naturally as nutrients return from the foliage to the bulb after it has flowered, and this process should not be interrupted. Sometimes, clumps of bulbs become congested and need to be lifted, split up, and replanted, singly or in smaller clumps, in revitalized soil. Wait until after flowering to do this.

Many bulbs, corms, and tubers can stay in the ground permanently; others are too tender to withstand winter temperatures or may simply be too delicate for year-round life in the open ground. In a small garden it can be convenient to use bulbs as seasonal bedding, lifted and replaced after they have finished flowering. You may question whether it is worth the bother of lifting and storing them, but if you do, make sure they are properly dried off, clearly labeled, and stored in suitable conditions away from pests such as rodents or aphids.

Many bulbs naturalize very well in grass. Particularly in a small space, this demands careful management and a mowing regime that minimizes untidiness while meeting the bulbs' needs. Early dwarf spring bulbs such as **winter aconites**, early **snowdrops**, **crocuses**, and **chionodoxas** are ideal, for their leaves will not be obstrusive and are likely to be quite well withered by the time the grass needs to be cut. For summer and fall varieties, mow the grass closely just before they are due to flower and then again in late fall if necessary. Careful planning when choosing varieties to plant together is also the key to success.

Crocus chrysanthus • Crocus speciosus • Narcissus 'Minnow' • Scilla bifolia • Tulipa linifolia • Tulipa tarda •

Bulbs for winter and spring

The sight of bulb shoots nosing their way through bare, cold ground in midwinter is surely the most eagerly awaited promise of spring. Bulbs continue to work their magic as days lengthen, never failing to surprise and delight when weather and light conditions allow their variously shaped, tight buds suddenly to open out into little explosions of much-needed color.

Iris danfordiae

A surprising number of bulbs come into flower well before winter's end, every one of them worth growing for their ability to brave harsh conditions and confirm the promise of a new season. Among the earliest is the little winter aconite, *Eranthis hyemalis* (zone 3–8). This is one of those puzzling plants that, for no apparent reason, will flourish and multiply in some gardens but will not grow at all in others. If you have not succeeded with ordinary bought bulbs, the best advice, as with other tricky bulbs, is to obtain a few plants "in the green," either begged from a friend who has thriving aconite colonies or purchased from one of the nurseries

Eranthis hyemalis

Iris 'Harmony'

that sell growing bulbs in spring. Plant them in a border initially—somewhere under a deciduous tree or shrub is fine. They seed readily when conditions suit them, and with luck they will begin to multiply in a year or two and you can

spread them around the garden by transplanting them after flowering. This is a perfect bulb for naturalizing in grass: each globular yellow flower, charmingly set in a ruff of leaves, makes its contribution to a golden flowering carpet, especially on fine days when the flowers open their petals to the sun.

Other gladdening flowers for late winter color include a group of beautiful little **irises** (zone 5–8). The earliest of all is yellow *Iris danfordiae*, soon followed by its blue and purple relatives, of which the best are *Iris* **'Harmony'** (a beautiful, early deep blue) and *Iris* **'George'** (purple, also early). Flowering a little later are the pale blue *Iris* **'Cantab'**, deep purple-blue *Iris reticulata,* and the fragrant reddish purple *Iris* **'J.S. Dijt'**. When you buy these bulbs it may be best to think of them as annuals. Although they are perfectly hardy, and will sometimes form good perennial clumps in the garden, not all can be relied on to

GOOD COMPANIONS: SPRING BULBS

Tulipa praestans (1) (z. 4–8) is perfect with *Euphorbia cyparissias* 'Fens Ruby' (2) (z. 4–8) in a dry, sunny border. The euphorbia's red-tipped, lime green foliage sets off the tulips' scarlet flowers, then smothers their withering leaves.

Tulipa 'Prinses Irene' (3) (z. 4–8) and *Ajuga reptans* (4) (z. 4–7) might have been made for each other: a stunning, unusual color combination of blue and orange, with more than a harmonizing hint of violet on the outside of the tulip's petals.

176

BULBS FOR NATURALIZING IN GRASS *Anemone apennina* • *Chionodoxa forbesii* • *Eranthis hyemalis* •

Crocus chrysanthus 'Ladykiller'

Muscari armeniacum 'Valerie Finnis'

flower in future years. However, bulbs of the common varieties are not expensive, and even if they do flower only once it is worth every penny to have such exotic-looking flowers so early in the season. Generously planted in shallow pots, they can be brought into the house or sunroom to be admired in comfort. In the garden, plant them quite deeply in a sunny, sheltered spot where you will see them every day—the base of a house wall is ideal.

Crocuses (zone 3–8) are among the more familiar spring bulbs and are widely available and inexpensive. Although their flowers are short-lived and open only on fine days, many types will self-sow once established, and it is worth trying a number of varieties in different parts of the garden (always where they will receive some sunshine) and allowing them to form colonies where they are happiest. For naturalizing, try the species *Crocus tommasinianus* and its cultivars, all in shades of purple and lavender (there is also a white form). *Crocus chrysanthus* is another reliable early crocus with many named hybrid offspring in various colors. Some of the best are *Crocus chrysanthus* 'Cream Beauty', *Crocus chrysanthus* 'Blue Pearl', *Crocus chrysanthus* 'Snow Bunting' (white), *Crocus chrysanthus* 'Ladykiller' (white and deep purple), and *Crocus chrysanthus* 'Zwanenburg Bronze' (yellow flowers with purplish shading on the outside of each petal). All are good for naturalizing in grass.

For something larger and more showy in pots and borders, or for naturalizing in coarser grass, buy the later-flowering **Dutch hybrid crocuses**: try white with yellow, or white and purple with the purple-striped *Crocus vernus* ssp. *albiflorus* 'Pickwick'.

Muscari (grape hyacinths, zone 3–8) are well-known spring flowers, but most of them seed abundantly, so deadhead the flowers to avoid a rash of seedlings. The common type, *Muscari armeniacum*, is a resilient plant of a very good blue, but can be rather coarse and invasive, so reserve it for difficult spots such as at the base of a hedge where little else will grow. More choice varieties include the pretty two-toned *Muscari latifolium*, the white-flowered *Muscari azureum* 'Album', and the pretty, powder blue *Muscari armeniacum* 'Valerie Finnis'.

Blue is a very useful color in the spring garden, giving a wonderfully fresh effect with white, new greens, and the ubiquitous yellows. **Scillas** and

CONNOISSEUR'S CHOICE: UNUSUAL EARLY BULBS

Very early flowers really earn their space in a small garden, instantly acquiring star quality and status simply because there are so few of them. You might have to obtain the following choice varieties from specialty nurseries, but the excitement of growing something unusual, especially at the bleakest time of the year, makes all the extra trouble worthwhile.

Cyclamen coum (left) (z. 6–8) If you can find the right place for it (well-drained, leafy soil with shade in summer), this little cyclamen will produce carpets of pink, sometimes white, flowers in early spring,

Galanthus reginae-olgae (z. 6–9) A plant for those who like their snowdrops to be early, this one from the eastern Mediterranean flowers from late fall.

Iris 'Katharine Hodgkin' (left) (z. 5–8) A distinguished, subtly colored hybrid of *Iris reticulata*, with cream and yellow flowers veined and stippled in blue.

Leucojum vernum (left) (z. 3–8) Shorter and earlier to flower than the summer snowflake (*Leucojum aestivum*), the spring snowflake is a good partner in shade for evergreen ferns, hellebores, and early scillas and narcissi.

Narcissus asturiensis (z. 6–7) A very select early, pale yellow miniature daffodil barely 4in. (10cm) high. Best in acidic or neutral soil.

Tulipa turkestanica (left) (z. 4–8) A species tulip with several nodding ivory flowers on each stem. They open wide in sunshine to reveal bright yellow centers. Plant in a dry, sunny, sheltered place.

Galanthus nivalis • Leucojum aestivum • Narcissus bulbocodium • Narcissus pseudonarcissus •

Anemone coronaria De Caen Group

Fritillaria imperialis 'Rubra'

Fritillaria imperialis 'Lutea'

Scilla siberica

Erythronium dens-canis

the related **chionodoxas** are very easy tiny blue flowers whose bulbs usually multiply well. For awkward, shady places, try to obtain the very early *Scilla mischtschenkoana* (zone 5–8). Its flowers are a pale, silvery blue with a darker stripe on each petal. Soon after it come *Scilla bifolia* (zone 5–8) and *Chionodoxa luciliae* (zone 5–8), both with star-shaped purple-blue flowers. The best known, *Scilla siberica* (zone 5–8), is later, but its little flowers are a truer blue. All these multiply well in borders or in gravel and are unobtrusive after flowering. Grow them in a mixed planting with the daisylike flowers of *Anemone blanda* (zone 5–8) or *Anemone apennina* (zone 6–9).

A different type of anemone, easy to grow and valuable for early color, is *Anemone coronaria* (zone 7–9). Common forms include the single *Anemone coronaria* De Caen Group

and the **Saint Bridgid Group**, with semidouble flowers. Both offer a range of jewellike colors: red, mauve, pink, and blue, with a velvety, blackish center. Soak the knobbly, dry tubers before planting them quite deeply in full sun.

Entirely different conditions—cool, damp soil in partial shade—are the preferred habitat of most **erythroniums** (zone 4–8). These are among the shapeliest of spring flowers, with dainty upturned petals. Generally available are the golden yellow *Erythronium* 'Pagoda' and the more choice cultivar *Erythronium californicum* 'White Beauty', with prettily patterned leaves. Mottled foliage is also a feature of two species with pink flowers, *Erythronium revolutum* (North American trout lily) and *Erythroniumdens-canis* (European dog's-tooth violet). Natural woodland plants, these both self-sow given the right conditions.

Damp meadows are the natural habitat of the delightful *Fritillaria meleagris* (snakeshead fritillary, zone 4–8). Even if you cannot persuade it to naturalize, it is worth planting a few bulbs to enjoy its extraordinary checkered bell-shaped flowers—mostly pinkish purple but sometimes white—at close range. An unlikely relative of these modest little flowers is *Fritillaria imperialis* (the crown imperial, zone 4–8). This stately plant is a true showpiece, in a pot or in a border. The tall, sturdy stems carry a cluster of downturned orange or yellow bell-shaped flowers topped, pineapple-style, by a large tuft of green bracts. Look closely inside the flowers to see the symmetrical collection of "teardrops"—but be prepared for the plant's strong, foxy smell. Unfortunately, crown imperials are prey to the scarlet lily beetle (see page 185), so if you spot these red pests destroy them at once.

Snowdrops (Galanthus)

Galanthus 'Atkinsii' with the lovely white-marbled, deep green leaves of *Arum italicum* ssp. *italicum* 'Marmoratum' is a classic early spring combination for the garden or in vases.

Almost everyone welcomes snowdrops as one of the first signs that spring is around the corner, and it is hard not to admire the resilience of these little flowers as they battle on through the worst of winter weather.

Snowdrops have attracted a large following of enthusiasts, collectors, and expert growers. Alongside 18 known species of *Galanthus*, around 400 different named forms now exist, and it is possible to have snowdrops in flower from fall through to late spring.

While in many gardens snowdrops appear in huge numbers, some gardeners find the bulbs difficult to establish. This will often be because they have dried out too much in the process of being harvested and packaged for sale. It is usually better to acquire them "in the green," that is shortly after flowering, with leaves still intact. Some mail-order nurseries sell them in this form. Alternatively, acquire a few bulbs in spring, after flowering, from a friend, or buy the bulbs that may be found for sale from the growing number of bulb societies. Plant them without delay, and keep them well watered in their first season. With most varieties, each single bulb will soon form a clump that can be split up, after flowering in spring, and replanted to form new colonies.

Galanthus nivalis (z. 4–8) is the common snowdrop: the most widely available kind, the most frequently seen, and usually the least expensive to buy, especially in large quantities. Buy them "in the green" if you can. Once established, they will multiply by both division and seeding.

Galanthus 'Magnet' (z. 4–8), a hybrid bred in the 1880s, is one of the prettiest snowdrops, generally agreed to be reliable. Each large, snowy white flower hangs from a slender, long, arching pedicel, or stalk, which enables it to sway gracefully in the wind.

You will probably have to buy your first few bulbs of *Galanthus* 'Atkinsii' (see top of page) (z. 4–8) from a specialty nursery, but it is worth the trouble and cost. It is a large, handsome, very early snowdrop. Each bulb soon grows into a clump, keeping you generously supplied for many years, with welcome bunches of winter flowers for the house.

The double snowdrop *Galanthus nivalis* f. *pleniflorus* 'Flore Pleno' (z. 4–8) is a choice plant to be viewed at close range, preferably at eye level so that its inner ruff of tightly packed frilly petals can be seen. Like most double flowers, it does not set seed but will slowly form clumps from individual bulbs.

OTHER GOOD SNOWDROPS

Galanthus elwesii (z. 5–8) Large-flowered, very early snowdrop with wide grayish leaves.

Galanthus nivalis 'Tiny' (z. 4–8) Miniature snowdrop; grows at most 4in. (10cm) high but is quite vigorous.

Galanthus plicatus ssp. *byzantinus* (z. 6–8) Very early and quite tall, with strong green markings on the inner tepals.

Galanthus 'S. Arnott' (z. 4–8) A shapely, comfortable-looking, well-scented snowdrop.

Daffodils (Narcissus)

There is never any shortage of daffodils in spring. It might be tempting, if space is very limited, to grow something more unusual instead and enjoy them in other people's gardens. However, no spring garden seems complete without them, and gardening in a confined space gives a good opportunity to try some of the many delightful smaller varieties instead of the conventional, large-cupped daffodils.

Choose narcissi that give the best value for space. Early flowers are an advantage: plants that bring spring forward are especially valuable in a small garden, and early-flowering narcissi tend to last longer and be appreciated more. Fragrance is another quality to look for—valuable if blooms are cut for the house and welcome surprise in the garden on those first war days of early spring (see pages 124–6).

Even compact daffodils need careful management in small garden if their fading foliage, which is untidy and hard to ignore, is not to spoil later displays. The leaves bulbous plants should not be cut off before they have withered, because the dying foliage restores food to the bulbs for flowering in subsequent years. The best way disguise it is to grow bulbs in an inconspicuous place the border, mixed with herbaceous perennials and beneath or behind deciduous shrubs, whose leaves open at the right time to hide the fading narcissi.

Narcissus 'Tête-à-Tête' (z. 5–7) is generally agreed to be one of the best small daffodils, early-flowering, very reliable, and usually multiplying well. Its size and earliness mean that its dying foliage is not obstrusive later in the spring. The miniature golden yellow flowers are good for picking.

Narcissus 'Jenny' (z. 5–7) has very elegantly shaped flowers with swept-back petals, opening very pale yellow and fading to white. It is happy in sun or semi-shade and is ideal for planting schemes that would not suit bright yellow daffodils.

The resilient little *Narcissus* 'Jack Snipe' (z. 4–9) is long-lasting, dainty, and good for picking. It multiplies quite well, even when grown in poor soil or with a fair amount of shade.

One of the best miniatures, **Narcissus 'Minnow'** (z. 4–9) is the ideal scaled-down narcissus for a small space. It carries several primrose yellow flowers on each stem. A sunny site will encourage it to flower more freely.

Narcissus 'February Gold' (z. 5–7) is a very popular, well-established early daffodil with compact, bright yellow flowers on a plant of medium height.

Narcissus cyclamineus (z. 5–7) is expensive to buy but very unusual: small and bright yellow, with strong swept-back petals.

Narcissus 'Hawera' (z. 4–9) is a very graceful, pale yellow narcissus with several pendent flowers on each stem.

Narcissus 'Jetfire' (left) (z. 4–9), a popular early-flowering hybrid, has bright yellow petals and an orange trumpet.

Narcissus 'Thalia' (right) (z. 4–9) is a pretty, popular mid-season narcissus with up to three pure white blooms per stem.

Narcissus 'Rip van Winkle' (z. 4–9) is a strange, rather dainty double narcissus with a starburst of narrow, ragged yellow petals.

Tulips (Tulipa)

With their formal structure and wide range of striking colors, tulips have always had a unique role in the spring garden. Since they tend to dominate, in a small space it is probably better not to have more than two or three types in flower at one time. If a collection of different kinds is chosen to flower successively, it is possible to have tulips in flower for many weeks.

Tulips are often used as spring bedding plants, to be lifted and dried off after flowering and replaced with other seasonal plants. If space is precious, it may be better to grow them in a border, integrated with other plants. In well-drained soil they may thrive for many years, or they may well dwindle and need replacing. Newly bought bulbs usually do well in pots their first year, after which they can be planted out in a border.

Tulips look best when grown in groups of a single type. Plant them quite deeply, and add a little slow-acting fertilizer to keep the bulbs flowering.

Invaluable for the earliest bright color in borders and containers, *Tulipa praestans* 'Fusilier' (left) (z. 4–8) is very hardy, free-flowering, and easy to grow. The closely related, more unusual *Tulipa praestans* 'Unicum' (z. 4–8) has similar scarlet flowers and variegated hostalike leaves.

Tulipa 'Prinses Irene' (z. 4–8) is a robust and attractive tulip, worth growing for its unique coloring of subtle orange with purplish tones. It looks especially good with deep blues and bronze, an unusual and striking color scheme for spring.

The sophisticated *Tulipa* 'Queen of Night' (z. 4–8) is almost the elusive 'black tulip'. Its deep, velvety maroon flowers look especially effective among plants with silver foliage, and with other tulips in shades of pink and mauve.

Tulipa 'Purissima' (z. 4–8) is a good, reliable, early-flowering white tulip, ideal to plant in drifts in a spring border with narcissi, pulmonarias, and primroses. It will tolerate partial shade and usually survives happily from year to year in well-drained soil.

OTHER GOOD TULIPS

Tulipa 'Ballerina' (z. 4–8) A tall, striking, slightly fragrant tulip with orange, lilylike flowers.

Tulipa 'Black Hero' (left) (z. 4–8) A tall, sumptuous double tulip with glossy, very dark petals.

Tulipa 'Giuseppe Verdi' (z. 4–8) Large, early flowers that are yellow with outer petals flamed red.

Tulipa linifolia (z. 4–8) A dwarf wild tulip for a well-drained, sunny site. The scarlet flowers are beautifully shaped when closed and flamboyant when open in the sun.

Tulipa linifolia Batalinii Group (z. 4–8) Small tulips (left, 'Bright Gem'), which come in a range of lovely shades of yellow and apricot.

Tulipa 'Maytime' (z. 4–8) Sturdy yet elegant lily-flowered tulip with purplish pink petals outlined in white.

Tulipa 'Peach Blossom' (left) (z. 4–8) A rose pink, early double tulip, pretty with forget-me-nots.

Tulipa 'West Point' (z. 4–8) Justly well known and widely grown; lily-flowered tulip with elegant yellow blooms.

Bulbs for summer and fall

It is perfectly possible to keep an effective garden display going all summer using shrubs, perennials, and annuals, but the addition of a few suitable bulbs, corms, or tubers can give even the smallest of spaces a tremendous boost. The great thing about bulbs is the surprise element: they can emerge from the soil unexpectedly and can prolong the season with bright color that lasts well into fall.

A well-planned garden planted with perennials alone will not need additional planting for color in midsummer, but there are a few unusual bulbous plants that might be added as a small indulgence. One is the delightful, easy *Triteleia laxa* 'Koningin Fabiola' ('Queen Fabiola', sometimes still found as *Brodiaea*) (zone 6–10). It resembles florists' freesia, with its modest habit

Babiana stricta

Triteleia laxa 'Koningin Fabiola'

and slender, wiry stems, but its funnellike flowers are a deep purple-blue that complements almost any other border plant. The species is found in the prairies, and the cultivar prefers a sunny site, where its bulbs will ripen for next year. It is a good plant for gravel.

Another unusual and compact purple-blue flower is *Babiana stricta* (zone 9–11). It is tender, flowering as a spring perennial in its native South Africa but marketed in colder zones as a corm for summer flowering.

It is hard to associate **wild gladioli** with the huge hybrids of flower shows

and florists, but there are several compact gladiolus species that are perfect for summer borders. The pretty, pure magenta flowers of *Gladiolus communis* ssp. *byzantinus* (zone 6–8) look good with silver foliage and with hardy geraniums in a well-drained soil. In the right conditions, the plants will multiply with great enthusiasm. Surplus corms may eventually need weeding out. Two useful white gladioli are the

tender but very beautiful *Gladiolus callianthus,* or *Gladiolus murielae* (zone 8–10), with slightly drooping, fragrant flowers that are borne in late summer and fall, and the attractive, earlier-flowering hybrid *Gladiolus* 'The Bride' (zone 6–8).

Related to gladioli and irises, **crocosmias** are another group of useful spiky summer plants for small spaces. In garden centers and nurseries, they are more frequently sold as pot-grown perennials than as dried corms, which is useful because you can be sure of the color if you buy them in flower. The stateliest is the well-known *Crocosmia* 'Lucifer' (zone 7–9), which is bright red and 4ft. (1.2m) tall, but there are many shorter cultivars in vibrant shades of red, yellow, and orange.

Dahlias are good companions for spiky plants such as crocosmias. Bright and brash, they integrate well into mixed borders and some are hardy enough to withstand most winters outdoors in milder areas. One of the best of these is probably now the most familiar of all, *Dahlia* 'Bishop of Llandaff' (zone 9–11). Deep red, semidouble flowers are backed by fern-like bronze-purple foliage that deserves garden space on its own merits, quite irrespective of the flowers. Dahlia breeders are producing new dahlias all the time, and with well over

Crocosmia 'Lucifer'

SOME BULBS THAT SELF-SEED *Allium* • *Chionodoxa* • *Crocus tommasinianus* • *Cyclamen* • *Eranthis hyemalis* •

Dahlia 'Bishop of Llandaff'

Cyclamen hederifolium

1,000 cultivars available there are dahlias of every color and size for every garden, however small.

Bulbs, corms, and tubers can provide some wonderfully uplifting surprises in late summer and fall, emerging from the ground fresh and colorful when many other plants have begun to look tired. Among the first to emerge are the distinctive flowers of *Cyclamen hederifolium* (zone 7–9). Their long-lived tubers are a great asset in a small garden. They are surprisingly tolerant of shade and drought, producing not only beautiful pink and white flowers but also, later in fall, lovely marbled leaves with many different patterns. The foliage lasts all through the winter and makes a good foil for snowdrops, ferns, and many other winter plants. Cyclamen like humus-rich soil and, if given the right conditions, will self-seed generously. Look for self-sown seedlings in the fall when the leaves of mature plants appear.

The first autumn rains after a dry period are usually the cue that **fall crocuses** have been waiting for. *Crocus speciosus* (zone 3–8) is always a pleasant surprise when it suddenly appears so late in the growing season, its delicate, veined, lavender blue goblets each framing a brilliant orange-

red stigma inside. This crocus looks good grown in borders or in grass. Its leaves are like those of an ordinary crocus, but they do not appear until early spring.

The leafless, showy flowers of **colchicums** resemble those of crocuses,

Colchicum autumnale

but they are unrelated. Colchicums need to be positioned with care in a garden, both on account of their strident mauve-pink coloring and because in spring they make huge leaves that tend to die off ungracefully. The British native meadow saffron, *Colchicum autumnale* (zone 3–9), is just one of a number of varieties. There is also an exotic-looking double form, *Colchicum* 'Waterlily' (zone 3–9), as well as beautiful white forms, one of which is *Colchicum speciosum* 'Album' (zone 3–9).

Nerines are tender natives of South Africa and so they like a dry, sunny climate. Many need a greenhouse but, with only the protection of a warm wall, *Nerine bowdenii* (zone 9–10) makes a truly grand finale to the bulb year with its exotic sugar pink flowers providing a fine show well into late fall.

Nerine bowdenii

COMBINING BULBS WITH OTHER PLANTS

When planting bulbs, try to picture them with their companion plants as they flower, considering the combination in terms not only of compatible color but also of contrasting structure. Many bulbs and corms, such as tulips, alliums, or crocosmias, have a strong, definite structure that is best partnered by plants with small, feathery flowers and foliage.

In existing borders, try to remember what else might be in the ground where you are planting bulbs, even if you can't see it at planting time. Many a new planting scheme is spoiled because of unintentional clashes with forgotten bulbs that were already in the ground.

When planting bulbs, it is a good idea to ensure that they will not spoil the show by being too conspicuous as their foliage withers. Deciduous shrubs and herbaceous perennials are your best allies here, especially with spring-flowering bulbs. A bit of clever organization will ensure that they can cover up (or at least distract attention from) dying bulb foliage.

Erythronium dens-canis • Fritillaria meleagris • Gladiolus communis ssp. *byzantinus • Lilium regale • Muscari •*

Alliums

Distinctive globular flower heads, often held aloft on tall, stiff stems, ensure that the ornamental onions or alliums have a valuable architectural role in the early summer garden. Many species continue to earn their space after flowering, retaining their seed heads for months. Most alliums also dry well for indoor arrangements and can be used to make magical holiday decorations.

The starry globes of *Allium cristophii* are always a talking point. Hardy geraniums make a good partner, hiding the alliums' fading leaves.

The taller alliums succeed in any good soil in a sunny position, preferably not too dry. They are fine partners for many other plants of contrasting shapes and colors. It suits them particularly well to grow among low shrubs and perennials, which help prevent them from drying out and also hide the lower leaves of the alliums. In many species, these are already dying off at flowering time and rather spoil the effect if they are visible.

Most alliums are very easy to grow, setting seed enthusiastically. The self-sown seedlings take a few years to reach flowering size, but they give colonies a comfortable, settled look that is worth waiting for.

The tall, sturdy *Allium hollandicum* 'Purple Sensation' (z. 5–9) is one of the most richly colored alliums. It looks best planted in generous groups and is a good foil for silver, lime green, and other purple and mauve shades.

OTHER GOOD ALLIUMS

Allium karataviense (z. 5–9) A dwarf allium for the front of a border or growing in gravel. Two broad, glaucous, furrowed leaves hug each flower globe.

Allium moly (z. 4–10) This little allium has yellow flowers in early summer.

Allium neapolitanum (z. 4–10) A compact, dainty, white-flowered allium which (in moderation) is a self-seeder.

Allium schubertii (z. 5–9) More tender but with an exquisite structure, like a sparkler captured in mid-spray.

Allium cristophii (z. 4–10) never fails to provoke admiration with its large, beautifully structured globular heads of metallic, pale lilac stars. Though the stems sometimes bend over at the base, the flower heads often retain their structure right through to winter.

All alliums are worth a look each day as their flowers open. Flowering later than most of the other alliums, *Allium sphaerocephalon* (z. 4–8) lifts a late-summer border with its solid, oval flower heads of purplish pink and green on tall, slender stems. It needs good drainage and full sun.

Nectaroscordum siculum (above) (z. 6–10) Highly fashionable plant, a close relative of alliums. Interesting structure, with seed heads turning from drooping to upright as they mature.

Lilies (Lilium)

For many people the lily is the queen of bulbs, a glamorous showpiece of the garden in summer. Dedicated breeders have produced lilies in a huge range of colors, shapes, and sizes, and with varying flowering times. Many are easy to grow, and there are numerous compact types that are suitable for pots and for the smallest of gardens.

For growing in borders, the species lilies are hard to beat, and provided you choose ones that are compatible with your soil type, they will usually settle in and give masses of flowers every year with little trouble. They are best grown among other plants such as low shrubs, which will protect their tender spring shoots from hard frosts. Never allow lily bulbs to dry out before planting.

If you grow lilies in containers, it is a good idea to repot them every other year, in early spring, storing the pots out of heavy rain and hard frost. Deadhead all lilies after flowering, but leave the stems to die down naturally, eventually cutting them down in fall.

An increasing problem for gardeners in the northeastern states is the scarlet lily beetle (*Lilioceris lilii*), which eats the foliage. Check the plants regularly and remove and destroy any beetles, eggs, or larvae.

The classic lily of cottage gardens is *Lilium candidum*, (z. 6–8) the Madonna lily, which is almost evergreen, with beautiful, highly fragrant white flowers. It needs a sunny position, sheltered from cold winds, and likes to be planted more shallowly than other lilies.

Lilium regale (z. 3–8) is one of the very best lilies for borders or large pots, combining stately, strong-stemmed white flowers with a very powerful fragrance. It carries several large, elegant white trumpets on each stem for quite a long season. It is tolerant of a wide range of conditions including alkaline soils.

Lilium 'Aphrodite' (z. 4–8) is one of many attractive dwarf cultivars bred for growing in pots. Its warm pink, double flowers are pollen-free, so it is a good lily for allergy sufferers.

OTHER GOOD LILIES

Lilium cernuum (left) (z. 4–8) Compact turkscap species with small pink or lilac flowers.

Lilium 'Fata Morgana' (z. 4–8) A double yellow, pollen-free lily.

Lilium longiflorum 'White American' (z. 7–8) Well-scented, large green-tipped white trumpets in midsummer, on a compact plant. Good for containers and for cutting.

Lilium 'Mona Lisa' (left) (z. 3–8) A fragrant, free-flowering dwarf hybrid in deep rose pink fading to pale pink. Good in a pot.

Lilium 'Orange Pixie' (z. 4–8) One of the Pixie lilies group, which come in various colors including orange, pink, and white. They are robust dwarf varieties perfectly suited to pots.

Lilium pardalinum (z. 5–8) Bears orange-red turkscap flowers. Naturalizes well in moist soil.

Lilium speciosum var. *rubrum* (left) (z. 4–8) Late-flowering lily, deep pink and fragrant. Dislikes alkaline soil.

Lilium martagon (z. 4–7) is another fairly reliable border lily. A hardy and long-lived turkscap, it flowers in midsummer and often naturalizes well. The species is purplish pink, and several color forms include the deep maroon *Lilium martagon* var. *cattaniae* and the lovely, pure white *Lilium martagon* var. *album* (right), which is good for a shady site.

Author's choice: top 20 performance plants

In a small space, especially, it is important to have something interesting to look at throughout the year. Some plants make a uniquely valuable contribution in at least one particular season. Others simply never go off duty, looking respectable whatever the month. The most successful all-year gardens usually combine plants of both types. The following selection from the many featured in this book represents tried and tested, reliable favorites that are relatively compact, easy to look after, and comfortable in the company of other plants. They are all worth considering for any small space.

SPRING

 Euonymus fortunei 'Emerald Gaiety' (pages 45, 46) (z. 5–8) Compact, white-variegated evergreen shrub that looks good all year in sun or shade.

 Clematis 'Frances Rivis' (page 77) (z. 3–9) Spring climber with a generous crop of elegant, blue, bell-shaped flowers, white inside.

 Pulmonaria 'Lewis Palmer' (page 84) (z. 3–7) Low herbaceous perennial for part shade, with spotted, ground-covering leaves and blue flowers.

 Narcissus 'Tête-à-tête' (page 180) (z. 5–7) Very early-flowering, miniature, bright yellow narcissus, often carrying several blooms on each stem.

 Euphorbia amygdaloides var. robbiae (page 46) (z. 7–9) Evergreen ground cover for difficult spots; dark green foliage and lime green spring flowers.

SUMMER

 Sambucus nigra f. porphyrophylla 'Eva' (page 52) (z. 5–7) Robust, deciduous shrub with deepest purple-black foliage that complements hot colors.

 Rosa 'Fru Dagmar Hastrup' (page 117) (z. 4–7) Healthy, easily manageable rose with single shell pink flowers followed by large red hips.

 Hebe 'Mrs Winder' (page 112) (z. 8–10) Compact evergreen shrub with slender purple bronze foliage and purple flowers in summer.

 Nigella damascena 'Miss Jekyll' (page 171) Useful self-sowing annual with fine, feathery foliage, blue flowers, and interestingly shaped seed pods.

 Lilium regale (page 185) (z. 3–8) Robust, alkaline-tolerant, fragrant white summer lily for borders or containers in sun or part shade.

FALL

 Crataegus persimilis 'Prunifolia' (page 56) (z. 4–7) Compact, round-headed deciduous tree with white spring flowers, autumn color, red berries.

 Perovskia 'Blue Spire' (page 114) (z. 5–8) Drought-tolerant silver shrub with long-lasting, purple-blue flower spikes in late summer and fall.

 Penstemon 'Andenken an Friedrich Hahn' (page 91) (z. 7–9) Hardy perennial with spikes of deep, coral red flowers for many weeks in summer and fall.

 Sedum 'Herbstfreude' (page 100) (z. 4–8) Succulent perennial with flat flower heads, pink in late summer turning chestnut and standing all winter.

 Verbena bonariensis (page 92) (z. 8–9) Tall, slender perennial with stiff, bare stems and purple flowers in late summer and fall. Good for butterflies.

WINTER

 Lonicera nitida 'Baggesen's Gold' (pages 39, 43) (z. 7–9) Dwarf evergreen shrub with small leaves of bright gold. Can be kept clipped or left informal.

 Buxus sempervirens 'Elegantissima' (page 39) (z. 6–9) Neat, small-leaved, variegated evergreen shrub which grows slowly and looks good all year.

 Sarcococca confusa (page 42, 124) (z. 6–8) Dense, compact evergreen shrub with slender, shiny leaves and very fragrant midwinter flowers.

 Stipa tenuissima (page 62) (z. 8–9) Fine, silky perennial grass, useful for textural planting. Lasts a long time and looks good for much of the year.

 Helleborus orientalis Hillier Hybrids (page 87) (z. 5–8) Shade-loving perennial with waxy flowers in pink, purple, and white, very early in the year.

Index

189

ACKNOWLEDGMENTS

AUTHOR'S ACKNOWLEDGMENTS

Clive Lane would like to thank Russell Lofkin, Pat Taylor and OutHouse Publishing for all their help and encouragement.

PICTURE CREDITS

The publishers would like to acknowledge with thanks all those whose gardens are pictured in this book.

The page number is followed by a second number in brackets indicating the position on that page. Numbers run across the page from left to right and from top to bottom.

Andrew McIndoe and John Hillier: front cover(top), back cover(btm), spine, 1(3), 12(2), 13, 22, 23(3), 24(1), 26, 28(all), 29(4/5), 30(all), 32(1), 34–5, 37(3), 39(2), 40(2/3), 42(1/2,4), 43(1/2/3/5/6/7), 44(3/5), 45(2/3), 46(1/2/4/8), 51(all), 52(1/2/4), 53(4/5/6/7), 54(1/3), 55(main), 56(2), 57(2/6), 58, 59(1,3), 60(3/4), 61(2), 62(2), 63(2/4/5/6), 69(9), 73(10/11/14), 74(2/3), 75(3), 77(1/2), 78(4/5/6), 79(3), 84(2/3/4), 85(1), 87(1), 88(3), 89(6), 90(2/3), 91(1), 92(1/2/3/4), 93(3), 94(1/3), 96(2), 97(1/3), 99(2/3), 102, 103(both), 104(3/4), 105(1/3), 106(2, rt), 107(2/3/4), 108(2/3), 109(1/3/4/5), 110(1/3/4), 111(1/2/4/6), 112(1/2/3), 113(2/5/6), 114(1/3/4/6), 115(1/2/4/5), 118(1), 119(1/2), 122, 123(6/7/10), 124(2/4), 125(1/6/7), 126(3/4/6), 127(all), 128(1), 129(6/9), 132(3), 135(all), 137(3), 141(4/6), 143(3), 151(4), 156, 174, 176(2/5/6/7), 177(1/2/3/6), 178(all), 179(3), 180(1/2/4/6/8/9), 181(2/3/4/5/6/7), 182(all), 183(1/2/3), 184(2/3/5), 185(1/6)

David Austin® Roses/www.davidaustinroses.co.uk: 73(12), 81(1/2/5/6/7/8/9/10/11/12/14), 114(5), 117(1/2/3/4/6/7/8/9/10/11/12/14)

Julia Brittain: 36(3)

Broadleigh Bulbs: 89(1/2)

Chiltern Seeds: 133(3)

David & Charles: front cover(btm rt), back cover(top), 93(1), 175/Michelle Garratt

Andrea Jones/Garden Exposures Photo Library/www.gardenexposures.co.uk: 4–5(page edge), 20(2), 72(1), 82–3(page edge), 94(2), 138, 148 (garden: The Lost Garden of Heligan, Cornwall, UK), 152(2, rt)

The Garden Picture Library: back flap(left)/J S Sira, back flap, rt/Howard Rice, 2(3)/John Glover, 3(2)/John Glover, 3(3)/Howard Rice, 4–5/Sunniva Harte (garden: Nan Goldman, Portland, Oregon, USA), 6–7/Sunniva Harte, 8(1)/Steven Wooster (garden: John Tordoff), 9/Suzie Gibbons (garden: Barbara Smith), 10/Marijke Heuff, 11(1)/Clive Nichols (designer: Arabella Lennox-Boyd), 11(3)/Marie O'Hara (garden: Chelsea Flower Show, The Knightsbridge Urban Renaissance Garden/designer: Phil Jaffa in assoc. with Patrick Collins), 14 & back cover(ctre)/Lynne Brotchie, 15(1)/Juliette Wade (garden: Pumpkin Cottage, Oxford), 15(2)/Juliette Wade, 18/Marianne Majerus, 20–1(top) & front flap/Howard Rice (garden: Toby Buckland & Lisa Davies), 21(lower rt)/Friedrich Strauss, 23(2)/Stephen Hamilton, 23(4)/Janet Sorrell, 24(2)/Ron Sutherland (designer: Duane Paul Design Team), 25(1)/Juliette Wade (garden: Overstroud Cottage, Buckinghamshire), 25(2)/J S Sira, 27/J S Sira (garden: Glen Chantry, Essex, UK), 29(3)/Marie O'Hara (garden: Cinderine Cottage/Daphne & John Chappell), 31(2)/Brian Carter, 31(3)/Mark Bolton, 31(4)/Stephen Hamilton, 31(5)/Mel Watson, 33(1)/NouN, 33(2)/Mark Bolton, 33(3)/Mark Bolton, 33(4)/Howard Rice, 33(5)/Stephen Hamilton, 36(1)/Will Giles, 36(2)/Frederic Didillon, 37(1)/John Glover, 38(1)/NouN (garden: Mme de Witte, Belgium), 38(2)/Anne Hyde (garden: Winslow Hall, Buckinghamshire, UK), 39(3)/Howard Rice (garden: Metherhall Manor, Cambridgeshire, UK), 40(1)/J S Sira, 44(1)/Neil Holmes, 44(2)/Lamontagne, 44(4)/Neil Holmes, 45(1)/David Askham, 47(1)/John Glover, 47(2)/Lamontagne, 47(3)/Sunniva Harte, 47(4)/Neil Holmes, 48(1)/Erika Craddock, 48(2)/Jerry Pavia, 49(1), 49(2)/Jerry Pavia, 49(3), 49(4)/John Glover, 50(1)/Ron Evans (garden: Abbotswood, Gloucestershire, UK), 50(2)/John Glover (the Dillon Garden, Dublin), 52(3)/John Glover, 52(5)/Neil Homes, 53(2)/Jerry Pavia, 57(1)/Howard Rice (Cambridge University Botanic Garden, UK), 59(2)/J S Sira, 61(1)/J S Sira, 61(3)/Will Giles, 61(4)/Marie O'Hara, 61(6)/Mark Bolton, 62(1)/Jerry Pavia, 63(1)/Howard Rice, 63(3)/Chris Burrows, 63(7)/Jerry Pavia, 63(8)/Andre Jordan, 63(9)/John Glover, 65(2)/Neil Holmes, 65(6)/Anne Green-Armytage, 68(1)/Jason Ingram, 69(3)/Mark Bolton, 70–1/Ron Sutherland (garden: Chelsea Flower Show, The Express Garden/designer: Peter Hogan), 72(2)/Howard Rice, 73(6)/David England, 73(15)/Howard Rice, 74(1)/John Beedle, 77(4/5)/John Beedle, 77(6)/Jo Whitworth, 77(8)/Howard Rice, 78(3)/Howard Rice, 79(1)/Howard Rice, 80/Clive Nichols (garden: Turn End, Buckinghamshire, UK), 82/John Glover, 83(1)/Howard Rice, 83(2)/Clive Nichols, 84(1)/Pernilla Bergdahl, 85(3)/J S Sira, 86(1)/Christopher Fairweather, 86(4)/David Cavagnaro, 89(8)/Didier Willery, 89(10)/J S Sira, 91(2)/Mark Bolton, 91(3)/David Dixon, 93(3)/Mark Bolton, 95(2)/Mark Bolton, 95(4)/J S Sira, 96(3)/Jo Whitworth, 98(1)/Lynn Keddie, 101(1)/Chris Burrows, 101(3)/Sunniva Harte, 101(4)/Brian Carter, 101(5), 104(1)/Howard Rice, 112(4)/John Beedle, 113(1)/Neil Holmes, 113(3)/Suzie Gibbons, 113(4)/Francois de Heel, 114(8)/J S Sira, 115(3)/Lynne Brotchie, 116(1)/Mark Bolton, 119(3)/Howard Rice, 120–1/John Glover, 123(1)/Jo Whitworth, 123(5)/John Glover, 123(8)/J S Sira, 124(1/3)/J S Sira, 125(2)/Pernilla Bergdahl, 125(8)/David Cavagnaro, 125(9)/J S Sira, 126(1)/Neil Holmes, 126(5)/John Glover, 126(7)/J S Sira, 126(9)/Howard Rice, 129(1)/Howard Rice (garden: Cambridge University Botanic Garden, UK), 129(2)/John Glover, 129(3)/Lynn Keddie, 129(11)/Mark Bolton, 130(3)/John Glover, 132(1)/Mark Winwood, 132(2)/Pernilla Bergdahl (garden: Downderry Lavender Nursery), 134(2)/Brian Carter, 136(1)/Eric Chrichton, 137(4)/Anne Green-Armytage, 137(5)/J S Sira, 139(1)/Howard Rice, 139(2)/Mark Bolton, 140(1)/Anne Green-Armytage, 140(3)/Jacqui Hurst, 141(1/3)/Jerry Pavia, 141(5)/Joanne Pavia, 141(7)/Chris Burrows, 142(4)/Chris Burrows, 143(2)/Juliette Wade, 144(1)/Howard Rice, 144(2)/Neil Holmes, 145(3)/Mark Bolton, 146–7/Mayer/Le Scanff (garden: Les Jardins des Bellevue), 149(2)/Marie O'Hara, 149(4)/Mark Bolton, 149(5)/J S Sira, 149(8)/John Beedle, 150/Marie O'Hara, 151(1)/Clive Nichols (garden: Turn End, Buckinghamshire, UK), 151(3)/Stephen Hamilton, 151(4)/David Cavagnaro, 152(1, left)/Graham Strong, 153(1)/Howard Rice, 154/David Cavagnaro, 155/Juliette Wade (garden: Pumpkin Cottage, Oxford, UK), 157(1)/Graham Strong, 164(5)/Clive Nichols, 165(4)/Friedrich Strauss, 165(5)/Juliette Wade, 166(4)/Jo Whitworth, 167(1)/Jo Whitworth, 167(2)/Howard Rice, 167(3)/David Dixon, 168(1)/Chris Burrows, 169(1)/J S Sira, 169(3)/Juliet Greene, 170(1)/Chris Burrows, 170(2)/John Glover, 172(3)/John Glover, 173(2) Frederic Didillon, 173(3)/Mark Bolton, 176(1/3)/Howard Rice, 177(4)/Lynn Keddie, 177(5)/Friedrich Strauss, 179(1)/Pernilla Bergdahl, 179(4)/John Glover, 179(5)/Ellen Rooney, 180(7)/Neil Holmes, 184(1)/Suzie Gibbons (garden: David Way & Anke van Diffelen), 185(2)/Chris Burrows, 185(3)/Jacqui Hurst, 185(5)/Mark Bolton

New Leaf Plants: 46(9)

Clive Nichols Garden Pictures: front cover(lower left) (garden: Swinton Lane, Worcestershire, UK), 16–17 (garden: Green Farm Plants/Piet Oudolf), 23(5) (designer: Jean Bird), 57(4) (RHS Garden Rosemoor), 76 (garden: Wollerton Old Hall, Shropshire, UK), 77(7), 95(1) & front cover(ctre btm), 95(3), 153(5) (garden: Lisette Pleasance)

Science Photo Library: 1(1)/Archie Young, 1(2)/Geoff Kidd, 2(1)/Adrian Thomas, 2(2)/Mrs Nina McKenna, 3(1)/Tony Wood, 8(2)/Malkolm Warrington, 12(1)/Joseph Malcolm Smith, 19/Adrian Thomas (RHS Garden Rosemoor), 23(1)/Geoff Kidd, 29(1)/Tim Rayner, 29(2)/The Picture Store, 31(1)/Mike Comb, 32(2)/Claude Nuridsany & Marie Perennou, 37(2)/Terence E. Exley, 39(1)/Geoff Kidd, 39(4)/Adrian Thomas, 41(1/3)/Geoff Kidd, 41(2)/Malcolm Richards, 41(4)/Adrian Thomas, 42(3)/Geoff Kidd, 43(4)/Malcolm Richard, 45(4)/Mike Comb, 46(3/5)/Geoff Kidd, 46(7)/Anthony Cooper, 53(1)/Geoff Kidd, 53(2)/Malkolm Warrington, 54(2)/Adrian Thomas, 55(inset)/Terence E. Exley, 56(3)/Adrian Thomas, 57(3)/Chris Dawe, 57(5)/Mike Comb, 60(1)/Bob Gibbons, 60(2)/Andrew Ackerley, 61(5)/The Picture Store, 64(1)/Science Photo Library, 64(2)/Ron Chapman, 64(3)/Adrian Thomas, 64(4)/Mrs W.D. Monks, 64(6)/Brian Gadsby, 65(1/5)/Archie Young, 65(3)/Malcolm Richards, 65(4)/Antony Sweeting, 66(1/3/6)/Adrian Thomas, 66(2)/Joseph Malcolm Smith, 65(4)/Brian Gadsby, 66(7)/Maurice Nimmo, 67(1)/Anthony Cooper, 67(2)/Joseph Malcolm Smith, 68(2)/Maurice Nimmo, 69(1)/Ron Bass, 69(2/4)/Archie Young, 69(5)/W. Broadbent, 69(6)/Neil Holmes, 69(7)/Malcolm Richards, 69(8)/Bjorn Svensson, 73(1/8/9/13)/Adrian Thomas, 73(2)/Malcolm Richards, 73(3)/Archie Young, 73(4/5)/Joseph Malcolm Smith, 73(7)/Geoff Kidd, 75(1/2)/Anthony Cooper, 75(3)/Joseph Malcolm Smith, 77(3)/Science Photo Library, 78(1)/Mrs W.D. Monks, 78(2)/Geoff Kidd, 79(2)/Adrian Thomas, 79(4)/Archie Young, 81(3)/J.B. Rapkins, 81(4)/Adrian Thomas, 81(13)/Science Photo Library, 85(2)/Geoff Kidd, 85(4)/A.C. Seinet, 86(2)/Ron Chapman, 86(3)/Malcolm Richards, 87(2)/Leslie J. Borg, 87(3)/Ian Gowland, 88(1)/Malcolm Richards, 88(2)/Glenis Moore, 89(2)/Chris Martin Bahr, 89(4)/Malcolm Richards, 89(5)/Geoff Kidd, 89(7)/Sally McRae Kuyper, 89(9)/Maxine Adcock, 90(1)/Adrian Thomas, 92(5)/Adrian Thomas, 92(7)/Malcolm Richards, 92(8)/Maxine Adcock, 93(2)/Tony Wood, 96(1)/Darryl Sweetland, 96(4)/Dan Sams, 97(2)/Archie Young, 97(4)/Geoff Kidd, 98(2/3)/Adrian Thomas, 99(1)/Adrian Thomas, 100(1)/Sally McRae Kuyper, 100(2)/Chris B.Stock, 100(3)/Maxine Adcock, 101(2)/Antony Sweeting, 104(2)/Geoff Kidd, 105(2)/Geoff Kidd, 106(1, left)/Archie Young, 107(1)/Bjanka Kadic, 108(1)/Geoff Kidd, 109(2)/Mrs Nina McKenna, 110(2)/Rosemary Greenwood, 111(3)/Adrian Thomas, 111(5)/Elsa M. Megson, 114(2)/Brian Gadsby, 116(2)/Bob Gibbons, 117(5)/Bob Gibbons, 118(2/4)/Adrian Thomas, 118(3)/Tony Wood, 123(2)/A.C. Seinet, 123(3/4)/Malcolm Richards, 123(9/12)/Adrian Thomas, 123(11)/Graham Jordan, 125(3/4/5)/Adrian Thomas, 126(2)/Matt Johnston, 126(8)/Sheila Terry, 128(3)/Ron Bonser, 129(4)/Geoff Kidd, 129(5)/Irene Windridge, 129(7)/A.S. Gould, 129(8)/Terence E. Exley, 130(1)/The Picture Store, 131(1)/The Picture Store, 131(3)/Archie Young, 133(1)/Adrian Thomas, 133(2)/Malcolm Richards, 134(1)/Malkolm Warrington, 134(4)/Mrs W.D. Monks, 136(2)/Geoff Kidd, 137(1)/Andrew Ackerley, 137(2)/Simon Fraser, 137(6)/Geoff Kidd, 140(2)/Dan Sams, 142(1)/Adrian Thomas, 142(2)/Bob Gibbons, 142(3)/Science Photo Library, 143(1)/Malcolm Richards, 144(3)/Adrian Thomas, 145(1)/Moira C. Smith, 145(2)/Archie Young, 145(4)/Adrian Thomas, 149(1)/Geoff Kidd, 149(2)/Mike Vardy, 149(8)/Geoff Kidd, 151(2)/Geoff Kidd, 153(2)/Mrs W.D. Monks, 153(3)/Tony Wood, 153(4)/A. Stennings, 157(2)/Geoff Kidd, 157(3)/Francoise Sauze, 158/Elsa M. Megson, 159(1)/K. Jayaram, 159(2)/Joseph Malcolm Smith, 159(3)/Simon Fraser, 159(4)/Archie Young, 159(5)/Tony Wood, 160(1, top)/Anthony Menzies-Shaw, 160(2, ctre)/Derrick Ditchburn, 160(3, btm)/Roger Standen, 161(1)/Archie Young, 161(2)/Chris B. Stock, 161(3)/Rosemary Greenwood, 161(4)/Irene Windridge, 161(5)/Mike Vardy, 162(1)/Rosemary Greenwood, 162(2)/Mike Danson, 162(3)/Adrian Thomas, 162(4)/Bjanka Kadic, 162(5)/Science Photo Library, 163(1)/Adrian Thomas, 163(2)/John J. Pettigrew, 163(3)/The Picture Store, 164(1)/Anthony Cooper, 164(2)/Dan Sams, 164(3)/S. Mansell, 164(3)/Adrian Thomas, 165(1)/Mike Vardy, 165(2/3)/Adrian Thomas, 166(1)/Mrs W.D. Monks, 166(2)/Adrian Thomas, 166(3)/Martin Stankewitz, 167(4)/Mike Danson, 167(5)/Science Photo Library, 169(4)/Brian Gadsby, 169(5)/Adrian Thomas, 171(1)/Malcolm Richards, 171(2)/Brian Gadsby, 172(1)/ David Nunuk, 172(2)/Ron Chapman, 173(1)/Sylvia O'Toole, 173(4)/Archie Young, 176(4)/Neil Davies, 179(2)/Annie Poole, 180(3)/Geoff Kidd, 180(5)/Adrian Thomas, 189(1)/Paul Shoesmith, 183(4)/Elsa M. Megson, 184(4/sequence)/Claude Nuiridsany & Marie Perennou, 185(4)/Darryl Sweetland

Suttons: 149(7), 168(2)

Thompson & Morgan: 128(2), 149(6)